Praise for *Foreign En*

"Arnaud Develay's new book is a must-read! This book shows how the corruption and lies of the liberal political establishment in the U.S. has inexorably led to the terrible war in Ukraine. Develay also demonstrates how democracy itself has been compromised and undermined, potentially fatally, in the process. This insightful book is a crucial antidote to the incessant media propaganda which is helping to prop up a corrupt political system leading us to the brink of nuclear war."

DANIEL KOVALIK, Professor, University of Pittsburg School of Law
and author of seven books

"An eye-opening account delving into the U.S. regime change scheme in Ukraine that masked high-level corruption and destroyed a country."

DR. CYNTHIA MCKINNEY, former Congresswoman
and Green Party Presidential Candidate

"Hard-hitting and comprehensive, Develay's investigative treatise uncovers the real nexus of Ukrainian and U.S. Democratic Party establishment corruption. For anyone interested in what really happened, this book should be at the top of their reading list."

PATRICK HENNINGSEN, journalist and founder of *21st Century Wire*

FOREIGN ENTANGLEMENTS

UKRAINE, BIDEN & THE FRACTURED AMERICAN POLITICAL CONSENSUS

Arnaud Develay

Clarity Press, Inc.

ISBN: 978-1-949762-93-8
EBOOK ISBN: 978-1-949762-94-5

In-house editor: Diana G. Collier
Book design: Becky Luening

Library of Congress Control Number: 2024930883

Clarity Press, Inc.
2625 Piedmont Rd. NE, Ste. 56
Atlanta, GA 30324, USA
https://www.claritypress.com

Table of Contents

PART III
Election 2024: Woe to the Vanquished | 125

INTRODUCTION

WASHINGTON IS IN TURMOIL.

In the wake of the 2022 U.S. midterm elections, the dynamics of American politics has shifted with the capture of the House of Representatives by the Republican party.

The Congressional investigation initiated by U.S. Rep. James COMER and U.S. Senator GRASSLEY into the influence-peddling scheme allegedly organized in Ukraine by then Vice-President Joseph BIDEN is at the heart of a ferocious battle involving all branches of the federal government.

As will be discussed further on, the FBI and the Justice Departments both played a central role not only in shielding Joe Biden and his family but in preserving the Ukrainian project which is dear to the neoconservatives who have managed to exert a stranglehold on the federal government.[1]

The question as to why no investigation was ever initiated in the U.S. despite the release of overwhelming incriminating information (going back as far as 2020 with the infamous DERKACH Tapes) baffles the mind of any neutral observer unless one begins to examine the role played by the former vice-president in masterminding the complete externalization of Ukrainian politics in order to facilitate the pillaging of that country before turning it into a battering ram against the Russian Federation.[2]

---

1 Philip Giraldi, "Neocons Poised to Join New Government," Strategic Culture Foundation, November 12, 2020. https://strategic-culture.org/news/2020/11/12/neocons-poised-to-join-new-government/

"It would not be overstating the case to suggest that the neoconservative movement has now been born again, though the enemy is now the unreliable Trumpean-dominated Republican Party rather than Saddam Hussein or Ayatollah Khomeini. The transition has also been aided by a more aggressive shift among the Democrats themselves, with Russiagate and other 'foreign interference' being blamed for the party's failure in 2016. Given that mutual intense hostility to Trump, the doors to previously shunned liberal media outlets have now opened wide to the stream of foreign policy 'experts' who want to 'restore a sense of the heroic' to U.S. national security policy."

2 Robert Parry, "Neocons and the Ukraine Coup," Truthout, February 25, 2014. https://truthout.org/articles/neocons-and-the-ukraine-coup/

In order to better understand the obsession of U.S. elites with Ukraine, it is useful to take a closer look at the individuals tasked with implementing the project.

As the main architect of the Maidan coup d'état organized in Kiev in 2014, Victoria Nuland can be said to be the driving force behind a conflict which has led to nearly half a million casualties (dead and wounded), including 120,000 deaths alone.[3]

U.S.-Chilean blogger Gonzalo Lira produced what can considered the definitive portrait of the person second-in-charge at the State Department.[4]

Victoria Nuland is to Ukraine what Paul Wolfowitz was to Iraq, with the sole difference that she holds a deep personal grudge against Russia which can only be understood by examining her own family history.

To be sure, this book will not endeavor to delve into the deeper motivations of Victoria Nuland's obsession with Russia.

Suffice it to say that owing to her influence at the State Department, she believes she can wield the power of the U.S. federal government to "forge reality."[5]

In so doing, she aims to carry out the neoconservative imperative which calls for U.S. full spectrum dominance over world affairs.

Owing to her husband's connections (noted arch-neocon Robert Kagan) with investment funds, Nuland has been able to deliver Ukraine to Wall Street on a silver plate.[6]

"Vice President Cheney and the neocons pursued a similar strategy during George W. Bush's presidency, expanding NATO aggressively to the east and backing anti-Russian regimes in the region including the hard-line Georgian government, which provoked a military confrontation with Moscow in 2008, ironically, during the Summer Olympics in China."

3 Helene Cooper, Thomas Gibbons-Neff, Eric Schmitt and Julian E. Barnes, "Ukraine War Casualties Near Half a Million, U.S. Officials Say," *The New York Times,* August 18, 2023. https://www.nytimes.com/2023/08/18/us/politics/ukraine-russia-war-casualties.html

4 Gonzalo Lira, "Victoria Nuland," March 27, 2022, livestreamed comnmentary, YouTube video, 1:51:44. https://www.youtube.com/watch?v=TzR---YDDIQ&t=1s

5 Ron Susskind, "Faith, Certainty and the Presidency of George W. Bush," *The New York Times Magazine,* October 17, 2004. https://www.nytimes.com/2004/10/17/magazine/faith-certainty-and-the-presidency-of-george-w-bush.html

6 Guy Faulconbridge, "Ukraine war, already with up to 354,000 casualties, likely to last past 2023 - U.S. documents," Reuters, April 12, 2023. https://www.reuters.com/world/europe/ukraine-war-already-with-up-354000-casualties-likely-

European Parliament Member Mick Wallace gave a sobering description of the stakes behind the conflict:

> The damage to Ukraine is devastating. Towns and cities that endured for hundreds of years don't exist anymore. We must recognise that these towns, cities and surrounding lands were long being stolen by local oligarchs colluding with global financial capital. This theft quickened with the onset of the war in 2014. The pro-Western government opened the doors wide for massive structural adjustment and privatisation programmes spearheaded by the European Bank for Reconstruction and Development, the IMF and the World Bank. Zelensky used the current war to concentrate power and accelerate the corporate fire sale. He banned opposition parties that were resisting deeply unpopular reforms to the laws restricting the sale of land to foreign investors. Over three million hectares of agricultural land are now owned by companies based in Western tax havens. Ukraine's mineral deposits alone are worth over $12 trillion. Western companies are licking their lips. What are the working-class people of Ukraine dying for?[7]

Arms manufacturing companies such as Lockheed Martin have seen the value of their shares soar on the stock market.[8]

---

drag-us-documents-2023-04-12/

"As many as 354,000 Russian and Ukrainian soldiers have been killed or injured in the Ukraine war which is grinding towards a protracted conflict that may last well beyond 2023, according to a trove of purported U.S. intelligence documents posted online."

7 Colin Todhunter, "The Damage to Ukraine is Devastating: 'What are the working-class people of Ukraine dying for?' MEP Mick Wallace," Global Research, June 28, 2023. https://www.globalresearch.ca/mep-mick-wallace-what-working-class-people-ukraine-dying-for/5823966

8 Guerre en Ukraine : le fabricant d'armes américain Lockheed Martin enchaîne les records en Bourse, Thales encore en dessous des siens malgré un gain de plus de 30%," Les Echos Investir, March 3, 2022. https://investir.lesechos.fr/actu-des-valeurs/la-vie-des-actions/guerre-en-ukraine-le-fabricant-darmes-americain-lockheed-martin-enchaine-les-records-en-bourse-thales-encore-en-dessous-des-siens-malgre-un-gain-de-plus-de-30-1857268

Republican Sen. Lindsay Graham expressed satisfaction that the U.S. had spent less than 3% of its annual military budget to aid Ukraine in its war against Russia, (leading) the Ukrainian Defense Forces to "have destroyed half of the Russian army."[9]

Against this backdrop, this book shall endeavor to examine how the mechanisms put in place in the wake of Ukraine's 2014 so-called "revolution of dignity" provided for the complete takeover of Ukraine by the American political establishment.

It will also be highlighted how attempts to conceal the ill-conceived imperial policies carried out against the interests and without the knowledge of the American people have led to the erosion of the American justice system and a breakdown of our system of government.

The Derkach Tapes

Andrii Derkach was a member of Ukraine's Verkhovna Rada.

Little known to the general public in the West, Derkach arguably stands today amongst the main enemies of the American establishment. Far removed from the cartoon-like characterization of America's usual bogeymen such as Al-Qaida, Kim Jong-Il, Saddam Hussein and consorts, the Ukrainian politician has managed to compile a significant amount of the proverbial dirt on the less than honorable activities carried out by some of Washington's most prominent figures in the wake of the so-called "Revolution of Dignity."

Despite the U.S. establishment's characterization of Derkach as a Russian agent bent on interfering in American politics, the impact of the material collected by the Ukrainian MP is hard to refute. Were some senior members of the Democratic Party of the United States today decided to compose a new "Axis of Evil," it stands to reason that Derkach would figure prominently on the list of those individuals slated for termination with extreme prejudice. His "crime": having dared to expose the scope of corruption implemented in Ukraine owing to a sophisticated system of external management of that country designed and operated by the Americans.

---

9 The New Voice of Ukraine, "Ukraine used 3% of US defense budget to destroy half of Russian army — Lindsey Graham," *Yahoo! News,* August 23, 2023. https://news.yahoo.com/ukraine-used-3-us-defense-203500822.html

Twice in a short time his name was mentioned in the speeches of high-ranking U.S. national intelligence officials.

The first time was in early August 2020. At that time, the U.S. presidential campaign was in full swing, and Joe Biden was to be confirmed as the Democratic nominee at that Party's convention. William Evanina, then director of the U.S. National Center for Counterintelligence and Security, mentioned Derkach in connection with the Kremlin's alleged use of a variety of measures to smear former U.S. Vice President Joe Biden and any individual deemed to belong to "the anti-Russian establishment."[10]

By means of illustration, Evanina pointed to "pro-Russian Ukrainian parliamentarian" Andriy Derkach spreading statements about the corruption of senior U.S. political figures. Specifically, Derkach was singled out for having made public former Ukrainian president Poroshenko's telephone conversations with then-U.S. Vice President Biden, the content of which was used in a campaign aimed at allegedly "undermining former Vice President Biden and the Democratic Party."[11]

We will return to the history of the tapes as well as to who exactly was interested in making them public but for now, let us just highlight the fact that Evanina did not even call into question the authenticity of the recordings between Biden and Poroshenko. Instead, Evanina merely referred to the material as "leaked phone calls." This somewhat demurred treatment of the allegations derived from Derkach's revelations could be construed in retrospect as an attempt by the national-security state to deprive the media of any pretext to fuel the

---

10 Mike Levine and Mark Osborne, "Russia working to boost Trump's reelection and 'denigrate' Biden, as China undermines Trump: US intelligence," *ABC News,* August 7, 2020. https://edition.cnn.com/2020/09/10/politics/treasury-sanctions-derkach-ukraine-election-interference/index.html

"'We assess that Russia is using a range of measures to primarily denigrate former Vice President Biden and what it sees as an anti-Russia 'establishment.'" This is "consistent with Moscow's public criticism of him when he was Vice President for his role in the Obama Administration's policies on Ukraine and its support for the anti-Putin opposition inside Russia," [Evanina added].

11 Ibid. "Providing an example of Russia's influence measures, the statement noted that 'pro-Russia Ukrainian parliamentarian Andriy Derkach is spreading claims about corruption -- including through publicizing leaked phone calls -- to undermine former Vice President Biden's candidacy and the Democratic Party.'"

emerging controversy ahead of the much-anticipated debates between then-U.S. President Trump and the Democratic nominee.

This strategy would however be completely abandoned once Biden won the election. From that point forward, the tone of statements emanating from U.S. officials resolutely turned hostile. In a manner reminiscent of the allegations bearing on Donald Trump's working as a Russian agent and despite these claims having been debunked by the Mueller Report, a report issued by Director of National Intelligence Avril Haynes, concluded that Russian officials had authorized and carried out "influence operations designed to smear President Biden and the Democratic Party, support former President Trump, undermine public confidence in the electoral process, and exacerbate the social and political divisions in the United States."[12]

Haynes emphasized that the Russian leadership "controlled the activities of Andrii Derkach, a Ukrainian lawmaker who played a prominent role in Russia's efforts to influence the election." The report added that Derkach "has ties to Russian officials as well as to Russian secret services."[13]

---

12 National Intelligence Council, Intelligence Community Assessment ICA 2020-00078D, *Foreign Threats to the 2020 US Federal Elections,* March 10, 2021. https://www.dni.gov/files/ODNI/documents/assessments/ICA-declass-16MAR21.pdf

"A network of Ukraine-linked individuals—including Russian influence agent Konstantin Kilimnik—who were also connected to the Russian Federal Security Service (FSB) took steps throughout the election cycle to damage U.S. ties to Ukraine, denigrate President Biden and his candidacy, and benefit former President Trump's prospects for reelection." (p. 3)

Key Judgment 2: "We assess that President Putin and the Russian state authorized and conducted influence operations against the 2020 U.S. presidential election aimed at denigrating President Biden and the Democratic Party, supporting former President Trump, undermining public confidence in the electoral process, and exacerbating sociopolitical divisions in the U.S. Unlike in 2016, we did not see persistent Russian cyber efforts to gain access to election infrastructure. We have high confidence in these judgments because a range of Russian state and proxy actors who all serve the Kremlin's interests worked to affect U.S. public perceptions. We also have high confidence because of the consistency of themes in Russia's influence efforts across the various influence actors and throughout the campaign, as well as in Russian leaders' assessments of the candidates." (p. 4)

13 Ibid. "We assess that President Putin and other senior Russian officials were aware of and probably directed Russia's influence operations against the 2020 U.S. Presidential election. For example, we assess that Putin had purview over the activities of Andriy Derkach, a Ukrainian legislator who played a prominent role in Russia's election influence activities. Derkach has ties to Russian officials as well as Russia's intelligence services." (p. 2)

To be sure, the DNI failed to produce a single shred of evidence to support such a claim as the talking points were reminiscent of the allegations at the heart of the Mueller commission's high-profile investigation (at the tune of $32 million of taxpayers' money) of Trump's ties to Russian intelligence.

One might be tempted to wonder why so much effort was expended to alter the reputation of a foreign politician unknown to the public. The answer was provided by Derkach himself in an op-ed piece published on the Ukrainian website *Strana*.

In it, Derkach pointed out that the materials he published did not interfere in the U.S. elections but merely exposed the level of corruption and external management of Ukraine. He asks:

In what way did American intelligence see a threat and facts of interference in the U.S. elections? Could it be about the issue of international corruption, when Alexeyevich (Poroshenko) removed people (who opposed) the company "Burisma" bringing in the Biden family? Or could it be about the issue of robbing Ukrainians as Poroshenko did when he raised tariffs on his own population by 100% just because one of Joe's friend asked for it in exchange for a billion in loan guarantees? Or could it be the issue bearing on the topic of external management, when Joe once again asked Petro to fire Prosecutor General Shokin before putting foreign overseers in charge of reversing Ukrainian gas in charge of state-owned companies? Or is it about the issue of subduing the Verkhovna Rada when Petro proceeded to guide the legislative agenda and secure the votes (endorsing the adoption of legislations compatible with U.S. business interests), all the while communicating with the prime minister of his own country through the vice president of the United States? Unlikely, for while every one of these issues point to corruption and foreign management, they cannot be characterized as instances of interference in the U.S. elections.[14]

_____

14 "Poroshenko boasted to Biden that he had raised tariffs by 100% instead of the required 75%, – a record of conversation was made public." *Ukrainian News,* May 19, 2020. https://ukranews.com/en/news/703227-poroshenko-boasted-to-biden-

For all intents and purposes, it bears noting that neither Biden nor Poroshenko ever sued Derkach over the allegedly falsified tapes nor did they ever call for an expertise purporting to call into doubt the authenticity of the recordings.

Rather, Poroshenko, who by that time was no longer the President of Ukraine, accused President Zelensky's office of leaking tapes of his conversations with Biden to the media.[15]

In effect, rather than prosecuting Derkach for defamation, the U.S. authorities opted to neutralize the Ukrainian MP along with individuals and companies associated with him through the imposition of sanctions on account of his allegedly working for the Kremlin.[16]

First, the Ukrainian deputy had his visa to the United States revoked. This was to be expected, since Derkach's revelations featured Marie Jovanovich (former U.S. ambassador to Ukraine), Christina Quinn (acting U.S. ambassador to Ukraine), several employees of the U.S. embassy in Kiev, their contacts in the National Anti-corruption Bureau of Ukraine, etc.[17]

---

that-he-had-raised-tariffs-by-100-instead-of-the-required-75-a-record

"'Petro Oleksiyovych confesses to Biden that he raised tariffs for ordinary Ukrainians, attention, not by 75% as requested by the IMF, but by as much as 100%. For the sake of a billion for himself, Poroshenko is ready to strip the Ukrainians naked and also make money on tariffs. By the way, tariffs really doubled,' Derkach said."

15 Yuras Karmanau, "Ukraine to investigate leaked tapes with ex-president, Biden," *AP News,* May 20, 2020. https://apnews.com/article/02895b0ffce2b6c6f11c20333fe7ba3d

"Zelensky, who carefully avoided taking sides in the U.S. impeachment inquiry, said his predecessor could be in trouble over the tapes. 'They governed the country in such a way that they could face many twists and convictions,' said Zelenskiy, who has repeatedly accused Poroshenko of corruption, accusations the former president has categorically denied. In a Facebook statement, Poroshenko said the tapes were fabricated and described their release as part of a Kremlin-driven effort to 'undermine bipartisan support of Ukraine in the United States.' He called Biden a 'friend and ally of Ukraine' and criticized Zelenskiy for eroding Western support for Ukraine to Moscow's benefit."

16 Adam Rawnsley, "Who Leaked Biden's Calls to Ukraine?" The Daily Beast, May 19, 2020. https://www.thedailybeast.com/who-leaked-bidens-calls-to-ukraine

"Andriy Derkach—a Ukrainian politician with a KGB background, a penchant for conspiracy theories, and a friendly relationship with Rudy Giuliani—released a host of conversations between former Vice President Joe Biden and former Ukrainian President Petro Poroshenko. The leaked talks purport to show the two discussing the firing of a Ukrainian prosecutor in exchange for American support for a billion dollar loan from the IMF."

17 U.S. Department of Justice, Office of Public Affairs, "Active Russian Agent

It was then the turn of Derkach's top-rated program "Good Morning, Country!" to be removed from the grid of programs of Ukraine's First National TV Channel.[18]

The show was produced by the Era Media production company (affiliated to Derkach). Pressure was exerted on the owners of Zurab Alasania (the channel) who themselves relied on American grants and were tetanized by the potential impact of Andrii Derkach's press conferences on the morning airwaves.

Finally, the U.S. Treasury Department at the request of two Democratic Senators proceeded to impose personal sanctions on Derkach for his meddling in American elections owing to his "close ties with the Russian secret services."[19]

In January 2021, in the wake of Biden formally taking office as U.S. President, certain Ukrainian nationals were immediately subjected to a barrage of sanctions.[20]

Andrii Derkach Indicted for Scheme to Violate Sanctions in the United States," December 7, 2022. https://www.justice.gov/opa/pr/active-russian-agent-andrii-derkach-indicted-scheme-violate-sanctions-united-states

"Moreover, in the years and months preceding his designation, the defendant spent significant time in the United States, including at the Subject Condominiums. In conducting that travel to, and spending time in, the United States, Derkach was actively involved in deceiving U.S. law enforcement and border authorities even prior to his SDN designation. For example, in December 2019 and February 2020, Derkach was in the United States to meet with U.S. persons and conduct media appearances. To obtain a U.S. visa, and to ostensibly attend meetings and conferences related to human rights issues in Ukraine, Derkach retained the services of a U.S.-based consulting firm (Firm-1)."

18 В США ввели санкции против украинцев и украинских компаний. Список (strana.news). https://strana.news/news/311291-ssha-vveli-sanktsii-protiv-dubinskoho-onishchenko-i-media-derkacha.html

19 Volodymyr Katsman, "Derkach tapes: will the U.S. sanctions list be expanded," *The Page,* February 15, 2021. https://en.thepage.ua/politics/derkach-tapes-will-the-us-sanctions-list-be-expanded

"A public investigation showed that in fact many more people were involved in the information operation to promote Derkach fake tapes, attempts to influence the elections in the United States and cause a quarrel between Ukraine and Americans, the Head of the NABU Civil Oversight Council Mark Savchuk assured. According to him, the activists have evidence that these people are not only interconnected, but also played different roles in the legalization of Derkach tapes in the information space."

20 Orion Rummler, "U.S. sanctions 7 more Ukrainian officials for 'Russia-linked' election interference," *Axios,* January 11, 2021. https://www.axios.com/2021/01/11/russia-election-interference-biden-trump-ukraine

"The Treasury and State Department identified former Ukraine officials Konstantin Kulyk, Oleksandr Onyshchenko, Andriy Telizhenko and Oleksandr Dubinsky — a

These were imposed on seven Ukrainian citizens for their association with an "active Russian agent," Andrii Derkach, per an official statement from the country's Ministry of Finance.

According to U.S. authorities, Derkach and his associates had since 2019 engaged through U.S. media, social media platforms, and influential American individuals in a concerted effort aimed at spreading "..misleading and unsubstantiated claims that current and former American officials are involved in corruption, money laundering, and illegal political influence in Ukraine."

In addition, the U.S. Treasury Department issued a statement claiming that all individuals subjected to the latest restrictions were likely to have been involved in Russian interference during the 2020 U.S. election.

The sanctions affected Alexander Dubinsky, a member of Zelensky's party Sluzhba Naroda, former Ukrainian officials Konstantin Kulik, Alexander Onishchenko, Andrey Telizhenko, as well as Dmytro Kovalchuk, Anton Symonenko and Petro Zhuravlya.

Furthermore, the companies deemed to own Internet websites such as Era Media, Only News, Nabuleaks, and Behemoth Media, which according to U.S. authorities belonged to Derkach, were also added to the list of entities subjected to U.S. sanctions.

Some of these individuals had participated in a multi-part documentary chronicling an investigation into the Biden family's financial interests in Ukraine co-produced by One American News (OAN) and Trump's lawyer Rudolph Giuliani.

Then in September 2022, Ukraine's SBU issued an arrest warrant against Derkach for treason.[21]

current member of the Ukrainian parliament — as part of a 'coordinated' effort to spread 'unsubstantiated allegations involving a U.S. political candidate.'"

21 Joshua Manning, "BREAKING NEWS: People's Deputy of Ukraine Andrii Derkach declared suspect of treason," EuroWeekly News, September 16, 2022. https://euroweeklynews.com/2022/09/16/breaking-news-peoples-deputy-of-ukraine-andrii-derkach-declared-suspect-of-treason/

"The activities allegedly included the discrediting of Ukraine in the international arena, deteriorating diplomatic relations with the United States of America, as well as complicating the integration into the European Union and NATO. Now the people's deputy is accused of committing crimes under Part 2 of Article 28, Part 1 of Article 111, Article 368-5 of the Criminal Code of Ukraine."

In December 2022, a Brooklyn federal court indicted Derkach on seven counts of seeking to evade sanctions placed upon him by the U.S. Treasury Dept. in September 2020.[22]

Finally, in January 2023, Derkach was stripped of his Ukrainian nationality.[23]

To this day, Derkach's whereabouts remain unknown.

The Tapes' Contents

On May 19, 2020, Andrii Derkach held the first of six press conferences purporting to expose the scope of the conspiracy engineered in Ukraine under the leadership of the U.S. Democratic Party led by Joe Biden.[24]

The "highlight" of the tapes featured a recording of Vice President Biden's conversation with Ukrainian President Petro Poroshenko dating from 2016, in which Biden appears to be giving direct orders calling for the firing of Prosecutor General Viktor Shokin, the official tasked with the investigation of Ukrainian energy company Burisma and its CEO, Ukrainian oligarch Nikola Zlochevsky.[25]

---

22 Colin Kalmbacher, "'Pro-Russian Propagandist' and Ukrainian 'Oligarch' Who Palled Around With Rudy Giuliani Is Indicted by U.S. Prosecutors," Law and Crime, December 7, 2022. https://lawandcrime.com/crime/pro-russian-propagandist-and-ukrainian-oligarch-who-palled-around-with-rudy-giuliani-is-indicted-by-u-s-prosecutors/

23 President of Ukraine | Volodymyr Zelenskyy, Official website, "Free world has everything necessary to stop Russian aggression; it is important for global democracy - address by the President of Ukraine," January 10, 2023. https://www.president.gov.ua/en/news/vilnij-svit-maye-vse-neobhidne-shob-zupiniti-rosijsku-agresi-80305

"Based on the materials prepared by the Security Service of Ukraine and the State Migration Service of Ukraine, and in accordance with the Constitution of our state, I have decided to terminate the citizenship of four persons: Andriy Leonidovych Derkach, Taras Romanovych Kozak, Renat Raveliyovych Kuzmin and Viktor Volodymyrovych Medvedchuk. If people's deputies choose to serve not the people of Ukraine, but the murderers who came to Ukraine, our actions will be appropriate."

24 Paul Sonne and Rosalind S. Helderman, "Ukrainian lawmaker releases leaked phone calls of Biden and Poroshenko," *The Washington Post,* May 19, 2020. https://www.washingtonpost.com/national-security/ukrainian-lawmaker-releases-leaked-phone-calls-of-biden-and-poroshenko/2020/05/19/cc1e6030-9a26-11ea-b60c-3be060a4f8e1_story.html

25 "A recording of a conversation between Poroshenko and Biden about a billion-dollar bribe has been released," *Baige News,* March 20, 2020. https://

Poroshenko for his part is heard replying that he found "a smart guy to replace Shokin. His name is Yuriy Lutsenko. If you want, you can appoint an American judge of Ukrainian origin to be an assistant prosecutor."[26]

On another tape, Biden is heard berating Poroshenko for the launching of an uncoordinated terrorist attack in Crimea in the summer of 2016.[27]

Biden is heard complaining that he had to call Obama as well, alluding to the fact that the Germans and the French had started asking questions. Not only had the sabotage team been intercepted by the Russians, Poroshenko had not even coordinated with Washington!![28]

Poroshenko is heard replying that he wasn't aware of anything, that he was visiting Southeast Asia at the time, before laying the blame at the feet of the head of Defense Ministry's Main Intelligence Directorate, Valery Kondratyuk.

Biden is then heard requesting Kondratyuk's dismissal.

---

baigenews.kz/news/obnarodovana_zapis_razgovora_poroshenko_i_baydena_o_vzyatke_v_milliard_dollarov/

"...The second material is dated March 22, 2016. On this recording, the former Ukrainian leader is already talking with Joe Biden. During the conversation, the then vice president offered Poroshenko a bribe. 'In the event that you have a new government and a new attorney general, I will be ready to publicly sign $1 billion in commitments,' the man said with Biden's voice."

26 "Joe Biden Leaked Call Transcript with Petro Poroshenko," *Rev,* May 20, 2020.   https://www.rev.com/blog/transcripts/joe-biden-leaked-call-transcript-with-petro-poroshenko

March 22, 2016 call transcript: "Petro Poroshenko: (05:22) And the second thing, I immediately invited Lutsenko and said that he should contact your embassy, and I would be very pleased if you will have a certain person who can come either from Washington or whatever. We have here, I don't remember his name, the Ukrainian origin American prosecutor. He is a little bit old. I sent to the, Jeffery his name, and he was ready to come and to be assistant and advisor."

27 "In Kiev, published a conversation between 'Biden and Poroshenko' about sabotage in the Crimea," *RBC,* July 9, 2020. https://www.rbc.ru/politics/09/07/2020/5f06fa8f9a794784ea09368e

"'As you know, we intervened once, before it happened, when we learned that the General Staff was taking certain steps. We have made it clear that we do not support this. You took a step back, but the next day it happened. I'll tell you frankly, he [Barack Obama] is not happy about it,' Biden said."

28 "Пленки Байдена-Порошенко - что нового стало известно о диверсиях Украины в Крыму 2016 года," *Strana News,* July 9, 2020. https://strana.news/news/277674-plenki-bajdena-poroshenko-chto-novoho-stalo-izvestno-o-diversijakh-ukrainy-v-krymu-2016-hoda.html

Later, Kondratyuk's career would take off as Zelensky appointed him head of the Foreign Intelligence Service in 2019.[29]

During the third press conference, Derkach exposed the wide-ranging scope of the U.S. Democratic Party's operations in Ukraine, a process he called "Democorruption."[30]

One of the most significant operations involved one of Biden's most trusted advisors: Amos Hochstein.

Hochstein proceeded to set up a gas-reverse scheme using the state-owned provider company Naftogaz in order to "rebrand" Russian gas into (more expensive) European gas. The reversed gas was then sold to gullible Ukrainian consumers.[31]

During this particular press conference, Derkach also provided lists of Ukraine's Members of Parliament, Members of the Cabinet, employees of the Office of the President and individuals sitting on the (state-owned companies) Supervisory Boards as being all in the pay of Open Society Foundation Founder, George Soros.

These recordings appeared to shed light on the control mechanisms at the heart of the external management of Ukraine.[32]

------

29 Daria Zubkova (editor), "Zelenskyy Appoints Balan National Guard Commander, Kondratiuk First Deputy Commander," *Ukrainian News,* June 14, 2019. https://ukranews.com/en/news/637048-zelenskyy-appoints-balan-national-guard-commander-kondratiuk-first-deputy-commander

30 Simon Shuster, "Exclusive: How an Accused Russian Agent Worked With Rudy Giuliani in a Plot Against the 2020 Election," *TIME,* May 28, 2021 (updated June 3, 2021). https://time.com/6052302/andriy-derkach-profile/

"'This isn't even the deep state. It's a state-run corruption machine,' Derkach said with mild frustration, as though repeating things that should be obvious. 'The machine is called DemoCorruption.' This is the term Derkach invented for his baroque conspiracy theory, which holds that Biden sits atop a vast system of graft that permeates the Democratic Party and colludes with George Soros and other Western billionaires."

31 Andrii Derkach, Member of Ukrainian Parliament, "New details in the case of Burisma bribe, as well as new records of conversations testifying to international corruption and the external governance of Ukraine," *Wayback Machine* Internet Archive, June 29, 2020. https://web.archive.org/web/20210921150435/https://www.derkach.com.ua/en/publications/new-details-case-burisma-bribe-well-new-records-conversations-testifying-international-corruption-external-governance-ukraine/

32 Andrii Derkach, Member of Ukrainian Parliament, "NEW FACTS ABOUT INTERNATIONAL CORRUPTION, BURISMA AND SCHEME TO BANKRUPT UKRAINE," *Wayback Machine* Internet Archive, 2019. https://web.archive.org/web/20200130005256/https://derkach.com.ua/en/publications/new-facts-international-corruption-burisma-scheme-bankrupt-ukraine/

To wit, Biden and Poroshenko are heard discussing "the unconstructive position" of the Samopomich faction (in Parliament).[33]

Poroshenko somewhat gently riles Biden over the fact that "your faction" had lost its edge, urging the VP to find some time in his schedule and talk to Andrei Sadov, because "when I call him, he doesn't pick up the phone."[34]

Another episode relates to the resignation of Prime Minister Arseniy Yatsenyuk.[35]

The recording reveals that "Arseniy" was so afraid of Poroshenko that he asked Biden for guarantees of personal immunity just in case he got fired.

Biden then strongly enjoined Poroshenko not to touch Yatsenyuk to which the "Chocolate King" replied: "I will never hurt a man who is practically my own!"[36]

---

33 Daria Zubkova (editor), "Poroshenko Asks Ex-U.S. Vice President Biden To Pressure Samopomich To Support Appointment Of Ex-Finance Minister Yaresko As Prime Minister In 2016 – Derkach Tape," *Ukrainian News,* May 20, 2020. https://ukranews.com/en/news/703342-poroshenko-asks-ex-u-s-vice-president-biden-to-pressure-samopomich-to-support-appointment-of-ex

34 Andrii Derkach, Member of Ukrainian Parliament, NEW FACTS OF INTERNATIONAL CORRUPTION AND EXTERNAL GOVERNANCE OF UKRAINE," *Wayback Machine* Internet Archive, 2020. https://web.archive.org/web/20211201151318/https://www.derkach.com.ua/en/publications/new-facts-international-corruption-external-governance-ukraine/

35 "Derkach's tapes: Poroshenko assured Biden there would be no criminal cases against Yatsenyuk," *UNIAN,* June 20, 2023. https://www.unian.info/politics/derkach-s-tapes-poroshenko-assured-biden-there-would-be-no-criminal-cases-against-yatsenyuk-11046767.html

36 Обнародованы аудиозаписи с голосом Порошенко, который просит Байдена повлиять на Яценюка," *TASS,* June 22, 2020. https://tass.ru/mezhdunarodnaya-panorama/8788763

".... Yatsenyuk is affected by two recordings released on Monday. The second concerns the consequences of his planned resignation. 'My opinion is that Arseniy [Yatsenyuk] is worried that with the loss of the post of prime minister, he will lose his immunity < ... >, he is afraid of criminal prosecution against himself,' says a man whom Derkach identifies as Biden and who asks to protect the head of government. In response, his interlocutor declares that he can give 'for his part any personal guarantees, including the new prosecutor general, that there is nothing on him.' In addition, he promises to 'develop a scenario for the resignation [of the prime minister], which will give him a positive perception' and will not bring risks."

Origins of the Tapes

When first queried about what he was going to do about the Derkach "tapes," Volodymir Zelensky was hosting a press conference dedicated to his first year in office. Obviously, the question caught him off-guard on two counts:[37]

First, Poroshenko had pointed to the leaks coming from the Office of the Presidency.

Second, Poroshenko had implicitly conceded that the material on the tapes was genuine.

To be sure, many theories are circulating as to the provenance of the recordings.

Ukrainian experts were quick to point out an important detail: While Poroshenko's voice can be clearly heard on the tapes, Joe Biden's "sounds" as if emanating from a speaker.

Per Derkach's own account, the tapes were given to him by some journalists, but this obviously is a cover story to cover the real source of the "leak."[38]

Biden's representatives of course had their own explanations as to who might have leaked the tapes and as if on cue, they adopted the "Russian connection" theory.

According to Biden's team spokesman Andrew Bates, the Rossiya Segodnya (RT) network was involved in the distribution of the tapes. "The tapes have been thoroughly edited, and the whole thing isn't worth a damn."[39]

---

37 Simon Shuster, "Exclusive: How an Accused Russian Agent Worked With Rudy Giuliani in a Plot Against the 2020 Election," *TIME,* May 28, 2021 (updated June 3, 2021). https://time.com/6052302/andriy-derkach-profile/

"Ukrainian investigators are still trying to understand how the alleged Russian agent got his hands on those recordings of Biden in the first place, and whether any crimes were committed as part of the apparent leak. 'This was the biggest problem,' Zelensky says. 'With whose permission was [Biden] taped? And how did those tapes get from the office of the President to someone else?'"

38 Valentyn Nalyvaichenko: Everything is not so clear in the scandal with "the Derkach tapes" – he was deported from Russia long ago. Interview," *Ukrainian News,* May 27, 2020. https://ukranews.com/en/news/705017-valentyn-nalyvaichenko-everything-is-not-so-clear-in-the-scandal-with-the-derkach-tapes-he-was

"We can get bogged down in conspiracy theories, look for new Melnychenko and the like. As a professional, I suppose that Poroshenko could record the conversations himself to play safe, defend himself or even blackmail the interlocutor."

39 "Audio of Biden and Poroshenko - who is its author?" *Strana News,* May 21,

This version however reflects the confusion on the part of the Biden campaign for the Daily Beast had already published an article which purported to establish that Biden's conversations with the former president of Ukraine were part of an elaborate system aimed at throwing would-be hackers off-track.[40]

Ukrainian pundits also speculated as to whether it was an inside job or the work of Russian hackers.

The *Washington Post* was prompted to draw parallels with 2016 while hinting at a "Russian trail":

> Events resonate with the 2016 presidential election, when Russian operatives hacked and released emails from Democratic candidate Hillary Clinton's campaign manager and Democratic National Committee officials, which American intelligence agencies later concluded turned out to be a staged operation by Moscow aimed at strengthening Trump's position.[41]

The newspaper seemed willing to conjure up the "RussiaGate" ghosts as it conveniently omitted to take into account the precedent involving former Trump campaign adviser Papadopoulos who had been approached by the now infamous Professor Mifsud who purported to offer him thousands of Clinton emails allegedly obtained by Russian hackers.[42]

2020.   https://strana.news/news/268427-audio-bajdena-i-poroshenko-kto-eho-avtor.html

40 Erin Banco, Sam Brodey, Spencer Ackerman and Asawin Suebsaeng, "U.S. Intel Repeatedly Warned About Andriy Derkach, Rudy Giuliani's 'Russian Agent' Pal," *The Daily Beast,* September 17, 2020. https://www.thedailybeast.com/us-intel-repeatedly-warned-about-andriy-derkach-rudy-giulianis-russian-agent-pal

41 Paul Sonne and Rosalind S. Helderman, "Ukrainian lawmaker releases leaked phone calls of Biden and Poroshenko," *The Washington Post,* May 19, 2020. https://www.washingtonpost.com/national-security/ukrainian-lawmaker-releases-leaked-phone-calls-of-biden-and-poroshenko/2020/05/19/cc1e6030-9a26-11ea-b60c-3be060a4f8e1_story.html

42 Brooke Singman, "Diplomat who helped launch Russia probe speaks out, defends role," *Fox News,* May 10, 2019. https://www.foxnews.com/politics/former-australian-diplomat-alexander-downer-defends-work-pushes-back-on-claims-he-tried-to-trap-papadopoulos

The *Post* also failed to mention the scandal in Italy involving Mifsud, a lecturer at the private Italian university Link University, which erupted after Papadopoulos 'infamous May 2019 interview during which, in the midst of incessant allegations bearing on the Trump campaign's alleged proximity with Russian intelligence, the former Trump adviser bluntly stated that "He (Mifsud- author) was a CIA spy, supported by the Italian services."[43]

Papadopoulos had come to this conclusion after Mifsud, who by then had become director of the London Center for International Legal Practice, hired him as director of diplomatic relations in September 2016. According to Papadopoulos, Mifsud seemed actually more interested in the confidential files he dealt with in Brussels, and the London center was just a CIA front.

This story was related to the question as to who might have actually hacked into the DNC server in order to accuse Trump of collaborating with Russia.

But back to the possible origin of the tapes:

Former Ukrainian President Petro Poroshenko whose voice can clearly be heard on the tapes ventured to issue a statement on this issue a full two days after Derkach first broke the story.

Visibly confused if not inherently contradictory in nature, Poroshenko's statement claimed that:

> The audio files that were produced yesterday by a graduate of the Dzerzhinsky Higher School of the KGB in Moscow (referring to Derkach) are crude forgeries which however contain genuine material likely leaked from the Office of the incumbent president (Zelensky).

---

43 "Simona Mangiante, wife of Papadopoulos: 'Mifsud? a CIA spy supported by Italian services,'" Chronicles, *DagoSpia,* October 5, 2019. https://www.dagospia.com/rubrica-29/cronache/ldquo-me-ci-sono-pochi-dubbi-mifsud-era-spia-cia-appoggiata-215530.htm

"..Above all, Simona Mangiante also worked for the enigmatic Maltese professor Joseph Mifsud, who blew Papadopoulos the news of the emails during the period in which he taught at Link University, the private university where a piece of the ruling class of the 5 Stars was formed (including the former Minister of Defense Trenta and the current Vice-Minister for Foreign Affairs Del Re). The American government has been looking for him since he disappeared in May 2018, and has returned to ask Italy to account in recent days."

Again, Poroshenko disputed the form but not the substance of the material.

Poroshenko's version does not however stand up to scrutiny. First of all, any leak by the Office of the Presidency could only have occurred if recordings of conversations between Ukrainian and foreign officials were official policy.

In such a case, the conversations would be recorded in a formal manner before being stored in the archives of the Presidency even after the incumbent president had left office. But there is no such policy at the Bankova. Former employees of the Ukrainian security services themselves confirmed to *Strana News* that there is no policy requirement for mandatory recording of conversations.

According to former employees of the presidential security service, Poroshenko would have either taken them with him or altogether destroyed the entire audio library when he left office.

Another version circulating is that the leak originated from the State Service for Special Communications and Information Protection. The SSSCIP is formally tasked with the organization of such calls.

Voices of officers of the State Special Communication Service could indeed be heard at the beginning of every conversation between Poroshenko and Biden. The agency at the time of the conversations was headed by Leonid Yevdochenko, a man appointed by then-Secretary of the National Security and Defense Council Alexander Turchinov in 2015.

However, a source in the State Service assured the *Strana* website that wiretapping of the communication channel by its employees must be excluded for "the protected communication channel is set up so that it is immediately disconnected when an attempt is made to tap the line," says the source.

At least, former employees of the Presidential Administration as well as employees of the Security Service of Ukraine and the State Security Directorate interviewed by *Strana* all agree on one point: the conversations were indeed recorded from the office of the President of Ukraine.[44]

Keeping that in mind, a source in the State Guard Department categorically opined to *Strana:*

---

44 Порошенко мог слить пленки Байдена в сеть, *Strana News,* May 21, 2020. https://strana.news/news/268497-poroshenko-moh-slit-plenki-v-set.html

It is clearly that the voice of the President of Ukraine sounds close and clear while Biden's voice is on speakerphone. That is, the recording came from Poroshenko's office. At the same time the probability of that it was not sanctioned by Poroshenko himself is minimal because it is difficult to imagine why Poroshenko would put his own conversations with Biden on speakerphone if he himself had no reason to record it. Therefore, it is with probability close to 100% that we can say that the recordings were made with the ex-president's knowledge.[45]

A former employee of the Presidential Administration went further in stating that he was sure that Poroshenko himself was the source of the leaks.

On the eve of the presidential election, in February-March 2019, Poroshenko made a desperate attempt through then Prosecutor General Yuri Lutsenko to gain Trump's support. Lutsenko, according to his published correspondence, established contact through American citizens Lev Parnas and Igor Fruman with Giuliani and promised him killer dirt on Biden and his son. At the same time, he publicly criticized U.S. Ambassador Yovanovitch, accusing her of demanding at a meeting with him not to prosecute the 'untouchable list.' Poroshenko could have promised through Lutsenko to give Giuliani recordings of his conversations with Biden. And then either Giuliani or Lutsenko sent these recordings to Derkach.[46]

Finally, experts also interviewed by the website, including one SBU officer, believed that the most likely scenario was that the tapes were leaked by a specific circle of people who had access to these tapes as well as the servers on which they were stored. As such, individuals tasked with protecting the former president could have leaked the tapes without the president's knowledge in retaliation for

---

45 Ibid.
46 "Audio of Biden and Poroshenko - who is its author?" *Strana News,* May 21, 2020. https://strana.news/news/268427-audio-bajdena-i-poroshenko-kto-eho-avtor.html

Poroshenko's being notoriously lax in handing out salaries to his personal bodyguards.[47]

In the final analysis, no one in Ukraine knows to this day who leaked the tapes and this includes U.S. intelligence. Faced with a lack of facts on the issue, all resort to speculations, the most common of which incriminates the Kremlin.

By that logic, all of Biden's opponents (including Trump and his supporters) can conveniently be referred as "Putin's agents."

---

47 Ibid.

"'The recording, indeed, could have been conducted with some of his goals by Petro Poroshenko. But these records and the servers on which they were stored must have had access to a certain circle of people. For example, the security guards of the ex-president. From them, a leak could go without the knowledge of the president. Let me give you an example. As part of the investigation of the criminal case of wiretapping of ex-Prime Minister Honcharuk, the SBU tested several dozen employees of the UGO who could be involved in the wiretapping. The results shocked everyone: it turned out that 80% of them leaked official information to third parties. So I would not rule out just a corruption moment either. And if soon there will be new recordings of other conversations of Poroshenko with some other persons, it means that someone simply sold the entire music library. As for the wiretapping case for Goncharuk, it is dead. In reality, no one is investigating it. Soon, apparently, they will finally be buried,' says a special services officer."

PART I

A Tale of Two Elections

Election 2016: Operation Crossfire Hurricane

The opening salvo of what would become known as Operation Crossfire Hurricane was fired in Kiev with an investigation targeting then-Trump campaign director, Paul Manafort. The operation was geared to lay the ground for the narrative that the investigation then carried out by the Federal Bureau of Investigation between May 2016 and May 2017 would eventually reveal that there existed myriad material links between Trump associates and Russian operatives conspiring to interfere in the 2016 U.S. Presidential election. Trump himself would eventually be targeted via the appointment of a Special Counsel when suspicions arose that the newly elected president was in effect aiming to obstruct justice when he decided to fire then-FBI Director, James Comey.[48]

It would eventually be made public that on January 5, 2017, Comey had held a meeting with then Director of National Intelligence, James Clapper, former CIA Director, John Brennan and NSA Director, Mike Rogers during which they proceeded to brief then-President Barack Obama, that there existed serious grounds to believe that the Russians had intervened in the election in order to help Trump get elected.

The briefing was provided at the request of Obama who had been calling for an inquiry into the matter back in December 2016.

More specifically, the content of the conversation was reported to have focused on the relationship between newly appointed National

---

48 Mollie Hemingway, "Obama, Biden Oval Office Meeting On January 5 Was Key To Entire Anti-Trump Operation," *The Federalist*, May 8, 2020. https://thefederalist.com/2020/05/08/obama-biden-oval-office-meeting-on-january-5-was-key-to-entire-anti-trump-operation/

"Not only was information on Russia not fully shared with the incoming Trump team, as Obama directs, the leaks and ambushes made the transition chaotic, scared quality individuals away from working in the administration, made effective governance almost impossible, and materially damaged national security. When Comey was finally fired on May 9, in part for his duplicitousness regarding his handling of the Russia collusion theory, he orchestrated the launch of a Special Counsel probe that continued his efforts for another two years."

Security Adviser Michael Flynn and the Russian Ambassador to the U.S., Sergey Kislyak in violation of the Logan Act.[49]

It was also during that meeting that the infamous and now-debunked Steele dossier first surfaced.[50]

Former National Security Adviser, Susan Rice would eventually refer to the meeting held between herself, Joe Biden, Obama and then-Deputy Attorney General Sally Yates in an email written shortly before effectively leaving office on January 20, 2017. The email related how Obama insisted that the "investigation should be handled by the book, while he was not in any way asking about, initiating, or instructing anything from a law enforcement perspective."[51]

On January 6, 2017, Comey, Brennan, Clapper and Rogers issued a briefing to then President-elect Trump about which Comey stated: "At the conclusion of that briefing, I remained alone with the president-elect to brief him on some personally sensitive aspects of the information assembled during the assessment."[52]

Comey revealed that he then had decided to brief Trump separately about the "Steele Dossier," although informing the winner of the election that he was not personally targeted by the investigation.

---

49 "Bombshell Admission: Clapper Says Obama Made Them Do It," iHeartRadio | *The Rush Limbaugh Show,* October 7, 2019. https://news.iheart.com/featured/rush-limbaugh/content/2019-10-07-pn-rush-limbaugh-bombshell-admission-clapper-says-obama-made-them-do-it/

Clapper: "The message I'm getting from all this is, apparently what we were supposed to have done was to ignore the Russian interference, ignore the Russian meddling and the threat that it poses to us, and oh, by the way, blown off what the then-commander in chief, President Obama, told us to do, which was to assemble all the reporting that we could that we had available to us."

50 Company Intelligence Report 2016/080, "US Presidential Election: Republican Candidate Donald Trump's Activities in Russia and Compromising Relationship with the Kremlin." https://www.documentcloud.org/documents/3259984-Trump-Intelligence-Allegations.html

51 Brooke Singman, "Declassified Susan Rice email shows Comey suggested 'sensitive' info on Russia not be shared with Flynn," *Fox News,* May 19, 2020. https://www.foxnews.com/politics/susan-rice-email-declassified-release-is-imminent-source

"Rice continued: 'From a national security perspective, Comey said he does have some concerns that incoming NSA Flynn is speaking frequently with Russian Ambassador [Sergey] Kislyak. Comey said that could be an issue as it relates to sharing sensitive information. President Obama asked if Comey was saying that the NSC should not pass sensitive information related to Russia to Flynn.'"

52 M. Dowling, "It Was Comey Who Asked for the Private Meeting on January 6th, Not Trump," Independent Sentinel, June 9, 2017. https://www.independentsentinel.com/comey-asked-private-meeting-january-6/

Of note, Comey still made sure to mention FBI General Counsel James Baker's concern that owing to the scope of the investigation, "Trump's behavior, his conduct will fall within the scope of that work."[53]

The investigation would soon be transferred to Special Counsel Rober Mueller, a former FBI Director. The investigation would lead to the release of a report in 2019 that concluded that while Russian interference occurred in a "sweeping and systematic fashion" and that there were substantial links between Russians and the Trump campaign, the evidence available to investigators did not establish that the Trump campaign had "conspired or coordinated" with the Russian government.

Trump and his team denounced the whole investigation as a political witch-hunt, a claim disputed by the release of a report published in December 2019, by then Justice Department Inspector General, Michael E. Horowitz.[54]

No to be deterred, Trump entrusted then-U.S. Attorney General William Barr to pursue the investigation into the origins of Crossfire Hurricane.

Barr appointed John Durham to look into the matter and a report would be released in late 2022, criticizing the FBI and Justice Department and stating that (these agencies) "failed to uphold their

---

53 Kyle Cheney and Racael Bade (*Politico*), "Collusion? FBI's James Baker was linked to reporter who broke Trump dossier story," *SOTT,* December 22, 2017. https://www.sott.net/article/372161-Collusion-FBIs-James-Baker-was-linked-to-reporter-who-broke-Trump-dossier-story

"House Republicans are investigating contact between the FBI's top lawyer and a *Mother Jones* reporter in the weeks before the left-leaning outlet broke the first news story about the existence of a disputed dossier alleging ties between President Donald Trump and the Kremlin, according to two congressional GOP sources who described documents linking the two men."

54 Lauren Toms, Guy Taylor and Lauren Meier, "John Brennan and James Comey, Obama intelligence chiefs, under fire after Mueller report," *The Washington Times,* March 28, 2019. https://www.washingtontimes.com/news/2019/mar/28/john-brennan-and-james-comey-obama-intelligence-ch/

"Special counsel Robert Mueller's finding that there was no Trump campaign conspiracy with Russia to steal the 2016 election has unleashed a tsunami of outrage toward Obama-era intelligence chiefs, particularly former CIA Director John O. Brennan and former FBI Director James B. Comey, who are accused of pushing the allegation during congressional hearings, in social media posts and in highly charged interviews on television over the past two years."

important mission of strict fidelity to the law in connection with certain events and activities described in this report." The report also concluded that a full investigation should never have been launched in complete contradiction with the findings of Horowitz's report on this issue.

The Manafort Smoking Gun

The start of what was to turn into a controversy plaguing much of the Trump presidency occurred in the midst of the U.S. presidential campaign on August 19, 2016.

Then, as the poll numbers indicated a real momentum for the New York billionaire, Paul Manafort, the then acting head of the Trump campaign suddenly resigned.[55]

The reason invoked bore on allegations that Manafort had received money from former Ukrainian President Yanukovych's Party of Regions for his work as a political consultant.

On August 2, 2016, Pulitzer Prize winner and regular columnist for the *Washington Post*, Anne Applebaum, signaled the start of the campaign based on allegations that Trump allegedly had ties with Russia during an interview she gave to the Ukrainian TV station Hromadske.[56]

---

55 Chloe Chaplain, "Donald Trump's campaign manager Paul Manafort steps down after two months," *The Standard,* August 19, 2016. https://www.standard. co.uk/news/politics/trump-s-campaign-manager-steps-down-after-just-two-months-a3325056.html

56 "'For some reason, Trump and his entourage are very interested in the issue of Ukraine'—Pulitzer winner," https://hromadske.ua/posts/trampa-ta-ioho-otochennia-chomus-duzhe-tsikavyt-pytannia-ukrainy-pulittserivska-laureatka

"It is important to understand who Trump surrounds himself, what kind of people are around him. As Ukrainians probably well know, one such person is Paul Manafort. It is known that he worked for Viktor Yanukovych. He was also linked to Yanukovych's business interests. In addition, he has ties to Ukrainian and Russian oligarchs. In particular, together with him he was engaged in various investment projects. For American politics, such a person is so unusual and corrupt that, I think, Americans have not even realized it yet. For example, the media do not yet know how to work with it. After all, American politics has not yet encountered such people at such a high level. Another person close to Trump is Carter Page. He has spent a lot of time in Russia over the past decades, investing in Russia. He has relations with both Gazprom and Russian oligarchs.In other words, Trump is surrounded by people close to Russia—and this is very unusual not only for American politics, but also for

Applebaum pointed to Manafort as the conduit between the putative Republican nominee and the Russian Federation.

Applebaum's interview was followed by somewhat of a lull on the issue, until August 14, 2016, when the *New York Times* published a comprehensive report compiled by the paper's Kiev correspondents.[57]

The article, citing unnamed NABU officials, claimed that "handwritten notes were found indicating $12.7 million in confidential cash payments intended for Manafort from Yanukovich's pro-Russian political party (the Party of Regions) between 2007 and 2012."[58]

The piece underlined Manafort's $18 million partnership agreement with Russian oligarch Oleg Deripaska related to the purchasing of assets of Ukrainian cable television as evidence of a "Russian trail."[59]

The next day, it was the *Washington Post*'s turn to publish its own feature story about Manafort and his alleged ties to the Russians.[60]

It too referred to Manafort's ties to Deripaska.

The story was then picked up by the Ukrainian English-language publication *Kievpost* before *Politico* stepped into the fray, suggesting

---

American business. There is no doubt about it. But that's only one part of the story."

57 Andrew E. Kramer, Mike McIntire and Barry Meier, "The Black Ledger in Ukraine Lists Cash for Trump's Campaign Chief," *The New York Times*, August 15, 2016. https://www.nytimes.com/2016/08/15/us/politics/what-is-the-black-ledger.html

"Before he fled to Russia two years ago, Mr. Yanukovych and his Party of Regions relied heavily on the advice of Mr. Manafort and his firm, who helped them win several elections," the story notes. "During that period, Mr. Manafort never registered as a foreign agent with the United States Justice Department — as required of those seeking to influence American policy on behalf of foreign clients — although one of his subcontractors did. "In the 400-page ledger kept at party headquarters, inside a room which contained two safes full of $100 bills, Manafort's name appeared 22 times over five years, according to Ukraine's National Anti-Corruption Bureau, which obtained the document and has an evidence-sharing agreement with the FBI. The Times says the purpose of the payments is not specified. Manafort lawyer Richard Hibey said his client never received the cash in question and did nothing illegal or corrupt."

58 Ibid.

59 Ibid.

60 James Hohmann, "The Daily 202: Can Trump chairman Paul Manafort survive new Ukraine revelations?" [analysis], *The Washington Post*, August 15, 2016. https://www.washingtonpost.com/news/powerpost/paloma/daily-202/2016/08/15/daily-202-can-trump-chairman-paul-manafort-survive-new-ukraine-revelations/57b0ec7ccd249a2fe363ba20/

that Manafort was at the heart of a Russian operation involving the hacking of the DNC server.[61]

The article proceeded to name Konstantin Kilimnik, Manafort's interpreter, as the acting liaison between Trump's campaign manager and Russian intelligence.[62]

Interestingly, the National Anti-Corruption Bureau of Ukraine (NABU) had prior to the media blitz proceeded on July 18, 2016 to publish 22 samples of receipts allegedly extracted from the secret accounting books kept by Viktor Yanukovych and the Party of Regions on its official website.[63]

NABU issued a statement pointing to the "receipts" as evidence and stated that these were confidential cash payments of $12.7 million, which Paul Manafort had allegedly signed off on between 2007 and 2012.

At this point, it is necessary to delve into the context and origins of NABU.[64]

The National Anti-Corruption Bureau of Ukraine was an agency created by the Obama/Biden administration with the stated aim of uprooting corruption and bringing Ukrainian oligarchs to heel.

61 Interfax-Ukraine, "NABU says Trump's campaign chief could get $12.7 million from Regions Party's 'black ledger,'" *Kyiv Post,* August 15, 2016. https://www.kyivpost.com/post/9713

62 Kenneth P. Vogel, "Manafort's man in Kiev," *Politico,* August 18, 2016. https://www.politico.com/story/2016/08/paul-manafort-ukraine-kiev-russia-konstantin-kilimnik-227181

"A Russian Army-trained linguist who has told a previous employer of a background with Russian intelligence, Kilimnik started working for Manafort in 2005 when Manafort was representing Ukrainian oligarch Rinat Akhmetov, a gig that morphed into a long-term contract with Viktor Yanukovych, the Kremlin-aligned hard-liner who became president of Ukraine."

63 "Clarification on mentioning Paul Manafort's name in the 'black ledger' of the Party of Regions," National Anti-corruption Bureau of Ukraine (NABU) [official website], August 18, 2016. https://nabu.gov.ua/news/novyny-rozyasnennya-shchodo-zgaduvannya-imya-pola-manaforta-u-chorniy-buhgalteriyi-pr/

64 "National Anti-corruption Bureau of Ukraine (NABU)," *Devex.* https://www.devex.com/organizations/national-anti-corruption-bureau-of-ukraine-nabu-131705

"On 16 April 2015 the President of Ukraine Petro Poroshenko signed two decrees: № 217/2015 – decree on founding the National Anti-corruption Bureau of Ukraine and № 218/2015 – decree on appointing Artem Sytnyk the Bureau's Director. This provided a starting point for a new state agency. The first order signed by the NABU Director on 23 April 2015 approved the Bureau's structure and stuffing. On 24 April Gizo Uglava was appointed First Deputy Director. Later two more Deputy Directors were appointed: Anatoly Novak and Tetyana Varvarska."

The agency was given the preeminent role of tackling corruption in Ukraine so as to pave the way for that country's future admittance into the hallowed halls of Western organizations such as the EU and NATO.

As it turns out, the NABU (as well as the subsequently created State Bureau of Investigation (GBI) and Specialized Anti-Corruption Prosecutor's Office (SAP)) became tools through which the Americans proceeded to implement their own comprehensive system of externalized control over Ukraine's internal politics as well as over the country's domestic law enforcement agencies.[65]

Beyond the questions centering on the means through which NABU managed to gain possession of Yanukovich's secret book-keeping, one is tempted to wonder: Why did they wait to do so until after Manafort was appointed as Trump's campaign director?

In order to begin understanding the underpinnings of this hatchet job, it is important to take a step back and examine who amongst some of the most unsavory characters operating in the Ukrainian national security state structure might have played a role in ferreting out the American businessman.

Once we have established the identities of these individuals, it will be highlighted to what extent the law was shirked in order to produce the kind of evidence normally deemed inadmissible in a court of law.

The individuals deemed to have played a role in framing Manafort and setting in motion the wheels of what would later be known the world over as "RussiaGate" are:[66]

---

65 "New Facts of International Corruption and External Governance of Ukraine," Andrii Derkach, Member of Ukrainian Parliament (archive.org), 2020. https://web.archive.org/web/20211201151318/https://www.derkach.com.ua/en/publications/new-facts-international-corruption-external-governance-ukraine/

66 "Kyiv court opens case against NABU chief, MP Leschenko on Manafort leaks," *Interfax-Ukraine,* October 24, 2017. https://en.interfax.com.ua/news/general/456824.html

"Kyiv District Administrative Court has opened a case pursuant to a complaint lodged by nonaligned Ukrainian MP Boryslav Rozenblat involving the National Anti-Corruption Bureau of Ukraine (NABU) chief Artem Sytnyk and Petro Poroshenko Bloc MP Serhiy Leschenko. According to the court's website, Rozenblat wants the court to recognize as illegal actions of NABU chief Sytnyk, who made public and disseminated information about U.S. citizen Paul Manafort, the chairman of U.S. President Donald Trump's election campaign. Manafort's name and alleged signature

- The head of the NABU, Artem Sytnik;

- Ukrainian MP Serhiy Leshchenko;

- First deputy director of the National Anti-Corruption Bureau Gizo Uglava;

- The head of the special investigation department of the Prosecutor General's Office Serhiy Gorbatyuk;

- The former deputy head of the Security Service of Ukraine, General Viktor Trepak.

Viktor Trepak is the individual who can be credited for having initiated the scandal which led to Paul Manafort's resignation followed by the launch of a campaign aimed at discrediting the winner of the 2016 U.S. presidential race, Donald Trump.[67]

Viktor Trepak had resigned as First Deputy Director of the SBU in April 2016 before recycling himself as a teacher at the SBU Academy. A couple of months later, he somewhat inexplicably took possession of the 585 hand-filled A4 pages "black book" featuring charts and columns showing the dates, names and descriptives next to payouts dished out in exchange for favors rendered to former Ukrainian President Yanukovych's Party of Regions.[68]

These hand-written entries altogether constituted the "black book" through which the Party of Regions purchased influence through the remunerating of dozens of politicians and journalists.[69]

---

appeared in the so-called black books [payment ledger] of the disgraced former Ukrainian President Viktor Yanukovych's Party of Regions in a pretrial investigation, leading to "interference in the 2016 U.S. election campaign and damaging Ukraine's interests."

67 "Clarification on mentioning Paul Manafort's name in the 'black ledger' of the Party of Regions."

"Among the names of persons on the list of the so-called 'black ledger of the Party of Regions,' which, according to V. Trepak, is being investigated by detectives of the National Anti-Corruption Bureau of Ukraine, is among others Paul Manafort. According to the lists, a total of more than USD 20.11 million has been allocated for expenses related to this person since 2007.12.7. The last entry in the "book" regarding P. Manafort dates back to October 5, 2012. We emphasize that the presence of P. Manafort's name in the "lists" does not mean that he really received these funds, because the recipients' column contains signatures of other persons."

68 Ibid.

69 "Riaboshapka appoints SBU ex-first deputy chief Trepak as his deputy," *Kyiv Post,* October 8, 2019. https://archive.kyivpost.com/ukraine-politics/riaboshapka-

The personal signatures of every single individual alleged to have been on the Party of Region's payroll featured in the column opposite the amount of monies received except that of Paul Manafort's.[70]

To be sure, Trepak was immediately confronted with having to publicly explain how he managed to get his hands on the "evidence" and his explanations to say the least were left wanting.[71]

Per Trepak's version, an "unknown person" had managed to enter his domicile before leaving a large envelope on the stairwell while escaping the concierge's scrutiny.

Trepak then explained that, rather than heading to his former office at the Security Services of Ukraine, he opted instead to head straight to the NABU headquarters where upon arrival, he signed off on the documents and issued a statement about the very nature of the materials.[72]

After Trepak's departure, NABU investigators immediately set out to interrogate the concierge at Trepak's domicile. The concierge promptly stated that she had not seen anyone.

Her statements were corroborated by CCTV footage which failed to reveal any individual entering the premises, although NABU never even bothered to mention that in their report.

In other words, no independent evidence nor witnesses existed to corroborate Trepak's written statement that he found a large envelope containing documents that was left by an individual at his domicile.[73]

---

appoints-sbu-ex-first-deputy-chief-trepak-as-his-deputy.html

"In the period after the Revolution of Dignity, Trepak was known for participating in the investigation into the case of 'diamond prosecutors' and transferring of the documents on the so-called 'black bookkeeping' of the Party of Regions to the National Anti-Corruption Bureau of Ukraine in May 2016."

70 Андрей Портнов, "Теперь Пол Манафорт может запросто пустить по миру главу НАБУ / Лента соцсетей / Страна" [opinion], *Strana News,* August 17, 2016. https://strana.news/opinions/27759-teper-pol-manafort-mozhet-zaprosto-pustit-po-miru-glavu-nabu.html

71 "No Manafort signature in Yanukovych Party's 'black ledgers' – Lutsenko," *UNIAN,* August 7, 2019. https://www.unian.info/politics/10642956-no-manafort-signature-in-yanukovych-party-s-black-ledgers-lutsenko.html

72 Ibid.

73 Volodymyr Boiko, "Artem Sytnyk's Terrible Vengeance: How Smuggler Alperin Suffered Because of Hillary Clinton," *Naspravdi.Today,* December 12, 2019. https://naspravdi.today/en/2019/12/12/artem-sytnyk-s-terrible-vengeance-how-smuggler-alperin-suffered-because-of-hillary-clinton/

"Of course, these records had no evidential value, and it is impossible to accuse

The dearth of evidence did not dissuade NABU from moving ahead and opening a criminal case based solely on the delivery by a former SBU official of a "notebook" of unknown origin.

The problem was compounded by the requirements under Ukrainian criminal procedure that in order to initiate a criminal case, the origin of the documents should be established independently in order for a court to call for an investigation.

As things stood, the "evidence" had been acquired in gross violation of the Code of Criminal Procedure and other laws of Ukraine, which in turn banned the use of said materials in future court proceedings.

This legal violation did not prevent the fact that based on a simple statement issued by Trepak on May 27, 2016, a criminal case was eventually filed purporting to involve the Party of Regions and its collaborators having engaged in crimes of corruption totaling more than 10 billion UAH.

Because Trepak's "notebooks" allegedly implied the disbursement of funds ranging from two to several million dollars and because Manafort's name was listed amongst the entries, nobody seemed to question why *entries featuring millions of dollars in payments pointed to services such as the purchase of paper and pencils.*[74]

---

that same Manafort of receiving cash from the President Yanukovych's 'black books' and evading taxes in his home country. But in March 2016, Manafort became the head of Presidential nominee Donald Trump's campaign, and his notoriety became a perfect target for compromising Trump himself."

74 "Yovanovitch's List," Хроніки Українських Йолопів (volodymyrboyko. com). https://volodymyrboyko.com/english/yovanovitchs-list/

"In May 2016, following Karen Greenaway's orders, the First Deputy Head of Security Service of Ukraine Viktor Trepak, who at that time had already been fired once from SSU because of outside affiliations with the U.S. Embassy (as it turned out, Trepak carried out Ambassador Pyett's and Deputy Chief of Mission Kent's very peculiar orders in order to force the Prosecutor General Viktor Shokin to close the criminal proceeding against Burisma company, where the son of the U.S. Vice President was employed), shared information about how he allegedly stumbled upon the 'Party of Regions black book' near his own house and handed it over to the National Anticorruption Bureau of Ukraine. At the same time, Kent handed over copies of a couple of pages from the 'black book' to Leshchenko for publishing with the intent of creating some fuss around Manafort. But since Leshchenko didn't bother to read what he was publishing in 'Ukrainska Pravda,' because of Kent's and Greenaway's negligence, he also shared the entry with the illegal money payment from the Party of Regions to 'Ukrainska Pravda,' where Leshchenko himself had been working at the time."

On May 30, 2016, a team of the bureau's detectives led by Roman Yegizarov registered criminal case 52016000000000166 in the Unified Register of Pre-Trial Investigations at Trepak's request.

The filing featured allegations about violations of Article 369, subsection 4 of the Criminal Code of Ukraine which in turn kickstarted a pre-trial investigation.

Again, issues of admissibility stood front and center for Article 214, subsection 1 of the Ukrainian Code of Criminal Procedure mandated that the registration of the application in the Registry be effected no later than 5pm on May 28, 2016 when in fact, the filing only took place on May 30, 2016.

This provision of the criminal procedure Code aimed at precisely avoiding the potential forgery of submitted documents and preventing interference by third parties.

In order to create the appearance of due diligence in their preliminary investigation, NABU investigators had proceeded to search the premises belonging to the building's management company, the lodge of the concierge as well as Trepak's own apartment following an order issued by investigative judge Andriy Makukha whose jurisdiction included the Solomensky District Court of Kiev.

These "diligences" did not however prevent NABU from coming up empty-handed in trying to establish the reliability of Trepak's statements bearing on someone dropping the documents at the concierge's lodge.

In the end, the "evidence" leveled against Manafort which led to his downfall never had any legal basis.

But back to our story.

At this point, NABU First Deputy bureau chief Gizo Uglava immediately took over the case.[75]

The background of this official is somewhat puzzling.

Uglava hailed from Georgia before settling in Kiev.

---

75 National Anti-Corruption Bureau of Ukraine, "Gizo Uglava assumes powers as acting NABU Director" [news release], April 18, 2022. https://nabu.gov.ua/en/news/novyny-povnovazhennya-dyrektora-nabu-vykonuye-gizo-uglava/

"From April 17, 2022, due to the expiration of the office of NABU Director Artem Sytnyk, the respective powers will be temporarily executed by his First Deputy Gizo Uglava. According to the Law 'On NABU,' in case of termination of office or dismissal of NABU director, the respective powers are exercised by their first deputy until a new director is appointed."

He first came to Ukraine in 2015 at the recommendation of former Georgian President Saakashvili, a man with whom Uglava had worked in Georgia.

Despite the fact that Uglava neither spoke Ukrainian nor had any knowledge of Ukrainian law, he miraculously became the first deputy of the NABU.

In order to get Uglava confirmed in this position in February 2015, Ukrainian MPs Yegor Sobolev and Serhiy Leshchenko proceeded to specifically amend the law bearing on the selection process of officials called to work at the National Anti-Corruption Bureau of Ukraine.

As the law initially mandated that putative candidates to NABU meet specific criteria such as fluency in Ukrainian and a requisite knowledge of that country's legal system, the amendment was necessary because Gizo Uglava, at the time still a citizen of Georgia, failed to fulfill either condition.[76]

Following Uglava's appointment, NABU Chief Artem Sytnik confided that the Georgian's candidacy had received the support of officials working at the embassies of the USA, Canada, Germany and France.[77]

Owing to his appointment as NABU's Number 2, Gizo Uglava instantly became the all-seeing eye of the U.S. embassy in Kiev.

This in turn explains why upon securing his position, Uglava immediately set out to turn General Trepak's "notebooks" into admissible evidence.[78]

---

76 Ibid.

"Gizo Uglava was born on Nov. 18, 1975 in Kutaisi, Georgia. Since 2015 he has been a citizen of Ukraine. Gizo Uglava started his career at the Prosecutor's Office of Georgia in 1998, where he worked until Nov. 7, 2012. During this period he went from an intern at the Imereti Regional Prosecutor's Office to the Deputy Chief Prosecutor of Georgia. Gizo Uglava is one of the persons behind the idea of launching NABU. In April 2015, he was appointed First Deputy Director of NABU."

77 ITTA Editorial Office, "G7 Ambassadors meet with NABU First Dpty Head Uglava," April 25, 2022. https://itta.info/en/g7-ambassadors-meet-with-nabu-first-dpty-head-uglava/

"'Ambassadors were pleased to meet with Ukraine's NABU Acting Head Gizo Uglava for a productive exchange on NABU's activity in wartime. The fight against corruption increases Ukraine's resilience. Ambassadors support protection of Ukraine's NABU's institutional independence under martial law,' the G7 said on Twitter on Monday."

78 "Who is Viktor Trepak, Ukraine's New Deputy Prosecutor General?," *hro* (hromadske.ua), October 9, 2019. https://hromadske.ua/en/posts/who-is-viktor-

To do so, the team of NABU detectives working under his authority proceeded to manufacture their own independent "evidence" by claiming that the "secret accounting book" was allegedly kept in the office of the Party of Regions located at 10 Lipska Street.

It should be mentioned that in the wake of the Maidan events, the offices of the Party of Regions had been completely destroyed by fire.[79]

With the offices having been thoroughly consumed by fire, one cannot help but wonder how the material miraculously escaped destruction before ending up in the hands of a good Samaritan.

This version is further called into question by the fact that fire-fighters never reported having found any papers.

A more plausible version is that the "notebooks" were crude forgeries manufactured by Trepak himself as he had belonged to the operational units of the SBU which were known to have experience in such matters.

On May 28, 2016, the Kiev newspaper *Zerkalo Nedeli* published a lengthy interview with General Trepak about the circumstances leading up to his getting his hands on the "evidence."

It bears noting that *Zerkalo Nedeli* is a publication financed by billionaire George Soros and is thus closely associated with the U.S. Embassy. It is therefore not surprising that the first article about the infamous "black box office" records of the Party of Regions appeared in this very newspaper.[80]

---

trepak-ukraines-new-deputy-prosecutor-general

"But Trepak wasn't about to go quietly. In May of 2016, Trepak found himself in possession of the so-called 'black ledger' detailing $2 billion of corrupt bribes and payoffs – including to Manafort– belonging to the previous ruling Party of Regions. He passed the ledger to the National Anti-Corruption Bureau (NABU), which was later leaked to the press."

79 "Ukraine: Man killed by fire in Party of Regions' office," Belarus news, *euroradio.fm,* February 18, 2014. https://euroradio.fm/en/ukraine-man-killed-fire-party-regions-office

"Several dozen protesters threw stones and Molotov cocktails at the office of the Party of Regions in Lipskaya Street in Kiev earlier today. Maidan protesters managed to seize the first floor of the building for 20 minutes. They took away state flags and some documents from the office."

80 UAWire, "Ukraine's National Anti-Corruption Bureau received more evidence tying former Trump adviser to Yanukovych regime," November 13, 2016. https://uawire.org/news/ukraine-s-national-anti-corruption-bureau-received-more-evidence-tying-former-trump-adviser-to-yanukovych-regime

According to *Zerkalo's* own editorial board, Trepak visited them on May 26.

Trepak was so thrilled about the "sensational discovery" of the "notebooks" that he thought it more important to give an interview to that specific media outlet *before* reporting his find to NABU the following day.

Journalists who know Trepak well have described him as not too subtle which is why many an eyebrow was raised when the content of the interview with the newspaper instantly turned to the topic of Paul Manafort and Ukrainian politicians connected with the Party of Regions.

As if acting on cue, Sergiy Leshchenko (a well-known journalist who had once worked on the team assigned to Sergey Lyovochkin, the then head of the presidential administration during Yanukovich's time), promptly joined in the campaign aimed at promoting the "notebooks."

Leshchenko had once been mandated to write a tell-all book about former Prime Minister Yulia Tymoshenko's gas scams on the instruction of Lyovochkin.[81]

He had actively supported the Maidan, and after the coup in Ukraine he joined George Soros' team and was promptly elected to the Verkhovna Rada of Ukraine.[82]

"'According to the weekly, recently NABU received additional evidence of payments for Manafort from the accounts affiliated with the former President of Ukraine, Viktor Yanukovych. The evidence was indicative of financial transactions in the European banks where Manafort received money,' Zerkalo Nedeli reported."

81 "MP Leshchenko: Manafort Should Be Questioned in Ex-Minister of Justice Lavrynovych Case," *Ukrainska Pravda,* August 19, 2016. https://www.pravda.com. ua/eng/news/2016/08/19/7118142/

"'There are documents that show that Mr. Manafort took part in writing a report by Skadden, Arps, Slate, Meagher & Flom LLP, which was justifying the criminal case against former Prime Minister Yulia Tymoshenko and the court decision in this case. The documents indicate that Mr. Manafort reviewed this report himself, edited it before publication and gave comments regarding the contents of this report,' Leshchenko said."

82 Sergii Leshchenko, Journalist and former Member of Parliament, Network participant, European Leadership Network. https://www.europeanleadershipnetwork. org/person/sergii-leshchenko/

"In 2013, Mr. Leshchenko was awarded a Press Prize by the German ZEIT Foundation and in 2014 he was honored with the NDI's Democracy Award. Sergii was Reagan-Fascell Fellow in the National Endowment for Democracy (Washington, DC). He is the author of two books about high level corruption in Ukraine."

Leshchenko set out to write a detailed article about the discovery of the "black box" alleged to incriminate the regionalists as well as its "sensational" content before publishing it on the website of the Internet edition of *Ukrainska Pravda*.

The content of the article was then used by NABU to issue search warrants for Trepak's apartment and the concierge's lodging.

As we have seen, while these searches yielded nothing, they provided the appearance of a criminal case upon which (by then) deputy Leshchenko decided to expound during a press conference held in Parliament on May 31, 2016.

And so it was that General Trepak's "notebook" came to assume a life of its own.

NABU and those standing to gain from promoting the story however felt that more steps were needed to fuel the scandal, and this led to the agency's decision to post 22 extracts of the "notebook" on its website on July 18, 2016 with the aim of linking Manafort to Yanukovych.[83]

NABU cynically accompanied the posting of the material with the following statement:

> We emphasize that the presence of P. Manafort's name in the "lists" does not mean that he really received these funds, because the column of recipients contains the signatures of other persons. The pre-trial investigation in this case continues.[84]

---

83 "Clarification on mentioning Paul Manafort's name in the 'black ledger' of the Party of Regions."

"Among the names of persons on the list of the so-called 'black ledger of the Party of Regions,' which, according to V. Trepak, is being investigated by detectives of the National Anti-Corruption Bureau of Ukraine, is among others Paul Manafort. According to the lists, a total of more than USD 20.11 million has been allocated for expenses related to this person since 2007.12.7. The last entry in the 'book' regarding P. Manafort dates back to October 5, 2012. We emphasize that the presence of P. Manafort's name in the 'lists' does not mean that he really received these funds, because the recipients' column contains signatures of other persons. The pre-trial investigation in this proceeding is ongoing."

84 Ibid.

Soon, the combined effect of the newspaper publications and references to the NABU website led to the story being picked up by the American mainstream media.

The fate of Trump's campaign manager was sealed.

Had the "notebook" been "uncovered" by an ordinary citizen, the public would never have believed in the whole story.

It had required the alliance of a former high-ranking SBU official and a prominent journalist to provide the scintilla of legitimacy needed to substantiate the general's claims about the "notebooks."

Moreover, nobody questioned how oddly the former first deputy of the SBU acted as a simple operative tasked with collecting evidence outside the scope of his own-mandated operational and investigative prerogatives without any grounds nor authority to do so.

To be sure, Ukrainian President Poroshenko would later for the sake of appearances publicly scold General Trepak for this violation.

In July 2019, Trepak decided to run for parliament and was featured in 10th position on the "Civic Position" list of candidates.[85]

It turns out that the leader of that party and its designated number one on the electoral list was Anatoliy Gritsenko.

Gritsenko had once served as Ukraine's defense minister in 2005–2007 and he was a perennial presidential candidate in the 2010, 2014 and 2019 elections.[86]

Prior to becoming minister, he underwent language training and training for foreign officers at the U.S. Air Force Academy while Gritsenko's wife, Yulia Mostovaya, worked as the editor-in-chief of the (Soros-financed) weekly newspaper *Zerkalo* to which Trepak

---

85 "Who is Viktor Trepak, Ukraine's New Deputy Prosecutor General?"

"His days of politics weren't behind him, however – he also joined the campaign team of Anatoliy Hrytsenko during the Ukrainian presidential campaign earlier this year."

86 Anatoliy Grytsenko, Former Defence Minister; Former Chairman of the National Security and Defence Committee in the Ukrainian Parliament, Network participant, European Leadership Network. https://www.europeanleadershipnetwork. org/person/anatoliy-grytsenko/

"From 2005 until 2007, Dr Grytsenko served as Defence Minister of Ukraine in the governments of Yulia Tymoshenko, Yuriy Yekhanurov and Victor Yanukovich. Grytsenko went on to serve as the Chairman of the National Security and Defence Committee at the Parliament of Ukraine (2007–2012), and as the Chairman of the subcommittee on fighting money laundering (201–2014)."

decided to grant the interview which would ignite the smear campaign leading to Manafort's resignation.[87]

While all this could be a coincidence, the development of the story about the "black" accounting of the Party of Regions looked like a well-orchestrated scheme designed to link the Trump campaign to the Russians, whether through Manafort or other ludicrous means.

Despite the lack of evidence, American and Ukrainian media kept the Manafort scandal afloat, which in turn caused considerable reputational damage to Donald Trump.

In any event, this perception of the events convinced Ukrainian MP Andriy Derkach to conclude that Ukraine had interfered in the 2016 U.S. presidential election owing to the manipulation of concocted evidence provided by Ukrainian officials operating at the behest of individuals associated with the Democratic Party.[88]

In April 2017, Derkach initiated a criminal case by sending a complaint to the Prosecutor General's Office.

In it, he demanded that light be shed on the circumstances surrounding the emergence of the "black accounting of the Party of Regions."[89]

Derlach also sought to draw attention to the illegal disclosure of the investigation materials.

As a result of Derkach's complaint, the Prosecutor General's Office of Ukraine registered criminal proceedings (№ 42017000000002470

---

87 Yulia Mostovaya [photo], *UNIAN*. https://photo.unian.info/photo/1669-yuliya-mostovaya

88 "Derkach was deported from Russia in 2017, – Nalyvaichenko. Document," *Ukrainian News,* May 27, 2020. https://ukranews.com/en/news/704997-derkach-was-deported-from-russia-in-2017-nalyvaichenko-document

"'As far as I know, the people who passed these tapes for disclosure to the Member of the Parliament Andrii Derkach wanted to draw attention to the horrible corruption and lies in the Ukrainian government at the highest level. And these people are located in Ukraine,' Nalyvaichenko said."

89 David Stern, "Ukrainian MP seeks probe of Ukraine-Clinton ties," *Politico,* August 16, 2017. https://www.politico.com/story/2017/08/16/ukraine-andrei-derkach-clinton-investigation-241704

"In the official registration of the criminal case — which Derkach posted on his Facebook page — officials said the investigation would look into whether Ukrainian authorities defamed Manafort by publicizing his possible connection to the black ledgers, "creating the impression of [Ukraine's] illegal interference in the U.S. elections."

of 01.08.2017) bearing on violations of Article 387, subsection 2 of the Criminal Code of Ukraine.

The complaint alleged interference of NABU and other Ukrainian officials in the 2016 U.S. Presidential elections.

Among those involved: Ukrainian MP Serhiy Leshchenko for his role in igniting the Manafort scandal, four high-ranking employees of the U.S. Embassy in Ukraine, the Ukrainian Ambassador to the U.S. Valery Chalyi, former deputy head of the SBU Viktor Trepak for his role in leaking the Leshchenko records regarding Manafort, and a number of other employees of the Ukrainian security services.

Republicans welcomed the initiative of the PGO and unaffiliated MP Andriy Derkach to seek prosecution of those it deemed responsible for Manafort's travails in Ukraine.[90]

At a U.S. congressional hearing, the new head of the FBI Christopher Wray promised to conduct a "thorough and comprehensive investigation of foreign, including Ukrainian, interference in the U.S. elections."[91]

This promptly led to NABU putting Derkach and his employees at the media holding company under surveillance.[92]

NABU hacked into the Wi-Fi network of Derkach's office as well as media editorial offices of the Era TV channel, Radio Era FM, the Era Media website, and other media outlets designed to carry out a

---

90 Ibid.

"A conservative watchdog group, Foundation for Accountability & Civic Trust (FACT), also filed a complaint with the Federal Election Commission, claiming Chalupa "knowingly solicited" damaging information on Manafort from Ukrainian officials."

91 "Did Ukraine try to interfere in the 2016 election on Clinton's behalf?," *CBS News,* July 13, 2017. https://www.cbsnews.com/news/did-ukraine-try-to-interfere-in-the-2016-election/

"Even Republicans who have been critical of the Trump administration over the Russia matter have recently talked about the story. On Wednesday, Republican Sen. Lindsey Graham pressed President Trump's nominee for FBI director, Christopher Wray, on whether he would look into any Ukrainian interference in the 2016 election."

92 Interfax-Ukraine, "MP Derkach complains about being followed by SBU, NABU," *Kyiv Post,* May 11, 2018. https://archive.kyivpost.com/ukraine-politics/mp-derkach-complains-followed-sbu-nabu.html

"'If actions by NABU or the SBU will endanger my life or the lives of my assistances and independent journalists, I will act in accordance with Article 39 of Ukraine's Criminal Code (extreme necessity),' the letter says. As earlier reported, in July 2017 the PGO opened a pretrial investigation into alleged interference by NABU in the 2016 U.S. presidential election."

number of provocations against journalists through the tapping of the phones of all employees and assistants.

Then on 16 August 2017, NABU raided the mobile studio of Radio "Era." The further pursuit of this operation was preempted by the PGO's published reply to the MP's request through which it became known that a criminal case was targeting Artem Sytnik, the head of NABU and some of his deputies. As a result, NABU detective units and the Bureau's assault team literally aborted an operation a dozen meters away from the MP's office before driving back to their base.

It was then MP Boryslav Rozenblat's turn to file a similar lawsuit in the District Administrative Court of Kiev.[93]

On December 11, 2018, the court issued a decision (No. 826/12998/17) holding that NABU head Artem Sytnik and MP and journalist Serhiy Leshchenko had illegally published unsubstantiated materials with the intent to interfere in the American election.

But the legal war did not end there as the Democratic Party's Ukrainian operatives retaliated by filing case against those who had exposed their machinations, which resulted in the dismissal of the Derkach complaint in January 2019 on recommendation of senior investigator Mikhail Nechitalyuk.

Throughout this flurry of lawsuits, the U.S. Embassy operated from behind the scenes.[94]

---

93 "Kyiv court opens case against NABU chief, MP Leschenko on Manafort leaks," *Interfax-Ukraine,* October 14, 2017. https://en.interfax.com.ua/news/general/456824.html

"According to the court's website, Rozenblat wants the court to recognize as illegal actions of NABU chief Sytnyk, who made public and disseminated information about U.S. citizen Paul Manafort, the chairman of U.S. President Donald Trump's election campaign. Manafort's name and alleged signature appeared in the so-called black books [payment ledger] of the disgraced former Ukrainian President Viktor Yanukovych's Party of Regions in a pretrial investigation, leading to "interference in the 2016 U.S. election campaign and damaging Ukraine's interests."

94 John Solomon, "As Russia collusion fades, Ukrainian plot to help Clinton emerges," *The Hill,* March 20, 2019. https://thehill.com/opinion/campaign/435029-as-russia-collusion-fades-ukrainian-plot-to-help-clinton-emerges/

"In our interview, Lutsenko accused the Obama-era U.S. Embassy in 2016 of interfering in his ability to prosecute corruption cases, saying the U.S. ambassador gave him a list of defendants that he would not be allowed to pursue and then refused to cooperate in an early investigation into the alleged misappropriation of U.S. aid in Ukraine."

In March 2019, a recording of a conversation featuring the head of NABU, Artem Sytnik, was made public in which he admitted having attempted to help Hillary Clinton during the 2016 election. Derkach was vindicated but the Ukraine PGO withdrew its investigation of Sytnik's role in the Manafort case.[95]

Despite his victory in the 2016 presidential election, Donald Trump failed to capitalize on the situation by removing the U.S. ambassador to Ukraine and replacing him with a hard-nosed supporter who could have quickly figured out how the revelations occasioned by Derkach's legal case could potentially pave the way for investigations and indictments of individuals associated with the Democratic Party.

Ukrainian authorities not only refused to investigate the Manafort scandal: every attempt was undertaken to cover up the story in the hope that Democratic Party candidate Hillary Clinton would win the election.

In a surreal twist of irony, NABU head Artem Sytnik would on June 6, 2017, declare that his agency had relented in pursuing an official investigation into Manafort owing to Trump's former campaign manager "not being a Ukrainian employee."!!![96]

And so it turns out that despite NABU's posting of materials personally implicating Manafort in the receipt of monies from the "black box," the investigation initiated at their own behest couldn't proceed on the ground that Manafort was a U.S. citizen!

---

95 Ibid.

"Ukraine Prosecutor General Yurii Lutsenko's probe was prompted by a Ukrainian parliamentarian's release of a tape recording purporting to quote a top law enforcement official as saying his agency leaked the Manafort financial records to help Clinton's campaign."

96 "NABU and SAPO are not authorized to investigate Paul Manafort's activities as a political adviser to the Party of Regions (Joint Statement)," National Anti-corruption Bureau of Ukraine, June 29, 2017. https://nabu.gov.ua/en/news/novyny-nabu-i-sap-ne-upovnovazheni-rozsliduvaty-diyalnist-pola-manaforta-yak-politychnogo/

"He has never been a Ukrainian official, and therefore cannot commit corruption acts, according to the Ukrainian laws. An assessment of the actions of the abovementioned person should be made by the competent authorities of other countries, whose jurisdiction extends to the investigation of the facts of probable offenses."

The most serious blow to the whole "notebook"/Manafort affair was struck by none other than the former head of the Central Election Commission, Mikhail Okhendovsky.

It bears noting that in an attempt to legalize Trepak's "notebooks," every effort was undertaken to highlight the role allegedly played by the former head of the Central Election Commission, Mikhail Okhendovsky.

The reasoning was that in order to lay the ground for a high-profile trial involving the payments of bribes from the "black treasury," Okhendovsky would have had to have been informed of the illicit payments.

This led to NABU immediately initiating a criminal case against Okhendovsky on suspicion of illicit enrichment.

Mikhail Okhendovsky was elected Chairman of the CEC in July 2013. Fluent in English, he had constantly participated in international forums and other events related to elections.

The CEC head was a regular guest at the U.S. Embassy when Jeffrey Pyatt was ambassador but following the latter's departure, there was a sharp downgrading of relations.

From that point on, the new U.S. ambassador in Kiev, Yovanovitch, and Deputy Ambassador for Political Affairs George Kent began avoiding contact with the CEC chairman.

In June 2016, it became apparent that Okhendovsky was selected as a target of the NABU's attempts to render Trepak's "notebooks" admissible and the former CEC Chairman was subjected to questioning.[97]

During his first audition, Okhendovsky voluntarily handed over samples of his handwriting to NABU detectives and in the summer

---

[97] "Head of Ukraine's CEC faces corruption charges in case of Party of Regions' 'black accounts,'" *UNIAN,* December 13, 2016. https://www.unian.info/politics/1677382-head-of-ukraines-cec-faces-corruption-charges-in-case-of-party-of-regions-black-accounts.html

"On May 30, the NABU launched an investigation at the request of the former first deputy chairman of the Security Service of Ukraine, Viktor Trepak. He said that he had handed to the NABU the documents which confirm illegal cash payments by the Party of Regions in the amount of nearly $2 billion to a number of former and current high-ranking officials, with head of the CEC Okhendovsky among them."

of 2016, the Bureau conducted a series of fruitless searches on the premises of the Central Election Commission.[98]

At the same time, proceedings targeting Okhendovsky were being leaked to the press, including the publication of court orders allowing NABU detectives access to his bank accounts.

NABU detectives also had their eyes on the wife of the CEC head, a private notary.

In December 2016, NABU officially charged Okhendovsky with "undue enrichment" in the form of cash, allegedly received in 2012 on the premises of the office of the Party of Regions on Lipska Street.[99]

The same evening, NABU detectives searched Okhyendovsky's house without a warrant, and with no evidence of the alleged crime being found, the entire case collapsed as the charges were downgraded to "illegally collecting travel allowance" from the "black box office."

The NABU investigation against the head of the CEC was carried out under the supervision of Gizo Uglava, whose appointment as NABU First Deputy was discussed above.[100]

When Uglava realized that Okhendovsky would defend himself ferociously against trumped up accusations, the Georgian transplant

98 UNIAN, "Okhendovsky hopes that the case against him closed," *Ukrainian Hot News,* December 17, 2016. https://ukrhotnews.com/2016/12/17/okhendovsky-hopes-that-the-case-against-him-closed/

"The CEC Chairman says that during the interrogation he and his defenders managed to deny all the factual circumstances underlying the notice of suspicion. For example, the lawyers allegedly failed to prove 'the futility of handwriting examination.'"

99 "The CEC head ohendovsky may become the first suspect in the case 'black accounting' of the Party of regions," *The good world change news.* https://runetor.com/the-cec-head-ohendovsky-may-become-the-first-suspect-in-the-case-black-accounting-of-the-party-of-regions/

"The Specialized Anticorruption Prosecutor's Office (SACPO) has dismissed the criminal case against former chairperson of the Central Election Commission, Mykhailo Okhendovskyi, over the expiration of terms of the pre-trial investigation."

100 Mykola Polishchuk (editor), "'Who are you, Mr. Kent?', – media," *Ukrainian News,* April 26, 2017. https://ukranews.com/en/news/494108-who-are-you-mr-kent-media

"'The group of people overseeing NABU activities use it as a political tool to fight against competitors and cause early parliamentary and presidential elections,' Martynenko said. A little later he clarified that he was talking about the 'Georgian mafia,' which according to him trumps-up Bureau cases (probably he referred to the Deputy Head of the NABU Gizo Uglava, close to Mikhail Saakashvili."

resorted to alternate means and called on Vano Nadiradze and the "Civil Corps of Donbass" to swing into action.

Nadiradze and his cohorts were often solicited to forcefully pressure and intimidate persons against whom the NABU leveled criminal charges.

On February 2, 2017, Nadiradze and his acolytes assaulted Okhendovsky's wife on the steps of her office in the center of Kiev.

She was then summoned to NABU headquarters by a text message sent by the Ukrainian Ministry of Justice where Nadiratze and his gang met her with threats of physical violence.[101]

Prior to this incident, in December 2016 and January 2017, the Civil Corps of Donbass had visited the school where Okhendovsky's three daughters were studying, expressing an interest in their class schedules.

At his trial, Okhendovsky was completely exonerated, and the court acknowledged the violation of the defendant's rights under Article 6 of the European Convention on Human Rights at the hands of NABU and the Specialized Anti-Corruption Prosecutor's Office (SAP).[102]

Moreover, an independent expert at the Kyiv Research Institute of Forensic Expertise, which operates under the control of the Ministry of Justice, admitted that it was impossible to authentically determine

---

101 "NABU refuses to execute ECHR's ruling – Ukrainian MP," *UNIAN*, July 9, 2020. https://www.unian.info/politics/nabu-refuses-to-execute-echr-s-ruling-ukrainian-mp-11068904.html

"'Rough disregard for human rights, norms and principles of European and Ukrainian legislation won't lead to anything good. One person, Artem Sytnyk, is ruining the relations that Ukrainian politicians and diplomats have been building with the European Commission and the European Parliament for years. We all understand that Europe does not need a visa-free regime, let alone close integration, with a country where such lawlessness is possible, where the decisions of the most important institution, the ECHR, are ignored, where witnesses are pressured, illegal surveillance is organized and family members of European Court judges are threatened. Other sanctions against Ukraine are not ruled out. In addition, Sytnyk's actions come as a huge reputational blow to NABU, from which the Bureau will be very difficult to recover,' Honcharenko said. 'Any application to the ECHR will now be considered through the prism of the lawlessness and disregard for the rulings by the European judicial system that Sytnyk allows himself.'"

102 Daria Zubkova (editor), "SACPO Dismisses Case Of CEC's Ex-Head Okhendovskyi Over Expiration Of Investigation Terms," Ukrainian News, January 24, 2020. https://ukranews.com/en/news/679478-sacpo-dismisses-case-of-cec-s-ex-head-okhendovskyi-over-expiration-of-investigation-terms

the authenticity of Okhendovsky's handwriting in the "notebooks" produced by Trepak.

After his trial, Okhendovsky gave an interview to the *Strana* website in December 2018 in which he confided that:

> It became clear to everyone that this case was purely political, ordered and bogus. In addition to the generally recognized goals of foreign policy, related to the 2016 U.S. presidential election, there is a conspiracy involving our diplomats in Washington, as reported by the foreign media. The NABU was probably instructed to come up with something against an official of the highest rank. My rank is enough. They were probably just afraid of going even higher. So it all came together... They were trying to achieve several goals with one action.

In support of its decision of February 9, 2017, the Kiev Court of Appeal explicitly stated that the NABU charges in the case of the "black box" were unfounded "owing to lack of evidence."

To this day, Mikhail Okhendovsky is still waiting for an apology from NABU.

During his interview with the *Strana* website, he noted that NABU director Artem Sytnik was strictly forbidden to do so "... through the actual head of the NABU... and obviously an official from a foreign embassy. Mr. Kent or Mr. Smith: what difference does it make?"[103]

George Kent was the head of the political department of the U.S. embassy in Kiev.[104]

---

103 "Secret conspiracy of 'anti-corruption officials' – who and how made a 'sacred cow' out of Sytnyk," *Lenta.ua,* April 29, 2020. https://lenta.ua/ru/taynyy-sgovor-antikorruptsionerov-kto-i-kak-sdelal-iz-sytnika-svyashchennuyu-korovu-48048/

"It is worth noting that the vast majority of publications and persons who are so advocating for the salvation of Sytnik are associated with 'grant' organizations that are confined to two structures – the U.S. Embassy in Ukraine and the funds of the American entrepreneur George Soros. It's a paradox, but the 'anti-corruptionists' – activists and even people's deputies (there are many of them in the Golos faction), as well as the media allied to them, cover up a natural corrupt official without a twinge of conscience. Moreover, they do it synchronously."

104 "'Who are you, Mr. Kent?,' – media."

Soon after Okhendovsky's trial, the General Prosecutor's Office opened a criminal investigation bearing on the circumstances surrounding the origins of Trepak's "notebooks" as well as potential abuse of power by NABU and SAP officers, deemed to have culminated in "pressure on a public figure" and leaking elements of an investigation.

One would think that following such a high-profile fiasco, NABU would have closed the case on the "black box" and apologized to all those involved.

Such was not to be the case.

In the spring of 2017, a decision was made to transfer the case from NABU to the Prosecutor General's Office's Department of Special Investigations headed by Sergei Gorbatyuk.[105]

The department had been tasked with investigating the circumstances surrounding the murders on the Maidan, and with no progress being made in solving the case Gorbatyuk was fired in the fall of 2019 owing to the investigation being stalled.[106]

In the light of the stalling of the Maidan investigation, one is left to wonder why the decision was made to transfer the "black box office" case to the PGO.

If the idea was to divert public attention away from the failures of the NABU, Gorbatyuk did not disappoint. He actually attempted to fabricate another case against Manafort!

"Storch and Kent attended Rada's Anti-corruption Committee hearing to select an independent auditor of the NABU. Talking about the procedure and candidates, Yegor Sobolev (Head of the committee) said that at first nobody applied, so he called the U.S. embassy asking them to suggest a candidate. They recommended Mr. Storch, and after the meeting Mr. Kent politely, but firmly said, 'The diplomatic mission did not invite anyone and Storch is a private person.' 'As far as I got it, Yegor missed the mark with this,' said the source."

105 "NABU continues pre-trial investigation of the so-called Party of Region 'black ledger' case," National Anti-corruption Bureau of Ukraine, September 29, 2017. https://nabu.gov.ua/en/news/novyny-nabu-y-nadali-bratyme-uchast-u-rozsliduvanni-spravy-chornoyi-buhgalteriyi-partiyi-regioniv/

"In June 2017 the NABU passed the materials of the pre-trial investigation of the so-called Party of Region 'black ledger' case to the GPO."

106 "In Ukraine, the head of the department of special investigations of the GPU was fired," *Teller Report,* October 23, 2019. https://www.tellerreport.com/news/2019-10-23---in-ukraine--the-head-of-the-department-of-special-investigations-of-the-gpu-was-fired-.rkJCj10tr.html

"'They called me from the personnel department and informed me that I was fired. I have not seen the order yet.' UNIAN quotes Gorbatyuk as saying."

The journalist-deputy, Sergei Leshchenko, this time around accused Manafort of receiving $750,000 in kickbacks.[107]

Leshchenko presented supposedly "tangible evidence" of these new allegations and Gorbatyuk was tasked with investigating the case. But like the Maidan investigation, this case quickly fell apart as it became obvious that the "tangible" evidence Leshchenko relied on was flimsy at best. None of the witnesses cited in the case ever confirmed that Manafort had indeed been paid those $750,000.

Ultimately, the Special Investigations Department of the Prosecutor General's Office failed in solving both the Maidan shootings case and the Yanukovych "black box" case.

While these cases in effect remained open, there is no evidence to support an investigation.[108]

Despite Trump being in power, the charges against the incumbent president's former campaign manager would not be allowed to be dropped for it was a part of the Russiagate narrative.

Any other outcome would de facto, albeit retroactively, vindicate the notion that Ukrainian authorities interfered in the 2016 U.S. election process.

In the end, the bogus Manafort case stood as evidence of the Democrats' willingness to use all their connections in Ukraine to cover up their own complicity in an effort to discredit the then-sitting U.S. president.

The case moreover highlighted the presence of elements working within the Trump administration to prevent him from turning the tables on the Democrats despite the evidence provided by the Derkach tapes.

Failure by the Republicans to act decisively in this matter also prevented the exposure of the system of external management installed in Ukraine by the Democrats following the Maidan coup d'état.

---

107 "Trump's ex aide Paul Manafort 'hid' $750,000 payment," *BBC News,* March 22, 2017. https://www.bbc.com/news/world-us-canada-39348265

108 Robert Mackey, "Republicans Smear Ukrainian Who Helped Expose Manafort," The Intercept, November 19, 2019. https://theintercept.com/2019/11/19/republicans-use-impeachment-hearings-smear-ukrainian-helped-expose-manafort/

"Leshchenko told Solomon that the ledger was not introduced as evidence in criminal proceedings because the chain of custody for the records was unclear."

Election 2020: Back in the Driver Seat Despite "The Laptop from Hell"

"I was getting a lot of death threats."

John Paul Mac Isaac, the Delaware computer repair shop owner who had alerted the FBI about Hunter Biden's infamous laptop before ultimately taking it to former New York Mayor and Trump attorney Rudy Giuliani, expressed concerns about his safety.[109]

Ever since finding himself embroiled in what by all account constituted a matter of national security, Mac Isaac confided that he had faced harassment from Big Tech companies, the Internal Revenue Services and a whole slew of other government agencies ever since going public with Hunter's laptop.

It had all started in October 2020 when in the midst of the General Election for the Presidency of the United States, the *New York Post* revealed the existence of a laptop alleged to belong to Hunter Biden, the son of the Democratic nominee Joe Biden.[110]

The *Post* related that the device had been abandoned at a Delaware computer shop in 2019.

The story went on to expose that three weeks before the 2020 U.S. presidential election, emails obtained from the laptop appeared to show evidence of influence-peddling connecting to Joe Biden.

A forensic analysis would eventually authenticate the data from the laptop, including emails purporting to proffer evidence of foul play.

---

109 Harriet Alexander, "Hunter Biden accused of 'intimidation' as it is revealed he was hit with $75,000 defamation lawsuit by Delaware laptop repairman five days BEFORE he demanded DOJ prosecute anyone who shared his hard drive," *Daily Mail,* February 3, 2023. https://www.dailymail.co.uk/news/article-11708809/Hunter-Biden-accused-intimidation-75k-defamation-suit-Delaware-laptop-repairman.html

"According to the lawsuit, the Post reports, Mac Isaac was forced to close down his computer repair shop near the Biden family homes in Greenville, Delaware following the CNN report – when people started throwing eggs, vegetables and even dog feces at his door."

110 Emma-Jo Morris and Gabrielle Fonrouge, "Smoking-gun email reveals how Hunter Biden introduced Ukrainian businessman to VP dad," *New York Post,* October 14, 2020. https://nypost.com/2020/10/14/email-reveals-how-hunter-biden-introduced-ukrainian-biz-man-to-dad/

"The shop owner couldn't positively identify the customer as Hunter Biden, but said the laptop bore a sticker from the Beau Biden Foundation, named after Hunter's late brother and former Delaware attorney general."

The Trump campaign attempted to exploit this "October surprise" and sway the election in favor of its candidate.

Against all expectations, the story was prevented from gaining traction.[111]

No fewer than fifty senior national security officials attested in writing that the Russian government was behind a disinformation campaign aimed at interfering with U.S. elections and that the laptop story was part of it.[112]

The FBI (who by then had taken custody of the laptop) proceeded to contact senior executives of every major Big Tech platform to enjoin them to suppress any and all reference to the story reported by the *Post*.[113]

These developments were made public when Facebook CEO, Mark Zuckerberg later on admitted to Joe Rogan "that the FBI had told (him) in the lead-up to the election that he should be 'on high alert and

---

111 Joseph A. Wulfsohn, "CNN's Jake Tapper insists he won't 'shy away' from covering Hunter Biden after avoiding laptop scandal in 2020," *Fox News,* July 11, 2023. https://www.msn.com/en-us/news/politics/cnns-jake-tapper-insists-he-wont-shy-away-from-covering-hunter-biden-after-avoiding-laptop-scandal-in-2020/ar-AA1dHFRJ

"Tapper's sentiments in July 2023 are certainly not the same as those in October 2020, in the days following the New York Post's bombshell reporting on Hunter Biden's infamous laptop that shed light on his shady foreign business dealings, including mention of '10% for the big guy,'... According to Grabien transcripts, in the days following the Post's laptop news, neither of Tapper's two CNN programs made any mention of the terms 'laptop,' 'New York Post' or 'Tony Bobuliski,' Hunter Biden's former business partner who came forward at the time confirming emails from the laptop and insisting the former vice president was involved in their business dealings."

112 Zack Budryk, "50 former intelligence officials warn NY Post story sounds like Russian disinformation," The Hill, October 20, 2020. https://thehill.com/homenews/campaign/521823-50-former-intelligence-officials-warn-ny-post-story-sounds-like-russian/

"Several of the signers have endorsed Democratic presidential nominee Joe Biden, according to Politico, which first reported the letter. The letter states that its signers do not have new information about the emails and their authenticity."

113 Jesse O'Neill, "FBI pressured Twitter, sent trove of docs hours before Post broke Hunter laptop story," *New York Post,* December 19, 2022. https://nypost.com/2022/12/19/fbi-reached-out-to-twitter-before-post-broke-hunter-biden-laptop-story/

"But The Post's story was suppressed by Facebook and Twitter, which temporarily banned the outlet in the wake of its publication. It was also ignored or discredited by mainstream outlets, many of whom quietly substantiated the report months later."

sensitivity'...if a trove of documents appeared that we should view that with suspicion, that it might be part of a foreign manipulation attempt."[114]

Then in early 2023, former CIA senior official Mike Morrell declared that Biden campaign director Anthony Blinken had been the individual responsible for having concocted the idea to gather all former National Security senior officials in order to convince them to sign the letter claiming that the laptop was part of a Russian disinformation campaign.[115]

The Twitter Files

The role played by the FBI in regulating social media content was made all the more explicit in the wake of Twitter's acquisition by billionaire Elon Musk.

In an unprecedented move aimed at exposing the (not so secret) interaction of Big Tech with federal agencies, Musk decided to make the company's internal files available to journalists Matt Taibi, Bari Weiss, Lee Fang, authors Michael Shellenberger, David Zweig and Alex Berenson shortly upon acquiring the Twitter platform on October 27, 2022.[116]

---

114 David Molloy, "Zuckerberg tells Rogan FBI warning prompted Biden laptop story censorship," *BBC News,* August 26, 2022. https://www.bbc.com/news/world-us-canada-62688532

Zuckerberg told Rogan: "The background here is that the FBI came to us – some folks on our team – and was like 'hey, just so you know, you should be on high alert. We thought there was a lot of Russian propaganda in the 2016 election, we have it on notice that basically there's about to be some kind of dump that's similar to that.'"

115 Miranda Devine, "Biden campaign pushed spies to write false Hunter laptop letter," *New York Post,* April 20, 2023 (updated April 21, 2023). https://nypost.com/2023/04/20/biden-campaign-pushed-spies-to-write-false-hunter-laptop-letter/

"Morell, identified as a potential CIA director under Biden, said he organized the letter to "help Vice President Biden ... because I wanted him to win the election."

116 Andrew Prokop, "Why the Twitter Files actually matter," Vox, December 15, 2020. https://www.vox.com/policy-and-politics/2022/12/15/23505370/twitter-files-elon-musk-taibbi-weiss-covid

"Many inclined to distrust what they see as Big Tech's liberal leanings have cried vindication. The documents show in detail how Twitter made key content moderation decisions that disadvantaged Trump, conservatives, and people who broke with the public health consensus on Covid-19. They say the evidence proves that, again and again, Twitter intervened to squelch speech that the liberal establishment didn't like."

The files revealed the extent to which Democrats angled to suppress expressed views considered inimical to the Democratic party's ideological and political views.

Musk moreover proceeded to fire Twitter's deputy general counsel, James Baker, whom we briefly discussed earlier in the context of what would come to be known as the CrossFire Hurricane scandal.[117]

Baker had once served as a senior federal employee with the U.S. Department of Justice where he occupied the position of General Counsel for the Federal Bureau of Investigation.[118]

While in the public sector, Baker had displayed staunch support for surveillance policies and was a strong advocate of the PATRIOT Act, so much so that he became known as Mr. FISA.[119]

In August 2020, Baker had joined Twitter as the 2020 Presidential Election was heading into its final stretch.[120]

---

117 Samantha Delouya, "Elon Musk confirmed the firing of Twitter deputy general counsel James Baker for allegedly interfering in the publication of the Twitter Files," Business Insider, December 6, 2022. https://www.businessinsider.com/elon-musk-fired-james-baker-deputy-general-counsel-twitter-files-2022-12

"The 'Twitter Files,' which were tweeted by Taibbi on Friday with the approval of Musk, revealed some of the inner workings of Twitter's content moderation practices, including the supposed suppression of a 2020 story about President Joe Biden's son Hunter Biden's laptop."

118 Devlin Barrett, Ellen Nakashima, and Carol Leonnig, "FBI's top lawyer said to be reassigned," *The Washington Post,* December 21, 2017. https://www.washingtonpost.com/world/national-security/fbis-top-lawyer-said-to-be-reassigned/2017/12/21/2ac76640-e6b5-11e7-833f-155031558ff4_story.html

"Baker told colleagues he will be taking on other duties at the FBI, according to people familiar with the matter. In recent months, Baker had been caught up in a strange interagency dispute that led to a leak probe and attracted the attention of senior lawmakers, but people familiar with the matter said the probe had recently ended with a decision not to charge anyone. The leak issue had not played a part in Baker's reassignment, these people said."

119 *Statement of James A. Baker, Counsel for Intelligence Policy, Office of Intelligence Policy and Review, United States Department of Justice, before the Subcommittee on Crime, Terrorism, and Homeland Security Committee on the Judiciary, House of Representatives, concerning The Foreign Intelligence Surveillance Act, Part I (USA PATRIOT Act §§204,207,214,225 & The "Lone Wolf" Provision), presented on April 26, 2005.* https://www.justice.gov/archive/ll/subs/testimony/042605-oipr-baker.pdf

120 Thornton McEnery, Jaclyn Hendricks, and Emily Jacobs, "Twitter hires former FBI chief counsel as deputy lawyer," *New York Post,* June 16, 2020 (updated June 17, 2020). https://nypost.com/2020/06/16/twitter-hires-former-fbi-chief-counsel-as-deputy-lawyer/

"Twitter has tapped former FBI general counsel James Baker, a central player in

Musk has since become a target of officials from the European Union and was recently warned that X (formely known as Twitter) would be excluded from operating in Europe if his service failed to abide by the regulations recently adopted by Brussels to counter "misinformation."[121]

In response, Musk fired the team in charge of "election integrity."[122]

---

the Russia collusion investigation, to serve as counsel to the tech giant."

121 Max Goldbart, "'We Will Be Watching What You Do': Elon Musk Warned By EU After Disinformation Report," *Deadline,* September 26, 2023. https://deadline.com/2023/09/elon-musk-x-warned-european-union-1235556331/

122 Ryan Grenoble, "Elon Musk Fires Twitter Election Integrity Team After Pledging To Grow It," *Huff Post,* September 28, 2023. https://www.huffpost.com/entry/elon-musk-twitter-election-integrity-team-fired_n_65158fb2e4b07cb570320406

PART II

The Biden Takeover of Ukraine

Burisma

The name of this company might not have ever penetrated public consciousness but for the revelations exposed by the Comer Committee related to the efforts initiated by this entity's CEO, Mykola Zlochevsky, to neutralize money laundering charges leveled against him between December 19, 2013 and January 22, 2014.

Owing to his ties with former Polish President Aleksander Kwasniewski, Zlochevsky set out to endear himself to senior Western officials, including former U.S. vice-president Biden.

This rehabilitation operation would later on help set the stage for a very close cooperation between Burisma and the Biden clan.

But first let us attempt to examine how the son of then U.S. vice-president Biden ended up sitting on the board of one of Ukraine's most prominent gas companies.

What could possibly connect the American lawyer with Burisma? On its face, nothing if one ignores the fact that he just happened to be the son of a powerful political figure.

People started to write about Biden's nepotism over 20 years ago. Wikipedia (not to be suspected of peddling conspiracy theories) gives a comprehensive characterization of the family: "...After graduating from Yale in 1996, Hunter got a job as a consultant at MBNA America Bank... Less than two years later, he would become a senior vice president of the company. Biden and his father established a relationship in which 'Biden wouldn't ask Hunter about his lobbying clients, and Hunter wouldn't tell his father about them.'"[123]

Hunter was indeed fortunate and former Polish President Aleksander Kwasniewski noted this when he confided in an interview with the Associated Press that: "If you don't have a name, you're nobody. It's not bad to be Biden. It's a good name."[124]

---

123 *Hunter Biden,* Wikipedia. https://en.wikipedia.org/wiki/Hunter_Biden

124 Vanessa Gera, "AP Interview: Ex-Polish president defends Biden and Burisma," AP News, November 28, 2019. https://apnews.com/article/37424b8a0a994c1a935c5831643a84e3

Shortly after the Maidan, Alexander Kwasniewski and Hunter Biden would end up working together at Burisma.

In order to understand how Kwaniewski got involved with Burisma, it is necessary to go back to 2012.

In 2012, a special commission featuring former head of the EU parliament, Pat Cox, and former Polish president Aleksander Kwasniewski began working in Ukraine under an agreement between the Ukrainian government and the leadership of the European Parliament.[125]

The Cox-Kwasniewski commission was tasked to find a compromise on the fate of convicted and later imprisoned former Ukrainian Prime Minister Yulia Tymoshenko. The commission carried out its work until Viktor Yanukovych's erstwhile opponent was eventually released from prison in the wake of the Maidan.

It is believed that the fate of the Ukraine-EU Association Agreement was conditioned by the work of the Cox-Kwasniewski commission. Therefore, the work of the commission was given the closest attention by the Ukrainian authorities, with then-Ukrainian Prime Minister Mykola Azarov personally supervising its work, while the Head of European Parliament Martin Schultz did the same.[126]

Ukraine quickly understood the importance of receiving foreign guests in a way befitting their status. In other words, Ukrainian hospitality should ensure that a guest be entertained, taken on a boat trip along the Dnieper, invited to fishing and hunting, treated with borshch, pampushki and salo, and feted with Gorilka.

While information about Pat Cox's time in Ukraine is scarce, Kwasniewski was known to be fond of all those traditional gatherings and feasts. Moreover, Kwasniewski spoke perfect Russian.

"I understand that if someone asks me to be part of some project it's not only because I'm so good, it's also because I am Kwasniewski and I am a former president of Poland," he said. "And this is all inter-connected. No-names are a nobody. Being Biden is not bad. It's a good name."

125 "The European Parliament's Diplomacy – a Tool for Projecting EU Power in Times of Crisis? The Case of the Cox–Kwasniewski Mission," *Journal of Common Market Studies* 55, no. 1 (2017): 71-86. https://core.ac.uk/download/pdf/79665709.pdf

126 Nikolay Azarov, Aleksandr Kwasniewski and Pat Koks [photo], *UNIAN*. https://photo.unian.info/photo/456509-nikolay-azarov-aleksandr-kwasniewski-and-pat-koks

Mykola Zlochevsky, deputy head of the National Security and Defense Council of Ukraine and CEO of the oil and gas company Burisma, rejoiced in playing the Ukrainian host. Burisma would later become the focus of the great emerging scandal surrounding Hunter Biden and his father Joe Biden.

In the meantime, Mykola Zlochevsky was happy to provide and pay for all the entertainment of the committee members out of his own pocket, which was no hardship for him since Burisma was one of Ukraine's largest private gas producers, with annual gas production of about 1 billion cubic meters.

The main asset of the company, Esko-Pivnich, produced about 37 million cubic meters of natural gas each month. Burisma also owned the gas production company Kub-Gaz, which Zlochevsky had acquired after the death of its previous owner, Polish businessman Jan Kulczyk.[127]

Mykola Zlochevsky himself had been in politics since the late 90s, having once served as Ukraine's minister of ecology and natural resources during Yanukovych's presidency.

While Zlochevsky could then hardly be labeled as an oligarch, his office managed quite well during the time when the Regionalists were in power.

To wit, his companies obtained two dozen special permits for oil and gas extraction located in the most promising areas of the Kharkov region.[128]

Later on, these licenses allowed Esko-Pivnich to grow tenfold so that from a very small gas producer with an annual production of 30

---

127 "Malczak: What do we know about Burisma Holdings?" [opinion], *CIRE. PL,* May 16, 2014. https://www.cire.pl/artykuly/opinie/88543-malczak-co-wiemy-o-burisma-holdings

"According to this information, the company obtained a lot of mining concessions by making acquisitions of other equally unknown entities: m.in. ESCO-PIVNICH (OOO 'ЭСКО-ПИВНИЧ') and PARI (OOO 'ПАРИ') or 'Krymtopenergoservis.' Journalist Wojciech Mucha links on Twitter an interesting article (http://gogetnews. info/economy/409-dobycha-2013-chastniki-sorvali-kush.html), which indicates that these companies are also controlled by Mykola Zlochevsky. Thanks to the support of Jakóbik from BiznesAlert.pl, it is also possible to identify several concessions, m.in in the Rakytnyanska, Karaikozovske deposits near Kharkiv or Niklovytske near Lviv. These are shale gas deposits, there is no data on their prospectivity."

128 Ibid.

million cubic meters in 2010, Burisma soon became a major player with an annual production of 400 million cubic meters in 2014.

Former "regionals" now find it difficult to recall exactly when Kwasniewski became friends with Zlochevsky but overtime the feasts turned from informal relations into quite businesslike ties during the Pole's time as co-head of the commission, so much so that by February 2014, shortly before the advent of the Maidan, Zlochevsky invited the former Polish president to join Burisma's board of directors.

As the Maidan events swept away Yanukovich's entourage, the victors descended upon the land and began hunting down former officials and businessmen associated with the old regime. Zlochevsky was no exception and in March 2014, he became the target of an investigation by Ukraine's General Prosecutor which soon turned into an international manhunt with the UK Interior Ministry's Serious Fraud Office accusing Zlochevsky of money laundering. Burisma's CEO opted to flee Ukraine.

What was to give rise to Biden's 2018 infamous speech at the Council on Foreign Relations boasting of his getting the Ukrainian prosecutor Derkach fired by threatening to withhold 18 billion in aid stemmed from Derkach's investigation into "tax evasion, money laundering and embezzlement of state funds" arising out of "funds obtained illicitly by way of purchase by Franklin Templeton Investments of state bonds to the total sum of $7.4 billion USD."[129]

Derkach "pointed to the findings of the GPO investigations, according to which the criminal money that belonged to Yanukovich's family and inner circle was transferred to offshore jurisdictions during 2013–2014, and then via Franklin Templeton Investments the money made its way back into Ukraine where it was spent on state bonds. Thus, as Dubynsky emphasizes, the beneficiaries of the scheme had first stolen funds from Ukrainian people, and then returned them to the country in the form of sovereign debt which paid bond holder a very high interest payment. This way, Ukrainian citizens were robbed

---

[129] "Hunting for Hunter: Evidence Reveals Biden, Burisma Ukraine Bond Scandal, Tied to U.S. Firm," *21st Century Wire*, November 26, 2019. https://21stcenturywire.com/2019/11/26/hunting-for-hunter-new-ukraine-evidence-reveals-biden-burisma-bond-scandal-tied-to-us-firm/

twice, and all with the help of one criminal scheme with Burisma Holdings at the center of it."[130]

On April 16 and May 28, 2014, the Central Criminal Court of London set out to impose restrictions on Zlochevsky's use of $23.5 million spread amongst four accounts belonging to Burisma and Brociti at BNP Paribas Bank.[131] All that time, Zlochevsky had never lost touch with his good friend Kwasniewski and through him, the Burisma boss devised a plan to gain the support of new patrons in the West. This plan did not look so unrealistic given Kwasniewski's wide range of connections. It appears that it was Kwasniewski who advised Zlochevsky to invite Joe Biden's son Hunter to join the Burisma Board of Directors, offering to personally take care of it for he knew Joe Biden well.

The evidence uncovered by the investigation revealed that between December 19, 2013 and January 22, 2014, some $35 million dollars were deposited on the corporate accounts of Burisma Holding Limited and Brociti Investments Limited (Cyprus), out of which 15 million were transferred to the personal accounts of Zlochevsky at Swiss bank LGT Bank.[132]

---

130 Ibid.

131 L. Todd Wood, "FLASHBACK: Former Ukrainian MP Alleges Biden Family Received $12M Kickback From Transaction With Burisma Owner To Kill London Criminal Cases, Provides Details To DOJ," *CDM,* June 16, 2023. https://creativedestructionmedia.com/investigations/2023/06/16/breaking-former-ukrainian-mp-alleges-hunter-biden-received-12m-kickback-from-transaction-with-burisma-owner-provides-details-to-doj/

"In further clarification of information provided, CD Media can now report that the $32M referenced below was sent to London, where it was seized by British officials and criminal charges were levied against Zlochevsky. Vice President Biden actively sought to have the charges thrown out in the United Kingdom for Zlochevsky in exchange for the $12M being diverted to Hunter Biden, according to Onyshchenko."

132 Paul Sonne, Michael Kranish, and Matt Viser, "The story of Hunter Biden's foray into Ukraine as a board member of Burisma," *The Washington Post,* September 28, 2019. https://www.washingtonpost.com/world/national-security/the-gas-tycoon-and-the-vice-presidents-son-the-story-of-hunter-bidens-foray-in-ukraine/2019/09/28/1aadff70-dfd9-11e9-8fd3-d943b4ed57e0_story.html

"Bringing aboard a son of the U.S. vice president was part of a broad effort by Burisma to burnish its credentials that had started before the 2014 uprising. The company tapped Alan Apter, an investment banker who has worked in the United States and Europe, as its board chairman, and the former president of Poland as a board member. Burisma had brought in a new executive team and hired established international firms to audit its reserves and financial results. The addition of prominent Americans and Europeans to the company's board in the weeks after Kiev's dramatic

On April 22, 2014, U.S. Vice President Joe Biden visited Kiev and held a meeting with government officials. Three weeks later, on May 12, 2014, his son Hunter joined the board of directors of Burisma. The prodigal son had overnight become a member of the Board of Directors of the oil and gas company.

To be sure, Zlochevsky's travails taught him to spare no expense in securing the support of influential lobbyists in the West. In that context, Joseph Cofer Black, former head of the CIA Antiterrorist Center in 1999–2002, and Devon Archer, a friend of former Secretary of State John Kerry's stepson, Devon Archer, also joined the Board.[133]

Hunter Biden's salary was set at $50 thousand a month although his principal place of business remained the headquarters of the law firm Schiller & Flexner LLP, located in New York.

Kwasniewski would later recall that following Hunter Biden's appointment, he held a brief phone conversation with him during which the Pole confided that one of Burisma's goals was to free Ukraine from Russian energy dependence.

The company produced an estimated 25-30% of Ukraine's gas and, according to the former Polish president, the company could manage to increase gas production and thus reduce dependence on Russia.

Burisma's management immediately commissioned the London-based PR agency Bell Pottinger with the task of handling media public relations. One of the Agency's founders, Lord Timothy Bell, had at one time served as an adviser to both former British Prime Minister

change in government sent a message internally in Ukraine that Zlochevsky had access to powerful people in the West, according to Bullough, who wrote about Zlochevsky in *Moneyland,* his book on tax havens and shell companies. 'Adding these people with these fancy names to the board made Burisma, [which] got licenses to extract gas in Ukraine through very suspicious means, look like a Western, legitimate company,' said Daria Kaleniuk, executive director of the Anti-Corruption Action Center. She described such 'whitewashing' as a common tactic for tycoons and officials who are looking to legitimize assets of questionable origin."

133 Toby Nwazor, "Former CIA Director Joins Burisma, and It Is Good News," HuffPost, February 22, 2017. https://www.huffpost.com/entry/former-cia-director-joins-burisma-and-it-is-good-news_b_58adf600e4b01f4ab51c75a4

"According to President of Burisma Group Nikolay Zlochevskyi, 'We are excited that Mr. Black has agreed to serve as a member of Burisma's Board... Burisma is expanding into new and emerging markets and is actively pursuing global energy projects.'"

Margaret Thatcher and former Russian President Boris Yeltsin. The wife of Syrian President Asma Al-Assad and the government of Belarus, among others, had also once been clients of the agency.[134]

The new PR agency stood up for its new clients, with *Deutsche Welle* reporting at the time that Bell Pottinger had left unanswered a written request bearing on the reshuffling of Burisma.

While it took almost three years to resolve legal problems in Britain, the reshuffling of personnel on the board of directors of Burisma ended up paying dividends. In January 2017, Zlochevsky was allowed to return to Ukraine and all lawsuits and criminal cases against Burisma were dropped.[135]

In January 2015, the British courts were convinced to unblock Zlochevsky's 23 million in the wake of the Ukrainian Prosecutor's Office refusal to provide documents deemed relevant to the investigation.[136]

The terms of the Poroshenko government's deal with the former Yanukovych minister were outlined in a Burisma press release.[137]

---

134 Roman Goncharenko, "Who owns Burisma?," *DW,* May 16, 2014. https://www.dw.com/en/who-are-hunter-bidens-ukrainian-bosses/a-17642254

"London-based PR firm Bell Pottinger handles Burisma's media relations, though they failed to respond to a DW request about Burisma. One of Bell Pottinger's founders, Lord Timothy Bell, once advised former British Prime Minister Margaret Thatcher, as well as the first Russian President Boris Yeltsin. Prominent customers in recent years include Asma Assad, the wife of the Syrian President, and the government of Belarus."

135 Alyona Zhuk, "Activists cry foul as courts, prosecutors clear Zlochevsky," *Kyiv Post,* January 19, 2017. https://www.kyivpost.com/post/10044

"Zlochevsky was among several top officials who fled Ukraine after the EuroMaidan Revolution that ousted Yanukovych on Feb. 22, 2014. Months later, some $35 million was found in his companies' bank accounts in the United Kingdom, prompting money laundering and illicit enrichment investigations in the UK and Ukraine."

136 Ibid.

"In the spring of 2014, after Yanukovych fled and the West started imposing sanctions against his associates, Andriy Kicha, Zlochevsky's lawyer and a top manager at the Burisma Group, tried to transfer some $23 million from accounts in the UK to Cyprus. The UK authorities blocked the operation, froze the accounts, and launched an investigation to determine the source of Zlochevsky's money, suspecting money laundering."

137 "Burisma: all cases against group and group's president Zlochevsky in Ukraine closed," *Interfax-Ukraine,* January 12, 2017. https://en.interfax.com.ua/news/economic/396015.html

"'It is reassuring that the independent Ukrainian court managed to take the

Complying with a British court findings dated January 21, 2015 that Zlochevsky was not involved in financial fraud, Ukraine withdrew the latter's name from the list of international fugitives.

European partners went out of their way to launder the image Burisma's CEO.

Kwasniewski insisted that amnesty for Zlochevsky and his business would help Ukraine to become energy independent and even linked the outcome of the case to the ideals of the Ukrainian revolution for which blood had been shed on the Maidan.[138]

Even Ukrainian President Petro Poroshenko could not hide the fact that it was Western lobbyists who had pulled Zlochevsky out of the clutches of British justice. This was confirmed by the so-called "Onishchenko tapes" that chronicled former MP Oleksandr Onishchenko's conversations with Poroshenko in the latter's office.[139]

One of these conversations specifically dealt with the issue of what to do about Mykola Zlochevsky. Dated January 2016, the voice

decision that is fully consistent with the decision made by the British court. For Ukraine, the decision on Zlochevsky and Burisma will be also instrumental in making the country energy sufficient, since it will allow Burisma to increase domestic gas production as well as payments to the national budget,' Independent Director of Burisma Aleksander Kwasniewski said."

138 Vanessa Gera, "AP Interview: Ex-Polish President Defends Biden and Burisma," *Business Insider,* November 28, 2019. https://www.insider.com/ap-interview-ex-polish-president-defends-biden-and-burisma-2019-11

"Aleksander Kwasniewski, a former Polish president and currently a board member for Ukrainian gas company Burisma, speaks to The Associated Press in his office in Warsaw, Poland, Thursday, Nov. 28, 2019. Kwasniewski says that when Hunter Biden was tapped in 2014 to join its advisory board, he told then–Vice President Joe Biden's son that the company was working to overcome a difficult past and was determined to be well-managed and transparent. Kwasniewski also said he also told the younger Biden that if Burisma succeeded in tapping into Ukraine's gas deposits, it would help Ukraine gain energy independence from Russia, a key part of its broader struggle to exist as an sovereign nation" [photo caption].

139 Betsy Swan and Adam Rawnsley, "Oleksandr Onyshchenko, Ukrainian Fugitive Who Claimed to Have Dirt on Burisma, Is Arrested," *The Daily Beast,* December 6, 2019. https://www.thedailybeast.com/oleksandr-onyshchenko-ukrainian-fugitive-who-claimed-to-have-dirt-on-burisma-is-arrested?ref=scroll

"As the impeachment proceedings against President Trump took hold in October, Onyshchenko claimed to have inside information about Hunter Biden and his work for Burisma. He told Reuters that his friend Mykola Zlochevsky, who founded Burisma, had placed the vice president's son on Burisma's board as insurance against criminal investigations. The claim echoes those made by Rudy Giuliani and former Ukrainian Prosecutor General Yuriy Lutsenko. 'It was to protect (the company),' he said."

audio purported to record Poroshenko's statement to the effect that "... Kolya [Zlochevsky – ed.] is a good guy. I will think about what can be done. It's just that the Americans have been getting excited about him lately."

Onishchenko is then heard replying: "In theory, they shouldn't have done anything against him, because Biden's son is on his company board. And so is Kwasniewski. Therefore, when I spoke to Kolya, there shouldn't have been any attempts on the West side from there."

Poroshenko was clearly lying since he evidently wasn't too keen on the fact that the shrewd Zlochevsky had obtained the trust of the Biden family and could thus work his way around him through Hunter.

Owing to support from American lobbyists, Burisma did well on the Ukrainian market. In 2016, the company Resano Trading Ltd, affiliated with Burisma, acquired the Ukrainian assets of Canadian Serinus Energy, namely, gas fields in the Dneprovsko-Donetsky basin.[140]

The acquisition would see the company being handed the task of carrying out the exploitation of the Olhivske, Makeyevske, Severo-Makeyevske, Verhunske and Krutogorivske gas fields all located in the Luhansk Region.[141]

Then in 2020, the Cyprus-based company of Nikolay Zlochevsky, Brociti Investments Limited, affiliated to Burisma, acquired 100% of the shares in the capital of the company Geounit, which specialized in seismic surveys of oil and gas fields.[142]

---

140 Serinus Energy, "Serinus Closes of Sale of Ukraine Interests" [news release], February 8, 2016. https://serinusenergy.com/serinus-closes-of-sale-of-ukraine-interests/

141 Ibid.

"Serinus sold all of the 70% of the outstanding shares of KUB-Gas Holdings Limited ('KHL') owned by the Company. KHL in turn, owns 100% of the shares of KUB-Gas LLC ('KUB-Gas'). KUB-Gas (directly and indirectly through its subsidiary, KUB-Gas Borova LLC) owns 100% of and operates the six licences/permits in Ukraine which contain the Olgovskoye, Makeevskoye, Vergunskoye and Krutogorovskoye gas fields."

142 Enkorr, "Burisma closes deal to buy service company Geounit," May 20, 2020. https://enkorr.ua/ru/news/burisma_zakryla_sdelku_o_pokupke_servisnoy_kompanii_geoyunit/241536

"From 2015 to 2018, Geounit signed 8 contracts with the state-owned Ukrgasvydobuvannya for seismic exploration or seismic data processing in the amount of UAH 350 million. The company's website says that it cooperates with almost all major Ukrainian gas companies, including Burisma."

Rumor has it that Poroshenko demanded that Zlochevsky supply gas to his glass factory free of charge. It was estimated that the "preservation of business and freedom" was deemed to be quite expensive. Zlochevsky went out of his way to demonstrate loyalty to his new Western partners and started providing financial support in the sponsoring of all kinds of events in Europe.

For example, he contributed to the financing of an energy forum organized under the patronage of Albert II in Monaco before bringing a Ukrainian government delegation there in the summer of 2017.

In 2015, Burisma had sponsored Europe's largest electric car marathon, which started in Kiev and finished in Monaco.[143]

But back to Hunter.

The appointment of Biden's son on the board of Burisma might not have caused such a storm of public reaction had it not been revealed that his appointment had become effective just a few weeks following his father's April 22 visit to Kiev.

Suspicion of nepotism was immediately aroused, and the German press started drawing comparison with former German Chancellor Gerhard Schroeder's involvement in Gazprom's management.[144]

A new term was coined for this type of lobbying: "Schroederism."

On the whole however, the media in Europe and the U.S. opted to ignore such a gross display of lobbying by the owner of Burisma as well as the role played by Kwasniewski.

Joe Biden publicly eluded this question by claiming that he never discussed with his son the nature of the latter's business with Burisma.[145]

---

143 Shmakov Valeriy, "Marathon electric cars, 'Kiev – Monte Carlo 2015'," [photo], *UNIAN.* https://photo.unian.info/photo/637071-marathon-electric-cars-kiev-monte-carlo-2015

144 Katrin Bennhold, "How the Ex-Chancellor Gerhard Schröder Became Putin's Man in Germany," *The New York Times,* April 23, 2022. https://www.nytimes.com/2022/04/23/world/europe/schroder-germany-russia-gas-ukraine-war-energy.html

"Three weeks before Russia launched its attack on Ukraine, Gazprom — the Soviet energy ministry turned Russian state-controlled gas company, which owns 51 percent of Nord Stream and all of Nord Stream 2 — announced that Mr. Schröder would join its board, too. (Mr. Schröder would not say whether he would accept the nomination.)"

145 Christopher Tremoglie, "Biden once denied knowledge of Hunter's business dealings; now, he's certain they were not illegal," *Washington Examiner,* April 4,

However bent on inquiring about Hunter's sudden promotion with Burisma, *Deutsche Welle* might have shown itself to be, the German news outlet was confronted with stone-cold silence from Burisma and the U.S. State Department.

The investigation in Washington did not yield any more result as the *DW* reporters were merely referred to a White House statement pointing out that Hunter Biden was only a private person. The German journalists decided to drop it the story and refrain from investigating the subject any further.

Lawyers familiar with the realities of energy companies in the former Soviet Union are known to list two main reasons for currying the favor of people of Western repute.

Firstly, it is about reputational achievements. Let's imagine that a gas production company needs to apply for a loan in a foreign bank. Not a Cypriot bank, but one of the top ten banks in the world. In order to do this, you have to go through the Know Your Customer procedure. It is reassuring for the bank to realize, as it conducts a cursory search online, that the first clicks reveal that the board of directors of the company petitioning for a loan includes "Western influencers."

Secondly, it is all about securing political ties, influence and support both in Europe and the U.S.

A clarification is at this point in order.

Edward Lucas, senior vice president of the Center for Analysis of European Politics and British journalist, stands amongst those who have long sounded the alarm about what he called "veiled bribery" of Western elites by post-Soviet kleptocrats.[146]

He distinguishes between so-called "schroederization" for the sake of real political influence in the West on the one hand, and the

---

2022. https://www.washingtonexaminer.com/opinion/biden-once-denied-knowledge-of-hunters-business-dealings-now-hes-certain-they-were-not-illegal

"'How many times have you spoken to your son about his overseas business dealings?' Doocy asked Biden. 'I have never spoken to my son about his overseas business dealings,' Biden replied. Biden even scolded Doocy for asking such a question."

146 PD Smith, "Deception: Spies, Lies and How Russia Dupes the West by Edward Lucas – review," *The Guardian,* February 15, 2013. https://www.theguardian.com/books/2013/feb/15/deception-russia-edward-lucas-review

"Welcome to the 'pirate state' of modern Russia, a nation ruled by a 'criminal conspiracy' of Soviet-era ex-spooks. Lucas tells a gripping story of organised crime, big business, corruption and, of course, espionage."

recruiting of people like Hunter Biden in order to whitewash the image of a company embroiled in legal troubles stemming from criminal cases filed against its owner.

Naftogaz

The Biden family's partnership with Zlochevsky was just the tip of the iceberg. Joe Biden had his sights set on the entire oil and gas sector of Ukraine. In order to accomplish these goals, it became paramount to promote Burisma for the oil and gas corporation business was Biden's instrument of choice in staking his claim in this most lucrative business.

While the events of the Maidan served as the foundation for such enterprise, it bears noting that as early as March 18, 2014, Joe Biden had visited Poland and discussed with then Prime Minister Donald Tusk the possibility of proceeding with reverse gas supplies to Ukraine.[147]

The new Ukrainian "authorities" selected by Washington had no inkling about the American vice president's avowed plans for "energy reform."

Biden's first order of business was to direct new Ukrainian Prime Minister Arseniy Yatsenyuk to immediately start working on replacing direct gas supplies from Russia with reverse ones from Eastern Europe.

The next U.S. presidential election campaign was fast approaching, and the Democrats victory was far from secured. As a result, Biden wished to accelerate the pace of Ukrainian "reforms" and this issue figured prominently during the three visits he made there in April,

---

147 The White House, Office of the Vice President, "Remarks to the Press by Vice President Joe Biden with Prime Minister Donald Tusk of Poland," Prime Minister's Chancellery, Warsaw, Poland, March 18, 2014. https://obamawhitehouse. archives.gov/the-press-office/2014/03/18/remarks-press-vice-president-joe-biden-prime-minister-donald-tusk-poland

"Mr. Prime Minister, we also spoke about energy. In the coming weeks, we'll be meeting with our European partners to discuss ways to further diversify their source and supplies of energy. This will help improve energy security and it will ensure that no nation can use the supply of gas as a political weapon against any other nation. Today, the Prime Minister and I spoke about steps Poland is taking to reverse natural gas flows into some pipelines to help the Ukrainians access additional supplies of gas if needed."

June and November 2014. Altogether, Biden would visit Kiev no less than six times leading up to his "farewell speech" in February 2017.[148]

In the span of his three visits, Biden would come to oversee the composition of a surrogate government in Kiev which would come to play a crucial role in the setting up of the external management system needed to exert control over the country.

A key piece of the edifice was put in place during a cabinet meeting chaired by Arseniy Yatsenyuk. Andrey Kobolev, once a former employee of the company, was confirmed as chairman of the board of Naftogaz.[149]

The *Wall Street Journal* couldn't help but highlight the fact that the Ukrainian gas giant would from now on be headed by a "newcomer." In so doing, the *WSJ* missed the point entirely for Kobolev's management skills weren't deemed as important as his supine character as the face of the gas scam being implemented by Biden and the State Department. The Derkach tapes chronicled this period with alacrity.[150]

At Biden's urging, Yatsenyuk had zealously begun his task of removing Russian gas lines. In October 2014, Naftogaz began to buy gas from Norway's Statoil, German EON and RWE, French GDF Sue

---

148 Rob Crilly, "Joe Biden visited Ukraine six times in eight years while vice president," *Washington Examiner,* October 10, 2019. https://www.washingtonexaminer.com/news/joe-biden-visited-ukraine-six-times-in-eight-years-while-vice-president

149 "Highlights of new Derkach tapes: Influencing Yatsenyuk, Groysman, Avakov; safeguarding Kobolyev (Video)," *UNIAN,* June 20, 2023. https://www.unian.info/politics/derkach-s-tapes-influencing-yatsenyuk-groysman-avakov-guarantees-for-kobolyev-11046770.html

"It follows from the records that in 2016, Biden explicitly demanded that Poroshenko provide Kobolyev with safeguards against criticism and actions of the then Prime Minister Arseniy Yatsenyuk who sought [Kobolyev] dismissal from Naftogaz. Moreover, the Supervisory Board of the Ukrainian state-owned gas company included a personal representative of Biden's interests – Amos Hochstein, Derkach says. Poroshenko promised the then U.S. Vice President that Kobolyev and his deputies would be immune. MP Derkach claims that Biden controlled Naftogaz of Ukraine in order to earn on the quasi-reverse supply of Russian natural gas (when gas is bought from Slovak companies with a EUR 50 mark-up per 1,000 cubic meters)."

150 Jeanne Whalen, "Rookie CEO Takes Over Ukraine Gas Monopoly, The Wall Street Journal, March 28, 2014. https://www.wsj.com/articles/SB10001424052702304688104579467610934906866

and American trader TrailStone by going through the Slovak operator Eustream.[151]

In April 2015, the law "On the Natural Gas Market" was adopted by the Ukrainian parliament.

The local press proceeded to hail Ukrainian energy independence for getting rid of Russian gas, although in practice these "reforms" did not reduce dependence on Russia for the simple reason that Europe did not produce enough gas to compensate for Ukraine's shortfall in kicking Russian suppliers out of the national market. All the same, Burisma had dramatically increased its portfolio of licenses to develop new gas fields in Ukraine.[152]

Burisma's Supervisory Board played a key role in the "reverse gas" scheme owing to a law adopted in Parliament granting boards of publicly owned companies expanded powers. This new legislation was heralded as a revolution in that it allowed management of these companies to adhere to the standards of the Organization for Economic Cooperation and Development (OECD).

Obviously, Biden's team couldn't care less about compliance issues.

---

151 "Naftogaz signed agreement with Statoil for gas deliveries in Slovakia: a breakthrough in line with diversification strategy," Naftogaz Group, October 3, 2014. https://www.naftogaz.com/en/news/ugoda-yaka-bula-pidpysana-naftogazom-ta-statoil-schodo-postavok-gazu-terytorieyu-slovachchyny-stala-proryvom-u-strategii-dyversyfikatsii-dzherel-postachannya-gazu

"Andriy Kobolyev, CEO of Naftogaz, commented on the deal: 'The agreement marks a significant breakthrough for Naftogaz. The multiple gas interconnectors that have been built over the last few years in Europe are substantially improving energy security, both for the EU and Ukraine. Working together, ensuring gas flows both ways, will significantly improve the liquidity and the stability of the EU market. We are committed to integrating Ukraine fully into the EU energy market and working with the European Commission and other key actors to do so.'"

152 CMS Cameron McKenna Nabarro Olswang LLP, "Ukraine: new 3rd Energy Package compliant gas market law," *Lexology,* April 17, 2015. https://www.lexology.com/library/detail.aspx?g=beaf7e79-338a-4223-9768-3b9b49d08d61

"10. Market Gas Pricing: The Law puts an end to the government's practices of cross-subsidisation and non-cost reflective prices. Once the Law comes into force, in theory neither wholesale nor retail prices will be regulated. However, it is likely that the government will impose PSOs for a period until the retail prices for some categories of consumers can reach average market levels. The Law also tries to find a balance between protection of gas consumers, especially 'vulnerable consumers,' which are households that are eligible for subsidies, and their right to freely select and change gas suppliers."

On one of the recordings featuring a Joe Biden and Petro Poroshenko conversation dated February 11, 2016, Biden is heard asking the "Chocolate King" whether the text of Law No. 3062 drafted by Ukraine's Minister of Economy Aivaras Abromavicius had been approved.

As mentioned earlier, Law No. 3062 "On introducing amendments to some legislative acts of Ukraine concerning management of state property" allows for the transferring of the levers of management of state-owned companies from ministries to New Administrative Boards (NABs).[153]

Biden was clearly nervous for he did not even react to Poroshenko's joke that the latter had only recently learned about Abromavičius, who had only arrived in Kyiv from Lithuania in March 2016 following his predecessor's sudden resignation a month earlier.[154]

All Poroshenko knew was that Aivaras Abromavičius was one of the select team of reformist ministers who had joined Arseniy Yatseniuk's government after the coup in 2014. This team had been assembled by the White House and Biden was the point man on this issue.

As such, he couldn't have cared less about the resignation of Abromavičius's predecessor. In the end, Biden's misgivings were not warranted for bill #3062 was eventually adopted by the Ukrainian Parliament in February 2016.

Biden was adamant about the adoption of a law which would pave the way for increased oversight powers of the team of managers waiting in the wings. These individuals would subsequently be introduced into the decision-making logjam of Ukrainian state companies through the Supervisory Boards.

Within a couple years, foreigners literally took over the Ukrainian public sector. By 2020, 5 of 7 members of the Supervisory Board of the railway company "Ukrzaliznytsia" were foreigners.[155]

---

153 "№3062 Draft law on amendments to certain legislative acts of Ukraine on public property management," date of registration September 9, 2015, Reanimation package of reforms. https://rpr.org.ua/en/draft-laws/3062-en/

154 "Как Байден спасал от увольнения Абромавичуса. Аудио разговора с Порошенко," *Strana News,* May 19, 2020. https://strana.news/news/268147-kak-bajden-spasal-ot-uvolnenija-abromavichusa-audio-razhovora-s-poroshenko.html

155 "Sevki Acuner, Chairman of Supervisory Board of JSC 'Ukrainian railways,' *Ukrinform.* https://www.ukrinform.net/rubric-economy/2641162-sevki-

Hailing from Turkiye, Sevki Acuner (a banker with many years of experience in finance around the world and former director of the EBRD office in Ukraine) was approved as the new head of the NAB Board.

It is noteworthy that Acuner simultaneously chaired the NAB Board of the company "Ukrenergo," which had nothing to do with the transportation or energy sector.

Swedish economist Anders Åslund, (who had been working as an advisor to the governments of Ukraine and Russia at the dawn of privatization and neoliberal reforms) and former IMF Boss, Dominique Strauss-Kahn, joined the Supervisory Board of the Credit Dnepr Bank, itself owned by Viktor Pinchuk, the Ukrainian oligarch who was well known as a big contributor to the Democratic Party.[156]

Through their control of the Supervisory Boards, the Americans managed to ingratiate themselves to their agents with sinecures and simultaneously create a system of shadow management of Ukraine's public sector. To be sure, Biden couldn't have cared about improving Naftogaz's finances.

In November 2017, Joe Biden's longtime partner Amos Hochstein was appointed as independent director of Naftogaz's supervisory board. Hochstein had worked for many years as a Democrat operator in the U.S. Congress. As a former lobbyist for Cassidy & Associates

acuner-chairman-of-supervisory-board-of-jsc-ukrainian-railways.html

"I have already mentioned some key elements of it, namely – changing the decision-making process, improving efficiency and capacity to attract additional financing resources for investments. Equally important is the fight against corruption and theft. Therefore, we fully welcome the work of the law enforcement bodies in this regard and encourage them to work closely with us to help eliminate any criminal and corrupt practices in the company. I asked for it in a letter to the authorities. While we are developing appropriate processes and measures to fight it, we are not a law enforcement body with the resources and powers that position carries. Fighting the organized crime element which constitutes the big majority of this malpractice against our company is neither within our capabilities nor power. Therefore, we are asking the state's law enforcement authorities to help us eliminate this crime that takes place against the company, thus against the people of Ukraine."

156 "Ex-head of IMF Strauss-Kahn, economists Aslund, Saltiel become members of supervisory board of Pinchuk's bank Credit-Dnepr," *Interfax-Ukraine,* February 3, 2016. https://en.interfax.com.ua/news/economic/322067.html

"Bank Credit Dnepr, under control of Ukrainian businessman Victor Pinchuk, has formed a new supervisory board consisting of six members, and famous international economists Dominique Strauss-Kahn, Anders Aslund, Jean-Pierre Saltiel and Alex Munteanu have become four independent members of the board."

in the 1990s, Hochstein had come under scrutiny while working with one of Africa's oldest dictators.

President Teodoro Obiang Nguema Mbasogo of Equatorial Guinea had been Biden's long-time collaborator despite being regularly condemned by international human rights organizations for his ferocious repression and suppression of political freedoms.

Speaking to the *Washington Post*, Hochstein attempted to smooth over the reputation of the regime. In 2011, he was appointed special envoy for international energy issues at the U.S. Department of State. There, he worked closely with Biden, accompanying him on numerous tours of various countries, including Ukraine, on behalf of which since 2014 he had been advocating against direct purchases of Russian gas.[157]

In that capacity, Hochstein had always been present during Biden's talks with Poroshenko, once telling the *New York Times:* "I was at almost every single meeting Vice President Biden had with President Poroshenko, I was on every trip, and I was present for most of the phone calls."

Hochstein was the perfect choice for the role of overseeing the Ukrainian gas market for not only did he possess an excellent grasp of the energy question;, he was also extremely cautious and had advised Biden against introducing Hunter to the board of directors of Burisma.[158]

---

157 Michael Grunwald, "A Conversation with Amos Hochstein" [Interview], *The Washington Post*, April 26, 2006. https://www.washingtonpost.com/archive/opinions/2006/04/23/a-conversation-with-amos-hochstein-interview-by-michael-grunwald/eaef2aa4-909d-4407-9fc6-d92a2b39c8a3/

"Our meetings have all been very businesslike. He's convinced me of his deep care for his people. And I've seen the changes. I know that he sent 120 Equato-Guinean nurses to Israel for training. I've seen the kids going to new schools in their blue pants and white shirts. Yes, he became president in a coup. But people forget that his predecessor [Francisco Macias Nguema] was the worst dictator ever in Africa. ... Secretary Rice isn't saying these positive things as a favor to me. She's saying it because it's real."

158 U.S. Senate Committee on Homeland Security and Governmental Affairs/ U.S. Senate Committee on Finance, *Hunter Biden, Burisma, and Corruption: The Impact on U.S. Government Policy and Related Concerns.* https://www.hsgac.senate.gov/wp-content/uploads/imo/media/doc/HSGAC_Finance_Report_FINAL.pdf

"Public reporting also confirms Hochstein's discussion with Vice President Biden. According to one report, 'Amos Hochstein, the Obama Administration's special envoy for energy policy, raised the matter with Biden, but did not go so far

Amos Hochstein would resign from the Naftogaz board in 2020 in the midst of the scandals surrounding Burisma.[159]

Back in 2016, Poroshenko pushed through parliament all the necessary laws necessary to legalize the gas contracts with Eastern European traders and proceedings related to the appointment of an American supervisor to Naftogaz. Soon thereafter, official gas deliveries from Russia began to drop sharply and were soon to be replaced with supplies from the European Union.

While Poroshenko proclaimed victory in Ukraine gaining its "energy" independence from Moscow, the real cost of Ukraine's "victory" was characterized by Andriy Derkach in less glowing terms: "The estimate of the corruption, according to experts, reaches at least $1.5 billion."[160]

In effect, Russian gas initially entered Ukrainian territory proper, then shortly bifurcated for one and a half kilometers onto the territory

---

as to recommend that Hunter leave the board. When Hochstein testified before the Committees, he declined on advice of counsel to testify about the substance of his conversation with Vice President Biden. *The New Yorker,* however, reported that Hochstein 'did not go so far as to recommend that Hunter leave the board.' It is unclear how Vice President Biden responded to this conversation. ... [Hochstein]: 'We were starting to think about a trip to Ukraine, and I wanted to make sure that he [Vice President Biden] was aware that there was an increase in chatter on media outlets close to Russians and corrupt oligarchs-owned media outlets about undermining his message—to try to undermine his [Vice President Biden's] message and including Hunter Biden being part of the board of Burisma.'"

159 "Ex-U.S. Diplomat Steps Down From Naftogaz Board, Citing Ukrainian Corruption Concerns," *Radio Free Europe/Radio Liberty,* October 13, 2020. https://www.rferl.org/a/ex-u-s-diplomat-steps-down-from-naftogaz-board-citing-ukrainian-corruption-concerns/30890034.html

"'Unfortunately, Naftogaz management's successful efforts to create a new corporate culture, transparent mechanisms, and an adherence to international standards, was resisted at every step of the way. The company has been forced to spend endless amounts of time combating political pressure and efforts by oligarchs to enrich themselves through questionable transactions,' Hochstein said."

160 "The Parliament Said That Ukraine Overpaid $1.5 Billion for Incoming Gas on Reverse," *Oreanda-News,* December 17, 2019. https://www.oreanda-news.com/en/finansy/the-parliament-said-that-ukraine-overpaid-1-5-billion-for-incoming-gas-on-reverse/article1294525/

"The deputy said that over 3.5 years (from 2015 to 2018), the average gas price in Europe was about $210 per thousand cubic meters, while Naftogaz purchased it at an average price of $245, so the difference was $35 per thousand cubic meters. And from July 2018 to April 2019, the average gas price in the EU was $238.5 per thousand cubic meters, while Ukraine imported an average of $288.5 per resource, and the overpayment amounted to $50 per thousand cubic meters."

of Slovakia before swerving back to the territory of Ukraine. At this particular point, it came back in as "European" gas.

What made it "European" was that during the transit on Slovakian territory, documents reveal is that pipeline companies associated with the schemers each took a share of the gas before tagging their commission—set at 50 Euros for each thousand cubic meters. "In so doing, these operators managed to 'snaftogaz' (to embezzle) USD 1.5 billion," said Derkach at a press conference.

Amos Hochstein supervised the whole scheme while Andriy Favorov, a Ukrainian with a U.S. passport, was tasked with handling the "colleagues" in Slovakia.[161]

At first glance, there is nothing criminal about Hochstein's scheme. If Kiev wants to pretend it consumes European gas that doesn't really exist, that's not illegal per se.

But the point here is different. As an indication, while in 2015–2018, the average price per 1,000 cubic meters of gas in Europe was set at 211 U.S. dollars, Naftogaz opted to pay on average 245.63 U.S. dollars, that is $35 over the market price.

From July 2018 to April 2019, the average price of gas in Europe was almost $238.5 USD, but Ukraine somehow imported it at a rate of $288.5 USD. The difference was 50 euros for every thousand cubic meters.

Andriy Derkach calculated that Ukraine overpaid almost $1.5 billion for so-called European gas over 5 years, and that's according to the most conservative estimates. In other words, in order to justify the surcharge, Biden demanded that Poroshenko increase gas prices for the population by 75%![162]

---

161 Naftogaz, "Andriy Favorov to lead Naftogaz's gas business" [news release], November 27, 2018. https://www.naftogaz.com/en/news/gazovyy-biznes-naftogazu-ocholyt-andriy-favorov

"Andriy Favorov worked as chief commercial officer at DTEK energy holding (Kyiv) between September 2010 and July 2014 and as business development director at ContourGlobal (Kyiv) between May 2009 and July 2010. Prior to that, he held managerial positions with AES Corporation. In 2005, Andriy Favorov obtained an MBA from Georgetown University (Washington D.C.)."

162 "'International corruption and treason' – Derkach unveiled conversations of voices similar to Poroshenko and Biden," Ukrainian News, May 19, 2020. https://ukranews.com/en/news/703200-international-corruption-and-treason-derkach-unveiled-conversations-of-voices-similar-to-poroshenko

"'Petro Oleksiyovych confesses to Biden that he raised tariffs for ordinary

Where did the difference of hundreds of millions of dollars between Russian and "European" reverse gas go? When Amos Hochstein joined Naftogaz's board of directors, the Ukrainian Energy Resources of Ukraine, or ERU, became the company's largest gas importer. It would be more accurate to say that behind this brand there existed a whole group of companies with "ERU" in their names.

Many of these affiliate companies were registered in Ukraine and offshore. ERU Trading, ERU Corporation, ERU Management Services LLC were all registered in Joe Biden's home state of Delaware. According to the data published by Andrii Derkach, the ultimate beneficiary of this web of shell-companies was Andrey Favorov, the deputy chairman of Naftogaz. This is not a coincidence since Favorov, a dual citizen (Russian-U.S.) was considered a proven and reliable manager who had once worked for the American energy giant AES in Third World countries, and he had since 2009 worked for AES-affiliated Contour Global at its Eastern Europe office.[163]

Under Viktor Yanukovych, Favorov had been appointed to oversee Rinat Akhmetov's DTEK energy holding company where he was officially tasked with the adjustment of gas imports from Europe. At the same time, he would supervise all reverse and offshore gas schemes. In 2013, he negotiated a natural gas supply contract between DTEK and the Polish company PGNiG, (PGNiG would later become a key partner of ERU).[164]

Ukrainians, attention, not by 75% as requested by the IMF, but by as much as 100%. For the sake of a billion for himself, Poroshenko is ready to strip the Ukrainians naked and also make money on tariffs. By the way, tariffs really doubled,' Derkach said."

163 Andrew Favorov | Speakers | Kyiv International Economic Forum. https://forumkyiv.org/en/speakers/andrij-favorov

"Andrew Favorov has vast experience in managerial positions with both American and Ukrainian companies, including DTEK ContourGlobal and AES Corporation where he implemented wide-scale projects with high capitalization. Having left the post of Commercial Director at DTEK energy holding, he founded Energy Resources of Ukraine (ERU)."

164 "Andrey Favorov Appointed Commercial Director of DTEK," *Oreanda-News,* April 26, 2012. https://www.oreanda-news.com/en/promyshlennost/article625372/

"'Setting up a unified centre of responsibility for the commercial activity will enable DTEK to enjoy all the benefits of the vertical integration. A strategic approach to this function will help us see bottle-necks well in advance and respond to challenges in time,' Andrey Favorov, DTEK's Commercial Director, commented. 'The new model systematizes our operations with the trading partners in and outside Ukraine.

In addition, he helped create DTEK Trading SA, a Swiss offshore entity conceived to import natural gas from Europe.

In retrospect, one better understands Biden's concerns (expressed in a conversation held with Petro Poroshenko on December 19, 2016), about the fate of "dedicated reformers" and "talented managers." Such concerns seemed justified as new Ukrainian Prime Minister Vladimir Groysman decided to fire Naftogaz head Andriy Kobolev.[165]

Realizing that his could put a stop to the entire scheme supervised by Hochstein, Biden commented: "In Europe this could be seen as a problem. I hope that you will ask the prime minister to slow down somewhat on this. This is not the right thing to do."[166]

Biden was making an explicit recommendation to Poroshenko that Kobolev not be fired.[167]

Another factor contributing to Biden's unease was that Donald Trump's chances of victory had increased dramatically and Biden

---

It will raise competitiveness of our commodities on external markets. I am sure Mr Favorov's experience will help efficiently use the Division employees' potential and implement the best commercial practices in the Company,' Maxim Timchenko, DTEK's CEO, said."

165 Oleksiy Sorokin, "Naftogaz head Kobolyev brands Groysman's move to oust him 'illegal,'" *Kyiv Post,* March 6, 2019. https://archive.kyivpost.com/business/naftogaz-head-kobolev-brands-gryosmans-move-to-oust-him-illegal.html

"'The main influence of the shareholder – the government – is appointing a professional supervisory board which will manage (Naftogaz),' Kobolyev said, stating that the supervisory board wanted to renew his contract."

166 Andrii Derkach, Member of Ukrainian Parliament, "Records of conversations testifying to international corruption," 2020. https://web.archive.org/web/20210921150435/https://www.derkach.com.ua/en/publications/new-details-case-burisma-bribe-well-new-records-conversations-testifying-international-corruption-external-governance-ukraine/

"'We hope the current leadership stays in place,' the lord says to his vassal. Biden will not let Kobolyev get hurt. And you know why? Because millions received from pseudo-European gas, which in reality is the reverse of Russian gas, are at stake. The price of interest was 50 euros per every thousand cubes."

167 Daria Zubkova (editor), "Biden Requested Poroshenko Not To Let Groysman Dismiss Naftogaz Board Chairperson Kobolev – Derkach's Records," *Ukrainian News,* June 23, 2020. https://ukranews.com/en/news/710373-biden-requested-poroshenko-not-to-let-groysman-dismiss-naftogaz-board-chairperson-kobolev-derkach-s

"This follows from the records of the talks between Biden and Poroshenko dated December 19, 2016 published by non-affiliated member of the Ukrainian Parliament, Andrii Derkach, Ukrainian News Agency reports. He added he knew that Groysman advocated Kobolev's dismissal. Poroshenko promised Biden to monitor the situation."

sought to preserve the entire system of influence he had created at Naftogaz. In January 2017, during his farewell visit to Kiev, Biden again reminded Poroshenko to appoint Hochstein as a director on the board of Naftogaz. Per Biden's logic, Hochstein would ensure continued control over the whole scheme of reverse gas supplies to Ukraine following the transfer of power in the United States.

While laying out the entire reverse gas scheme during his press conference held on June 22, 2020, Ukrainian MP Derkach explained that between 2015 and 2018, the revenue of ERU Trading was 15.6 billion hryvnia ($700 million). Part of this money was withdrawn offshore. For example, from July 2016 to June 2017, almost UAH 348 million were withdrawn from ERU Trading and transferred to the account of American ERU Management Services LLC. Then from May 2017 to July 2017, another UAH 274 million underwent the same route. This adds up to more than $25 million. Hopefully, evidence will someday be presented bearing on revenues from the reverse scheme finding their way to accounts Stateside. Until then, discourses on these schemes will likely keep being characterized as Russian disinformation.

State Dept., Inc.

Loan guarantees served both as carrot and stick in the wrangling of Ukraine.[168]

Admittedly, the process of developing an external management system bearing Joe Biden's imprimatur did not always go smoothly as one recalls the controversy surrounding the dismissal of Prosecutor General Viktor Shokin. Similar cases lined the path of Joe Biden's takeover of Ukrainian politics. Groiman's conflict with Kobolev stood as another notable episode.

Biden's main instrument of pressure on Kiev took the form of financial support from the IMF and USAID. Biden made that clear during a January 2018 panel held at the Council on Foreign Relations. The then–Vice President gave a speech he would later come to regret:[169]

---

168 Congressional Research Service, *U.S. Foreign Assistance: USAID Loan Guarantees,* updated July 18, 2017. https://crsreports.congress.gov/product/pdf/IF/IF10409/5

169 "Joe Biden Brags About Withholding Ukraine Aid in Council on Foreign

I went to Kiev 12 or 13 times, and at the end I had to announce that we were offering another billion dollars in loan guarantees. I got promises from Poroshenko and Yatsenyuk that they would take steps on the attorney general, but they didn't. I told them: "We're not going to give you a billion dollars." They told me, "But you don't have that authority, you're not the president, and the president said he would." I said, "Call him. I'm telling you you're not getting a billion dollars." I looked at them and said, "I'm leaving in six hours, and unless your attorney general gets fired, you don't get the money until then." Son of a bitch! And they fired him. And they put someone in his place who was suitable at the time.

The Biden team's statement to the effect that the "Derkach tapes" were "a hole in a bagel" fabricated by the Russian special services does not sound very convincing, for Biden actually conceded having discussed the fate of Prosecutor General Shokin with Poroshenko.

The first U.S. senior official recorded to have expressed concerns about Shokin was former Secretary of State John Kerry, who in on December 3, 2015, stated:

I would like to urge you to consider a solution to replace Attorney General Shokin, because he has, in my opinion, blocked the reform of the purification of the Prosecutor General's Office.[170]

Back then, Poroshenko ignored his request, but following the Ukrainian Prosecutor General's issuance of a subpoena for questioning Hunter, Biden Sr. decided that a red line had been crossed. In a March 22, 2016, conversation with Poroshenko, Biden explicitly stated that

Relations," YouTube video [1:00] posted by jRon's Two Cents, December 12, 2019. https://www.youtube.com/watch?v=u27qy5YViFs

170 Ibid.

"One of the conversations on the said issues was allegedly recorded on December 3, 2015, where the voice that's purportedly John Kerry's is heard saying: 'I wanted to try to urge you to see if there's a way to get by that problem of replacing the prosecutor general, you know, (Viktor) Shokin because per my perception, he's blocked the cleanup of the Prosecutor General's Office,' said Kerry."

as a condition for providing $1 billion in financial aid to Ukraine, a change at the Prosecutor General's Office had to be implemented. "If you have a new government and a new attorney general, I will be prepared to publicly sign off on the $1 billion" Biden said.[171]

U.S. State Department's Special Representative for Ukraine, Kurt Volker was a high-ranking witness to the story of the Prosecutor General's resignation. In his testimony to the U.S. House Intelligence Committee, Volker confirmed the existence of pressure on Kiev: "There is clear evidence that Biden suggested that the president of Ukraine fire Shokin." According to Volker, the motivation for such pressure was not, however, linked to Biden's affairs but to the fact that the prosecutor general was himself corrupt and as such "interfered with the reform of the prosecutor's office."[172]

Petro Poroshenko disagreed with Volker's assertion. He recalled telling Biden in a recording dated February 18, 2016, that: "Yesterday, I met with Prosecutor General Shokin, and despite the fact that there are no accusations of corruption or misconduct against him, I still asked him to resign. And an hour ago, he brought me his letter of resignation."

In effect, Poroshenko fired Shokin, about whom he had no complaints, only because the then U.S. Vice President did not hesitate to use American taxpayers' money to carry out his own agenda.

Natalia Jaresko, a U.S. citizen of Ukrainian descent, came to play an important role within the scheme of U.S. external control over Ukraine.[173] Fluent in Ukrainian, she was on friendly terms with

---

171 "Joe Biden Leaked Call Transcript with Petro Poroshenko" (March 22, 2016), *Rev Transcripts,* May 20, 2020. https://www.rev.com/blog/transcripts/joe-biden-leaked-call-transcript-with-petro-poroshenko

"Well, I'm on Air Force Two, and I think we're going to stay connected. We just took off and I'm hoping this connection will stay open... Tell me that there's a new government, and a new Prosecutor General. I am prepared to do a public signing of the commitment for the billion dollars. Again, I'm not suggesting that's what you want or don't want. I'm just suggesting that's what we're prepared to do, and again, it wouldn't be finalized until the IMF pieces are written."

172 Kurt Volker Testimony, October 3, 2019, contributed by Brandon Carter (NPR).   https://apps.npr.org/documents/document.html?id=6540391-Kurt-Volker-Testimony

173 "Minister Natalie A. Jaresko, EY-Parthenon Managing Director, Turnaround Restructuring and Strategy, Ernst & Young LLP," EY Parthenon. https://www.ey.com/en_us/people/natalie-a-jaresko

representatives of the financial world both in the U.S. and abroad. Jaresko would go on to serve as head of Ukraine's Ministry of Finance from December 2014 to April 2016, a position she owed to the patronage of Joe Biden. Jaresko is remembered in Ukraine for her role in issuing $3 billion in Eurobonds under U.S. guarantees, and then setting up the restructuring of the country's foreign debt, which ended up driving Ukraine into a debt hole.

In 2016, as Arseniy Yatsenyuk's tenure as Prime Minister was coming to an end, Biden had tried to promote Jaresko to replace him owing to her U.S. citizenship, which exempted her from being targeted in any criminal prosecution. However, Poroshenko promptly granted her Ukrainian citizenship before she committed to start the procedure of renouncing American citizenship, as was required under Ukrainian law. The circumstances surrounding Jaresko almost becoming prime minister illustrate Biden's system of external management in the most caricatural fashion.

In another one of Derkach's recordings, Biden is heard defending Yatsenyuk who was threatened with removal owing to his disagreements with the Samopomich faction.[174] In the spring of 2016, a political crisis in parliament escalated as Samopomich, but also Fatherland and Lyashko's Radical Party all opted to leave the coalition. By law, Poroshenko was obliged to dissolve parliament and call on new elections. As he prepared to dissolve Parliament, Poroshenko had no plans on keeping Yatsenyuk as prime minister.

Petro Poroshenko: "As expected, the Batkivshchyna and Samopomich factions have left the coalition. There are now less than 226 votes left in the coalition, so we don't have a majority. I personally, together with the Prime Minister, invited Lyashko's Radical Party to join the majority, so that formally we could maintain our eligibility. But we have no formal strength in parliament or support in society."[175]

Biden: "...If I understand correctly, the resolution of no confidence in the government did not pass, you blocked it? Arseniy still remains. But then, there was a vote for the reform package that the

---

174 Andrii Derkach, Member of Ukrainian Parliament, "New Facts of International Corruption and External Governance of Ukraine," 2020. https://web.archive.org/web/20211201151318/https://www.derkach.com.ua/en/publications/new-facts-international-corruption-external-governance-ukraine/
175 Ibid.

government proposed, and 247 votes were against it. So in terms of moving forward and additional reforms that you have to implement, you don't have a majority in parliament, you don't have a coalition for that, right? Is that what you're talking about?"

Poroshenko: "...no, not really. First, the parliament had to evaluate the work of the government, and it gave an unsatisfactory evaluation to the Cabinet. That was the first event. It does not mean an urgent resignation of the government, it is just a political assessment of its actions. Then, when the resolution of no confidence was put to a vote, I organized in such a way that there were not enough votes in my faction and in other factions. The Prime Minister had a hand in that, too, of course, but I personally blocked the resignation of the government, because I promised you that. But now that two of the four factions have left the coalition, we do not have a majority in parliament."[176]

Judging by this dialogue, Biden was struggling to absorb the subtleties of political life in Ukraine in his drive to keep Yatsenyuk as Prime Minister. He recommended that Poroshenko make an alliance with Lyashko's Radical Party, but Poroshenko explained that Lyashko's votes would not be enough to save the coalition and hinted at the possibility of buying the votes of the deputies.

And then Natalia Jaresko's name popped out.

Biden: "...Just recently on her Facebook page, Jaresko said she was ready to be prime minister and lead a government of technocrats. And I know you need 226 votes either way. Tell me what's going on, if you can?"

Poroshenko pointed out that after discussing her candidacy with the Samopomich faction, the latter was putting out too many political conditions in order to green light the nomination. He then begged Biden to press Samopomich into a compromise, suggesting that Biden exert leverage not only on Samopomich, but also on other parties:

> Please don't give grants to Samopomich, don't give them money because this is not funding an opposition party, but funding an absolutely irresponsible political leader who is doing very bad things for the future of my country, for Ukraine and for security and stability.[177]

---

176 Ibid.
177 Ibid.

In effect, Poroshenko was thrusting the issue of forming a coalition under Jaresko's premiership into Biden's hands, pleading for Biden to allow him to assume his duties as president of Ukraine and micro-manage the political crisis down to its last details. It is no coincidence that Derkach's tapes generated such a backlash from the Democrats as they regained control of the White House in late 2020.

Jaresko had worked for many years for the U.S. Agency for International Development (USAID), and before that at the U.S. State Department. From 1992 to 1995 she had served as the first chief of the economic section at the U.S. Embassy in Ukraine. In 1995 she started working as a regional investment manager for the Western NIS Enterprises Fund (WNISEF), a private equity fund created by the U.S. Congress and funded by the U.S. government through USAID.[178]

In 2001, Jaresko became the head of WNISEF. In 2006, she became the co-founder and head of the management company Horizon Capital. Under the auspices of Horizon Capital, the Americans launched the Emerging Europe Growth Fund (EEGF), which received 132 million dollars. The purpose of the program was to finance invest-ment projects in Ukraine. In 2008, an EEGF II program was launched with 370 million dollars, followed by an EEGF III program, created with 200 million dollars in investments.[179]

Upon becoming Ukraine's finance minister, Jaresko started work on preparing loan guarantees. In the Loan Guarantee Agreement dated May 18, 2015, the Ukrainian Finance Ministry pledged to make changes to gas market legislation and to the management structure

---

178 Western NIS Enterprise Fund, *Advancing Change that Lasts: Annual Report, 2017.* https://wnisef.org/wp-content/uploads/2018/09/2017-WNISEF-AR_ENG_FINAL.pdf

179 "Horizon Capital closes third Ukraine fund at 200 million-U.S. dollar hard cap," *Emerging Europe,* January 25, 2019. https://emerging-europe.com/business/horizon-capital-closes-third-ukraine-fund-at-200-million-us-dollar-hard-cap/

"U.S. private-equity firm Horizon Capital, which invests in high growth and export-driven companies in Ukraine and the near region, has closed its third fund, Emerging Europe Growth III (EEGF III), as its 200 million U.S. dollar hard cap, far surpassing the 150 million U.S. dollar target. In what marks the largest private equity fund raised for Ukraine in a decade, Horizon's EEGF III received strong backing from existing and new investors, attracted by the excellent value, fast growth and abundance of opportunities that Ukraine offers. Horizon manages over 850 million U.S. dollars in assets from investors with a capital base exceeding 350 billion U.S. dollars. Its Ukraine-focused funds have invested over 650 million U.S. dollars in 140 companies employing over 46,000 people."

of Naftogaz Ukrainy. These were exactly the same changes that had allowed the supervisory board to expand its powers and exert control over Ukrainian state property, primarily in the oil and gas sector. In addition, the Agreement mandated that Ukraine had to provide USAID with a schedule for the increase of tariffs in the energy sector by 75% by 2017.

Poroshenko would exceed his mandate and report to Biden that he had eventually increased tariffs by 100%. In order to provide credit guarantees, Poroshenko and Biden had opted to reach into the wallets of Ukrainian citizens. The issue was chronicled in one of Derkach's tapes as follows: "In the last three weeks, we have shown significant progress on reforms. We voted for 100 percent on tariffs despite the fact that the IMF expected only 75 percent."

Poroshenko is heard reporting this to Biden who welcomes the decision since it was necessary to justify the surcharge on the reverse gas.

The crowning achievement of Natalia Jaresko's tenure as finance minister was to be the scheme at the heart of Ukraine's restructuring of its foreign debt. At Jaresko's urging, Ukraine concluded an agreement to restructure its foreign debt of $15 billion in August 2015. The creditors included the Franklin Templeton Foundation, which stood as the largest holder of Ukrainian government debt.[180]

The agreement provided for a 20% reduction in external debt, i.e., 3.6 billion dollars, which the Ukrainian and foreign press hailed as a phenomenal accomplishment.

In practice, this was not debt forgiveness.[181] Rather, Ukraine issued special securities to the creditors, the so-called GDP-warrants

---

180 Robert Parry, "How Ukraine's Finance Chief Got Rich," *Truthout,* November 13, 2015. https://truthout.org/articles/how-ukraine-s-finance-chief-got-rich/

"Last December, Ukrainian President Petro Poroshenko named Jaresko Finance Minister after awarding her instant Ukrainian citizenship. At that point, she quit WNISEF and has since become the face of Ukrainian 'reform,' representing the US-backed government at international banking events at Davos, Switzerland, and elsewhere while appealing for billions of dollars in Western financial aid which she oversees."

181 "Ukraine completes debt restructuring of around $15 billion," *Reuters,* November 12, 2015. https://www.reuters.com/article/us-ukraine-crisis-debt-idUSKCN0T12FT20151112

"'The successful conclusion of our debt restructuring process, completed while or "Value Recovery Instruments," the income of which was linked to the economic growth of the country.[182] For example, if the GDP growth rate reached up to include 3%, the payout would be zero percent; if the economy grew between 3% and 4%, the payout would be fixed at 15% of one percent of GDP growth and if the growth rate exceeded 4%, Ukraine would then have to pay out 40% of each additional percentage of economic growth.

Jaresko's method of tying debt payments to economic growth is unprecedented. Assuming that Ukraine's growth did not suffer unexpected obstacles, Jaresko's GDP-warrants, which were to be effective from 2021 to 2040, endeared her to owners of debt securities. Sergiy Marchenko, Jaresko's successor, echoed the general optimism: "Potential payments on state derivatives by 2040 with a moderate growth of GDP may reach more than 22 billion dollars and Natalia Jaresko should be thanked for that."[183]

In recognition of her work in obtaining such favorable terms for the U.S. resolution of the debt crisis in Ukraine, Jaresko was sent to oversee the implementation of economic reforms in Puerto Rico where a political crisis erupted shortly after her arrival.

USAID Money

The story of how the Ukrainian government, maneuvering with the tacit complicity of U.S. officials and diplomats, misappropriated U.S. taxpayers' monies displays all the hallmarks of a criminal scheme reminiscent of a Martin Scorsese picture. Derkach devoted entire press conferences to this topic.

---

avoiding default, leaves Ukraine's economy in a much stronger position and is an important prerequisite for our return to growth,' Finance Minister Natalia Yaresko was quoted as saying in a statement."

182 Sujata Rao, "Ukraine's growth-linked bonds – when recovery becomes painful," *Reuters,* September 15, 2017. https://www.reuters.com/article/uk-ukraine-bonds-gdp-analysis-idUKKCN1BQ1UY

"But Kiev made one crucial omission: unlike other warrant issuers, it did not cap future payouts, possibly making itself liable for big annual payments after 2025."

183 "Payments on GDP warrants of $40 mln in 2021 with moderate GDP growth potentially could reach $22 bln by 2040 – Finance Minister," *Interfax-Ukraine,* September 9, 2020. https://en.interfax.com.ua/news/economic/686624.html

According to Derkach, the National Police of the Ministry of Internal Affairs filed a case involving an international embezzlement scheme with the Unified Register of Pre-Trial Investigations at the Anti-Corruption Center.

The case revolved around the head of the Anti-Corruption Center, Vitaly Shabunin (26.11.1984), and the founder of the Anti-Corruption Center, Dmitry Sherenbey (21.02.1977), very effectively "sawing away" international financial aid. Sherenbey and Shabunin were close friends. Of note, not only was Sherenbey a friend of Ukraine's chief anti-corruption official, he was also rumored to be romantically linked with then acting U.S. Ambassador to Ukraine, Christina Quinn. Finally, Sherenbey was a repeat offender, having been convicted 4 times from 1992 to 2002.[184]

Anti-corruption: The Ukrainian Version

Derkach: "…they (Shabunin and Sherembey) organized a scheme to embezzle international technical assistance through the charitable organization 'All-Ukrainian Network of People Living with HIV/AIDS' founded by Sherembey."[185]

Between 2015 and 2017, it is estimated that $142.9 million were funneled through this network of organizations, with Derkach highlighting that Sherembey and Shabunin had lobbied commercial

---

184 "Виталий Шабунин и Кристина Квин. Что известно об этой паре," *Strana News,* September 16, 2020. https://strana.news/articles/private-life/290074-vitalij-i-kristina-chto-izvestno-ob-etoj-pare.html

185 "Int'l donors asked not to send aid to Ukraine though corrupt structures led by Sherembei, Shabunin both close to NABU chief Sytnyk," *UNIAN,* April 14, 2020. https://www.unian.info/politics/10958189-int-l-donors-asked-not-to-send-aid-to-ukraine-though-corrupt-structures-led-by-sherembei-shabunin-both-close-to-nabu-chief-sytnyk.html

"'We believe that representatives of the All-Ukrainian Network of People Living with HIV ("100% Life"), the Anti-corruption Action Center, the Light of Hope NGO and some other organizations affiliated with them have no moral right, until the results of the investigation are received and truth is established in these cases, to occupy elected positions in bodies like the "Stop tuberculosis, Ukraine" Partnership,' activists say. 'We also believe the said organizations cannot be the main recipients of grants of international assistance provided to Ukraine. We are not aware of any examples in a civilized democratic international community that people representing organizations that are suspected of embezzlement and misuse of funds occupy posts, that these organizations and people representing these organizations are listened to and respected in society.'"

companies for the procurement of medical equipment and medicines from "fictitious companies as well as companies known for their negative business reputation." said the MP.[186]

According to Derkach, "Since the U.S. government money was used, I believe that the investigation should take advantage of the possibilities of international legal assistance within the framework of existing treaties" the MP summarized.[187]

The two friends' so-called charity organization, All-Ukrainian Network of People Living with HIV/AIDS was set up in 2015. Between 2015 and 2017, using the Global AIDS Foundation as their main donor, they managed to collect $133,881,757 and funnel the funds to the organization's accounts. This scheme, entailing the embezzlement of international financial aid, was organized very simply: large sums of money (from $33,324 to $7,821,215) were transferred to front companies, which then issued fake reports on the use of the received funds. Subsequently, investigations revealed that a number of such firms and organizations featured in the process had previously engaged in the embezzlement of international financial aid along with other criminal violations.[188]

As an example, the "Farmasko" company received $2,721,279 from the Shabunin-Sherembey Foundation for allegedly supplying equipment. Farmasko was defendant in a criminal case bearing on the misappropriation of funds belonging to the international charity fund International Alliance Against HIV/AIDS in Ukraine. The scam involved disguising the origin of funds obtained by fraudulent means under color of law.

Optima Pharm Ltd is another example. The firm received $942,139 and has been repeatedly involved in criminal cases related

---

186 "Шабунин и СПИД - уголовное дело против Центра противодействия коррупции," Strana News, March 12, 2020. https://strana.news/news/253984-shabunin-i-spid-uholovnoe-delo-protiv-tsentra-protivodejstvija-korruptsii.html

187 Ibid.

188 "U.S., Soros-Funded Ukrainian HIV Charity Under Criminal Probe for Embezzlement," *Judicial Watch,* February 26, 2020. https://www.judicialwatch.org/u-s-soros-funded-ukrainian-hiv-charity-under-criminal-probe-for-embezzlement/

"Ukrainian authorities have launched a criminal investigation into an HIV nonprofit that receives huge sums of money from the U.S. government as well as leftwing billionaire George Soros. The foreign probe exposes one of many outrageous collaborative efforts between Uncle Sam and the Hungarian philanthropist who funds a multitude of projects worldwide aimed at spreading a radical globalist agenda."

to "the creation of shady and corrupt schemes to conceal the real cost of drugs."[189]

Another charity, Light of Hope, received $5,399,355 for its own program. This "charitable organization" was also well known to Ukrainian law enforcement. Its representatives had managed to obtain a grant from the European Union worth 10,000.40 euros in order to "provide assistance to internally displaced persons," i.e., refugees from Donbass.[190] The investigation established that not a single euro ever reached the IDPs. The Poltava Regional State Administration was also involved in the scheme.

Christina Quinn, as acting U.S. Ambassador in Kyiv, personally selected and approved the lists of organizations to which grants and USAID funds were to be distributed to these entities alleged to work on behalf of the public interest.[191]

Another of the embassy's tasks entailed oversight of the program bearing on the reform of the Ukrainian Prosecutor General's Office. In April 2020, Andrii Derkach claimed to have unearthed more acts of corruption in his statement filed with the Prosecutor General's Office of Ukraine (case №12020800000000444). The allegations this time targeted officials of the IDLO office in Ukraine and Psymetrics-Ukraine LLC, whom Derkach claimed had engaged in "embezzlement of international technical assistance funds." According to the procurement plan, over $7,380,000 were allocated for the "Support for reform of criminal justice of Ukraine" project, a program aimed at reforming the prosecutorial organs in Ukraine. Derkach alleged that $744,000 of

---

189 "Optima-Pharm LTD," Organizations | *DevelopmentAid.* Supplier from Ukraine; Funding agencies UNDP, other; Health sector. https://www.developmentaid. org/organizations/view/97414/optima-farm-ltd

190 Sergii Slukhai, *Ukraine: Light of Hope's Work Improving Social Services for Marginalized Groups* (October 2016). https://ssrn.com/abstract=2926625

191 Irina Schiller, "Hard Crisis Manager: Who is Christina Quinn, replacing Marie Yovanovitch at the U.S. Embassy in Ukraine," *ForumDaily,* June 1, 2019. https://www.forumdaily.com/en/zhestkij-krizis-menedzher-kto-takaya-kristina-kvin-zamenivshaya-mari-jovanovich-v-posolstve-ssha-v-ukraine/

"According to the political observer, a person specializing in economic and military issues has been appointed to replace Jovovich. In particular, she is able to effectively and competently talk with businessmen, including with Ukrainian oligarchs, in a language they understand, and, in turn, well understanding her counterparts. While in the status of a temporary attorney, Quinn has the maximum freedom of action, nd given her growth in comparison with the previous position, she is maximally motivated for success."

this amount had been spent by the "reformers" on hotels, cocktail parties, as well as the publishing of ads "looking for new prosecutors."[192]

Deputy Prosecutor General Vitaly Kasko and the head of the PGO's International Cooperation Department, Polina Chizh, were tasked to carry out the reform of the PGO.

Polina Chizh is known for her involvement in the NABU scandal. While working as head of the patronage service under the first deputy director of the Bureau, Gizo Uglava, Chizh was alleged to have leaked confidential information related to ongoing criminal investigations to the U.S. Embassy, which included elements of the investigation concerning Burisma's Zlochevsky: a case of the utmost interest to Joe and Hunter Biden.[193]

Kasko and Chizh selected the International Development Law Organization in Ukraine (IDLO), headed by Levan Duchidze, to execute the re-certification program. Registered in Rome with a branch in Den Hag, Netherlands, the organization had notoriously been embroiled in claims of inefficient use of funds, lack of tangible work, and false representation.[194]

---

192 "Ukraine," *Where We Work,* International Development Law Organization. https://www.idlo.int/where-we-work/eastern-europe-and-central-asia/ukraine

"Ukraine has embarked on a wide-ranging process of reform. Much of the region's future stability depends on success in this 45-million strong country. The momentum is there to overcome a legacy of bureaucratic stagnation, arbitrariness and corruption. But efforts to complete the transition to a modern, prosperous state must contend with a crippling economic crisis and the persistence of conflict in the east of the country. As of 2015, IDLO is working at both the national and regional level to facilitate justice sector reform and promote integrity. We particularly focus on criminal justice reforms, which are critical to strengthening of the rule of law and democratic institutions in Ukraine. Our work is aligned with Ukraine's own laws and policies – chiefly the National Justice Sector Reform Strategy, the amended Law on the Public Prosecutor's Office and the Deregulation Strategy – as well as with Ukraine's international obligations on combatting corruption."

193 Andrii Derkach, Member of the Ukrainian Parliament, "The Billion Dollars Corruption: How the Top Officials of Ukraine and the USA Have Been Stealing the Public Money," 2019. https://web.archive.org/web/20220313193748/https://www.derkach.com.ua/en/publications/billion-dollars-corruption-top-officials-ukraine-usa-stealing-public-money/

"Shokin just doesn't know yet, that while the NABU buggers him around, the first NABU deputy Gizo Uglava through his assistant Polina Chyzh leaks the case files of these criminal proceedings to the U.S. Embassy."

194 "Evaluation of the project 'Supporting Justice Sector and Anti-Corruption Reforms in Ukraine – Phase 1,'" *What We Do: Initiatives,* International Development Law Organization. https://www.idlo.int/what-we-do/initiatives/evaluation-project-

In Afghanistan, internal investigations had led to an unfavorable review of the IDLO project. An investigation into the Justice Training Transition Program (JTTP) project in Afghanistan had been initiated after U.S. Senator Claire McCaskill had approached the office of the U.S. government's Special Inspector General for Afghanistan Reconstruction (SIGAR) to conduct an investigation into the disappearance of $47.8 million.[195]

This investigation did not prevent the IDLO from being entrusted with the execution of programs aimed at "reforming" the prosecutor's office in Ukraine. To make matters worse, the IDLO opted to subcontract its work to LLC "Psymetrics-Ukraine." The contract called for the anonymous testing of prosecutors staffing the Prosecutor General's Office which essentially served as a tool to evaluate the staff's professional aptitude. Normally, the proctoring of such an exam should have been entrusted to a reputable and certified body holding significant and extensive experience owing to the paramount importance of carrying out a proper evaluation of the personnel working out of the Prosecutor General's Office.[196]

---

supporting-justice-sector-and-anti-corruption-reforms

195 Charles S. Clark, "State Department Faulted for Lax Oversight of Afghanistan Justice Contract," *Government Executive,* January 24, 2014. https://www. govexec.com/oversight/2014/01/state-department-faulted-lax-oversight-afghanistan-justice-contract/77510/

"State Department contracts totaling $223 million to help train Afghani justice administrators, prosecutors, attorneys and case managers suffered from requirements that 'were poorly defined, resulting in useless deliverables,' as well as expenses that are difficult to track, according to the audit report released Friday by the Special Inspector General for Afghanistan Reconstruction."

196 Yakov Stashynskyi, "U.S. Department of State representative George Kent contributed to the embezzlement of U.S. taxpayers' money through a shell company – Derkach," *Ukrainian News,* April 14, 2020. https://ukranews.com/en/news/696542-us-department-of-state-representative-george-kent-contributed-to-the-embezzlement-of-us-taxpayers

"'449kg of materials related to attestation of prosecutors and investigators of the Prosecutor General's Office of Ukraine has been destroyed on behalf of the Prosecutor General's Office of Ukraine. Psymetrics-Ukraine LLC was the actual executor of attestation. This company has not conducted any activities earlier and has never submitted tax reports. Moreover, during attestation in October 2019, the company changed its owner. Instead of the psychologist and wife who founded this company, the person whose main activity is non-store retailing became the owner,' Derkach wrote."

However, "Psymetrics-Ukraine," created in 2018, had never engaged in carrying out any such assignments. Upon completion of the "tests," Prosecutor General Ryaboshapka destroyed all documentation pertaining to the program and the company proceeded to change ownership.

Another U.S. Embassy-sanctioned program was called "Improving Public Trust." This whistleblower program received a $52 million budget and the "Ukrainian Confidence Initiative," was awarded the contract before "disappearing" $36 million.

The "Democratic Salvation of Eastern Europe" program received $57 million.

All these programs received funds from the U.S. Agency for International Development (USAID).

As the sole authority tasked with selecting organizations for the awarding of substantial grants, the U.S. Embassy in Kiev was deemed responsible for guaranteeing their integrity, but disastrous results never led to accountability as Christine Quinn kept sending laudatory reports about "Ukraine's steady progress on the path to reform" to the State Department.

One crucial element which might shift the focus to Joe Biden is USAID's possible funding of the Burisma holding.

In late June 2014, U.S. Senators Edward Markey, Ron Wyden, Gene Shaheen, and Christopher Murphy approached U.S. President Barack Obama with a proposal to strengthen the dialogue on energy efficiency and development of domestic energy resources in Ukraine. For this purpose, USAID specifically developed the "Municipal Energy Reform in Ukraine" program with a budget of $16.5 million. Importantly, these funds were allocated on a grant basis, unlike other programs with repayable funding. Tasked with supervising the project, Ukraine's Ministry of Regional Development reported that "in Ukraine, the American company International Resources Group and its international and local partners are in charge of implementing it."[197]

International Resources Group (IRG) is a subsidiary of the non-profit organization RTI International, whose senior director is Paul

---

197 U.S. Senators Edward J. Markey, Ron Wyden, Jeanne Shaheen, and Christopher S. Murphy, letter to U.S. President, June 27, 2014. https://www.markey. senate.gov/imo/media/doc/2014-06-27_PresidentObama_Ukraine_energy.pdf

Weisenfeld. Before working at RTI, Weisenfeld worked as a foreign service officer for USAID.[198]

The IRG has a pool of U.S. companies and organizations associated with donor structures and Ukraine was not the IRG's first foray. The Foundation had extensive experience in countries once targeted by U.S. intervention as it had once mastered a grant for the reconstruction of Iraq within the framework of the corresponding USAID programs. The organization also carried out activities in Liberia, Pakistan, and Afghanistan.

The Ministry of Regional Development of Ukraine released a communiqué listing Burisma Holdings amongst the "local partners" of USAID in Ukraine. This occasioned a major conflict of interest since by then, Joe Biden had already signed a memorandum of understanding with USAID as part of the "Municipal Energy Reform in Ukraine" program.[199]

It was listed as program number 2926-09 by the Ministry of Economic Development of Ukraine and its budget was set at $16,496,928, featuring $8.8 million in direct funds by USAID while the difference would be provided by the World Bank and the EBRD. In typical fashion, the items listed for expenditure failed to show any capital investments allocated for the purchase of equipment or software.

---

198 "Paul Weisenfeld, Executive Vice President, International Development" *Experts | RTI International.* https://www.rti.org/expert/paul-weisenfeld

"Before joining RTI, Mr. Weisenfeld served as a foreign service officer for the United States Agency for International Development (USAID), achieving the highest rank of career minister in the Senior Foreign Service, and led high-profile initiatives across various international development sectors. During this time Mr. Weisenfeld directed the Bureau for Food Security at USAID, which leads Feed the Future, the U.S. Government's global hunger and food security initiative. He also led the Haiti Task Team, charged with coordinating relief and reconstruction planning following the devastating earthquake in 2010, and served as USAID Mission Director in Peru and Zimbabwe. Mr. Weisenfeld received the USAID administrator's Distinguished Career Service Award, the agency's highest award. He served in Africa, the Middle East, and Latin America."

199 USAID, *Municipal Energy Reform Project (MERP), Seventh Quarterly Report, April 1, 2015–June 30, 2015.* https://pdf.usaid.gov/pdf_docs/PA00MD15.pdf

"The GOU and Presidential Administration developed and approved National Sustainable Development of Ukraine 2020. The Plan has 62 reform measures including energy reforms. The Plan aims to increase energy efficiency and to substitute imported Russian gas by local alternative fuels."

Instead, $6.3 million went to consulting services while another $2.4 million was spent on seminars, conferences, PR, and advertising.

In June 2015, USAID and Burisma Holdings held a contest devised to promote the best stories on energy efficiency.[200] An awards ceremony for the winning journalists was organized.[201]

This publicity stunt allowed for the public to be sold on the idea of a partnership chiefly concerned with responsible social and environmental policies.

As USAID Ukraine Economic Growth Office Director Steven Gonier commented at the time: "The media play an important role in providing unbiased and objective information on why and how energy sector reforms and energy efficiency improvements will help develop Ukraine's economy. And that means that a sum equivalent to two months of Hunter Biden's salary can easily be written off under such an important event."[202]

---

200 Burisima Group, "USAID and Burisma Holdings Award Best Journalists" [news release], June 24, 2015. https://web.archive.org/web/20210121053454/ https://burisma-group.com/ru/media/usaid-i-burisma-holdings-nagradili-luchshih-zhurnalistov-po-teme-energeticheskoj-reformy/

201 Ibid.

"The Project conducted a formal awards ceremony for the winning journalists in the contest for best published materials. Topics included energy efficiency, alternative and clean energy, advantages of condominiums, tariff reform and social protection for the population. The OEG Director of the USAID Mission in Ukraine, Steve Gonyea, opened the event and outlined the importance of transparency in the municipal energy sector. The contest was organized by the Project together with the Center for Ukrainian Reform Education (CURE) and with corporate sponsorship from Burisma. The contest was conducted among journalists from Chernihiv, Dnipropetrovsk, Ivano-Frankivsk, Kherson, Kyiv, Vinnytsia, and Zaporizhzhya oblasts, all of which are implementation partners in USAID MERP pilot programs. The contest took nominations for the best material in the categories of printed and online media, best TV and best radio materials. One hundred thirty-two materials arrived from more than 30 journalists in different parts of Ukraine – just 10 of them were recognized as winners."

202 Ibid.

"At the same time, Mykola Zlochevsky, President of Burisma Holdings, believes that energy efficiency technologies and the search for alternative and clean energy sources are issues that are now focused not only on Ukraine, but also on our international partners. 'To raise awareness of the population of Ukraine on these issues, the USAID Municipal Energy Reform in Ukraine Project conducted a large-scale educational campaign through the media. Such an important initiative was supported by the Burisma Holdings team. We are interested in the qualitative development of Ukrainian journalism and professional coverage of the topic of energy efficiency, since the latter is the basis of energy security and energy independence of the country,' he said."

In 2017, the Accounting Chamber published a report titled "On the results of the analysis of the effectiveness of the use of international technical assistance by public administration bodies."[203]

The report concluded that while 440 international technical assistance projects worth a combined $5.3 billion had been implemented in Ukraine since 2015, the effectiveness of the use of international aid was extremely low as the Ministry of the Economy "did not properly act as a coordinator and supervisor of the spending of foreign money."[204]

In other words, the ministry had not received a single report and 5.3 billion simply vanished in the hands of "volunteers" like Vitaly Shabunin and Sherembey.

Effectively, billions of U.S. taxpayers' monies were deliberately left unsupervised by American authorities, thus allowing for the embezzling of the funds by local parties. Ukrainian volunteer organizations and Western foundations popped up out of nowhere to provide legal cover of schemes involving the pilfering of upwards to five billion dollars in taxpayers' monies.

No outlet covered these facts in the European press. They did not even look into the matter. There appeared to be an unspoken ban on all unsightly facts which might have existed in Ukraine. This omerta

---

203 Andrii Derkach, Member of Ukrainian Parliament, "The first meeting of Giuliani in Kiev was held with the People's Deputy Derkach," 2019. https://web.archive.org/web/20200814142907/https://derkach.com.ua/en/publications/first-meeting-giuliani-kiev-held-peoples-deputy-derkach/

"As the People's Deputy recalled, according to the report of the Accounts Chamber of Ukraine from 2017, at the beginning of 2015 there were 440 projects of international technical assistance (ITA) with a total value of more than $5.2 billion. As of July 1, 2017, the number of ITA projects decreased to 390 with an increase in cost up to $ 5.3 billion dollars. This assistance was not aimed at strategic directions of development of our country. Moreover, the effectiveness of the implementation of projects and the effectiveness of the use of aid by state structures were not evaluated."

204 Andrii Derkach, Member of Ukrainian Parliament, "The corruption pyramid. What will be the result of the theft of American aid to Ukraine, which is alleged by Giuliani?," 2020. https://web.archive.org/web/20220122014200/https://www.derkach.com.ua/en/publications/corruption-pyramid-will-result-theft-american-aid-ukraine-alleged-giuliani/

"'The Accounts Chamber in Ukraine discovered an alleged abuse of $5.3 billion during the Obama's administration, while Joe Biden was an "inside man." The Obama's Embassy had urged the Ukrainian police not to investigate!' commented Giuliani."

extended both to American corruption in the country as well as to events in the Donbass.

The documents issued by investigators of the Prosecutor General's Office of Ukraine showed that corruption schemes in Ukraine were built up over a short period of time. The Russian FSB had nothing to do with it. While Ukraine suffered reputational damage, the pilfering was largely carried out thanks to American politicians, officials, diplomats, all acting in coordination with a slew of American foundations of dubious reputation, all involved in the large-scale theft of funds from the U.S. budget.[205]

The U.S. had methodically built a system of external administration of Ukraine with the result that Kiev lost its sovereignty, becoming a puppet in the hands of Washington. The bribe paid by Burisma was the result of Biden's efforts to hush up all criminal cases against that company and discredit potential witnesses such as Trump's own lawyer, Rudy Giuliani.[206]

WMDs in Ukraine

During her testimony in front of the Senate Foreign Relations Committee about the Russian Special Military Operation in Ukraine, Undersecretary of State for Political Affairs Victoria Nuland was questioned by Sen. Marco Rubio (R-FL) about whether Ukraine hosted chemical and/or biological weapons facilities.

---

205 Yakov Stashynskyi (editor), "U.S. Department of State representative George Kent contributed to the embezzlement of U.S. taxpayers' money through a shell company – Derkach," *Ukrainian News,* April 14, 2020. https://ukranews.com/en/news/696542-us-department-of-state-representative-george-kent-contributed-to-the-embezzlement-of-us-taxpayers

206 Andrii Derkach, "The corruption pyramid."

"According to Giuliani's version, the corruption pyramid looks like this: Soros-Biden, three U.S. ambassadors in Ukraine (Payette, Jovanovic, Taylor), George Kent (former U.S. deputy ambassador in Ukraine, and now a senior State Department official), Poroshenko and Yatsenyuk, Sytnik (head of NABU), as well as Kasko, the former Deputy Prosecutor General of Ukraine. 'Evidence of corruption by the past Ukrainian government and excessive spending on non-State humanitarian organizations can cause a criminal case against Poroshenko and can lead to the end for many grant recipients. In the U.S., Democrats are accused of using the state apparatus for their own purposes and of creating a network of NGOs that "protect" corruption.' Giuliani said during interview with *Strana.*"

She replied: "Ukraine has biological research facilities, which, in fact, we are now quite concerned...Russian forces may be seeking to gain control of," at which point Rubio interrupted her, forestalling any further blundering revelations. She then refuted allegations that Ukrainians were plotting to use biological weapons, and averred that if such an attack happened in Ukraine, "there is no doubt in my mind (that) it would be caused by Russian forces."[207]

Biological laboratories have existed inside Ukraine since 2005 in the context of "preventing" the production of biological weapons. The United States has financed a number of such institutions, presenting its actions as philanthropic ventures.[208]

To Tucker Carlson, however, these remarks from an American official stood as proof that these labs were indeed conducting biowarfare research.[209] Carlson pointed to an interview with Robert Pope, the director of the Pentagon's Cooperative Threat Reduction Program. The CTRP was created to assist countries of the former Soviet Union to secure or eliminate nuclear and chemical weapons. Carlson observed: "As Pope put it, scientists are scientists, they don't want to destroy all the bioweapons... Instead, they're using them to conduct new bioweapons research — that's what he said."[210]

As for Nuland's follow-up remarks, Carlson scoffed at the notion that "...we are working with the Ukrainians on how they can prevent any of those research materials from falling into the hands of Russian forces should they approach."

As he scathingly remarked:

207 "Undersecretary of State for Political Affairs Testifies on Ukraine," *C-SPAN,* March 8, 2022. https://www.c-span.org/video/?518355-1/undersecretary-state-political-affairs-testifies-ukraine&live=

208 Linda Qiu, "Theory About U.S.-Funded Bioweapons Labs in Ukraine Is Unfounded," Fact Check, *The New York Times,* March 11, 2022. https://www.nytimes.com/2022/03/11/us/politics/us-bioweapons-ukraine-misinformation.html

"There are biological laboratories inside Ukraine, and since 2005, the United States has provided backing to a number of institutions to prevent the production of biological weapons."

209 "Tucker Carlson: Someone needs to explain why there are dangerous biological weapons in Ukraine," *Fox News,* March 9, 2022. https://www.foxnews.com/opinion/tucker-we-have-right-know-this

210 Linda Qiu, "Theory About U.S.-Funded Bioweapons Labs in Ukraine Is Unfounded."

Why would we fund something like that in Ukraine, and why didn't you secure the contents of these bio labs before the Russians arrived as you knew they would? And then why did you go out of your way to lie to the American public about all of this? If the "research materials" in these labs were to escape somehow and you seem very concerned about that, what would be the effect on Ukraine and then on the rest of the world? How can we prepare for the consequences of that, this thing that you're worried about? Shouldn't we be preparing? Because as it turns out, we've just spent the last two years living with the pathogen that began in another foreign bio lab funded by the United States government secretly.

The Cooperative Threat Reduction Program

After the collapse of the Soviet Union, concerns grew about its nuclear weapons arsenal falling into the wrong hands. As a countermeasure, the Nunn-Lugar Act saw the creation of the Cooperative Threat Reduction (CTR) program. The CTR was initiated as a control mechanism intended "to secure and dismantle weapons of mass destruction and their associated infrastructure in former Soviet Union states."[211] In 2009, the program's scope was extended "to secure and dismantle weapons of mass destruction and their associated infrastructure in former Soviet Union and beyond."[212]

---

211 William M. Moon, "Beyond Arms Control: Cooperative Nuclear Weapons Reductions – A New Paradigm to Roll Back Nuclear Weapons and Increase Security and Stability," *Journal for Peace and Nuclear Disarmament* 3, no. 1 (2020): 92–114. https://www.tandfonline.com/doi/full/10.1080/25751654.2020.1732516.
"From 1991–2013, the United States and Russia worked closely together to eliminate and secure thousands of Russian nuclear weapons at dozens of sites across Russia. Under the Cooperative Threat Reduction (CTR) program, teams of U.S. and Russian nuclear weapons and security experts worked together to drastically cut nuclear weapons delivery systems, reduce and consolidate nuclear weapons storage sites, and eliminate nuclear warheads beyond the limits established by formal arms control treaties."
212 U.S. Defense Threat Reduction Agency, *Fiscal Year 2011 Budget Estimate: Cooperative Threat Reduction Program,* February 2010. https://comptroller. defense.gov/Portals/45/Documents/defbudget/fy2011/budget_justification/pdfs/01_Operation_and_Maintenance/O_M_VOL_1_PARTS/CTR_FY11.pdf
"The New Initiatives program was established with additional funding in the FY

The CTR pursued four objectives:

- Dismantle former Soviet Union (FSU)'s weapons of mass destruction (WMD) and associated infrastructure.

- Consolidate and secure FSU WMD and related technology and materials.

- Increase transparency and encourage higher standards of conduct.

- Support defense and military cooperation with the objective of preventing proliferation.[213]

The Defense Threat Reduction Agency (DTRA), as both a defense and a combat support agency affiliated with the U.S. DOD, emerged as the key organ tasked with countering the proliferation of WMDs (chemical, biological, radiological, nuclear and high explosives) and supporting the nuclear enterprise. On the agency's website, it is stated that "DTRA provides cross-cutting solutions to enable the Department of Defense, the United States Government, and international partners to Deter strategic attack against the United States and its allies; Prevent, reduce, and counter WMD and emerging threats; and Prevail against WMD-armed adversaries in crisis and conflict."[214]

Initially established on October 1, 1998, as a result of the 1997 Defense Reform Initiative, the DTRA consolidated several DoD organizations, including the Defense Special Weapons Agency (successor to the Defense Nuclear Agency), the On-Site Inspection Agency, the Defense Technology Security Administration and the Nunn-Lugar Threat Reduction Program (itself answering directly to the Secretary of Defense's Office)

2008/ 2009/2010 Defense Appropriations Acts and DoD completed an assessment of where CTR assistance would best support the effort to counter the threat from WMD transiting or in potential partner countries. Potential nuclear, chemical and biological threats were assessed. Pakistan, Afghanistan and select countries in Asia and Africa have been identified as high priority partners."

213 Center for Arms Control and Non-proliferation, *Fact Sheet: The Nunn-Lugar Cooperative Threat Reduction Program,* March 29, 2022. https://armscontrolcenter. org/fact-sheet-the-nunn-lugar-cooperative-threat-reduction-program-2/

214 "Mission," U.S. Defense Threat Reduction Agency. https://www.dtra.mil/ About/Mission/

Slightly over one tenth of the workforce operate at the following testing sites: Kirkland Air Force Base, White Sands Missile Range in New Mexico and the Nevada National Security Site (formerly called the Nevada Test Site). An additional 15% of the workforce is stationed at locations in nearly a dozen countries including Ukraine.

DTRA shares liaison offices with each of the U.S. military's regional Combatant Command Centers as well as the National Guard and the FBI. In 2005, the Commander, United States Strategic Command (USSTRATCOM) assumed the leading role of Combatant Command tasked with the integration and synchronization of the Department of Defense's efforts to pursue "Combating WMD" objectives. DTRA recently requested a base budget of $2 billion for fiscal year 2023 (FY23). As part of this, $998 million goes to Operation and Maintenance, another $654 million is to carry out Research, Development, Test and Evaluation activities.[215]

In 2008 the DTRA awarded Black & Veatch the first of its Biological Threat Reduction Integrating Contracts (BTRIC) in Ukraine, considered a "vital part" of the CTR mission.[216] For the next five years, B&V would go on to administrate the laboratory facilities in coordination with the Ukrainian Ministry of Health.

In the wake of the so-called "Orange Revolution" of 2004, Black & Veatch set out to build and modernize no fewer than 8 biological facilities in Ukraine, including one in Odessa conceived since 2011 to engage in "the study of pathogens likely to be used in terrorist attacks," rather than carry out the dismantling of the military biological infrastructure per CTR's original mandate.[217]

---

215 U.S. Defense Threat Reduction Agency, *Fiscal Year 2023 Budget Estimates: Defense Threat Reduction Agency,* April 2022. https://comptroller.defense.gov/Portals/45/Documents/defbudget/fy2023/budget_justification/pdfs/01_Operation_and_Maintenance/O_M_VOL_1_PART_1/DTRA_OP-5.pdf

216 "Black & Veatch to Coordinate Armenia's National Biological Threat Reduction Program," *Business Wire,* June 2, 2011. https://www.businesswire.com/news/home/20110602006066/en/Black-Veatch-Coordinate-Armenia's-National-Biological-Threat

"In 2008, Black & Veatch was awarded the first Task Order under BTRIC – prime integrating contractor for DTRA's CBEP in Ukraine, a five-year, more than $100 million project under which Black & Veatch is designing, engineering and deploying systems, processes and technologies to further strengthen reporting, detection and response capabilities."

217 "Interim Central Reference Laboratory Opens BSL-3 Facility," *Tradeline,*

In 2010, B&V commissioned Ukraine's first BSL-3 laboratory for the DTRA in Odessa. Designed by Black & Veatch "to renovate a decades-old facility into a state-of-the-art diagnostics laboratory that will become the nexus of Ukraine's biosurveillance network... (and train) Ukrainian personnel in molecular diagnostics, biosafety, operations and maintenance, and laboratory management techniques," its personnel would undergo training for the next three years so as to "provide Ukrainian scientists with the necessary resources to manage the BSL-3 laboratory and the Ukrainian biosurveillance system."[218]

Starting in 2000, major U.S. companies with ties to the military-industrial complex angled to set up military biological research facilities in Ukraine. These included USAID, the EcoHealth Alliance, the Bill and Melinda Gates Foundation, and Metabiota.[219]

In 2007, Nathan Wolfe, then working for the U.S. Dept. of Defense, set up the Global Viral Forecasting Institute (GVFI), a

---

June 22, 2010. https://www.tradelineinc.com/news/2010-6/interim-central-reference-laboratory-opens-bsl-3-facility

"The Interim Central Reference Laboratory opened its BSL-3 facility in Odessa, Ukraine, in June of 2010. Created in alliance with the Nunn-Lugar Cooperative Threat Reduction program, the biocontainment facility will enable scientists to secure and eliminate weapons of mass destruction in former Soviet states. The Interim Central Reference Laboratory will also support research on infectious diseases and pathogens. Other BSL-3 facilities are under construction in Kazakhstan, Azerbaijan, and Georgia."

218 "State-of-the-Art Diagnostics Laboratory Helps Make the World Safer," Black & Veatch. https://www.bv.com/projects/state-art-diagnostics-laboratory-helps-make-world-safer

"Bradley Karn, DTRA BTRP Program Manager, added, 'More important was the quality of the effort. Black & Veatch was able to renovate a decades-old facility into a state-of-the-art diagnostics laboratory that will become the nexus of Ukraine's biosurveillance network.' The BSL-3 laboratory was specifically designed and constructed to support work with especially dangerous pathogens that can be naturally occurring or introduced through a bioterrorism attack. It serves as a central location for research, consolidation and training on the proper handling of dangerous pathogens. The lab also provides the Ukrainian Ministry of Health a safe environment to confirm diagnosis of suspected dangerous pathogens, enhancing public health while deterring bioterrorism."

219 Tony Sifert, "U.S. Biological Research Co. in Ukraine Tied to EcoHealth Alliance, Wuhan Lab," *Headline USA,* March 23, 2022. https://headlineusa.com/us-biological-research-co-in-ukraine-tied-to-ecohealth-alliance-wuhan-lab/

"Both EcoHealth Alliance and Metabiota, a San Francisco-based biological research company said to be the 'main player in the Ukrainian labs,' has partnered with the United States Agency for International Development (USAID) to fund incredibly risky bioweapons research throughout the world [according to] *The Exposé.*"

bio-medical company whose stated mission was to produce a not-for-profit study of transborder infection, notably in China.[220] GVFI then underwent a name-change and became Global Viral (GV), now designated as a not-for-profit organization with the mission to study infectious diseases and their modes of transmission across species.[221]

Wolfe had long conducted research on pathogens. Having spent over eight years conducting biomedical research in both sub-Saharan Africa and Southeast Asia, Wolf also founded Metabiota: a company specialized in the evaluation of biological threats.

Wolf's resume indicates that he holds a seat on the board of reputable scientific reviews such as *EcoHealth* and *Scientific American* while also serving as a member of DARPA's Defense Science Research Council, an agency of the DOD specialized in cutting edge research on new technologies compatible with military applications, reporting directly to senior Department of Defense management and in charge of about 250 research and development programs.

In 2008, Wolfe warned that the world was unprepared for a pandemic. To give an idea of his stature and expertise, the website of the World Economic Forum entry on Wolfe states that:

> Dr. Nathan Wolfe is the Founder & Chair of Metabiota. Metabiota is the provider of a unique data analytics platform for risk. The company's analytics platform combines proprietary real-time and historical data, machine learning and economic/risk modeling to enable companies, insurers, and sovereign entities to assess risk accumulations...

---

220 "Dr. Nathan Wolfe/GVFI.ORG, The Global Viral Forecasting Initiative," Lightray. https://lightray.com/2010/12/gvfi-2/

"Founded by world renowned scientist Nathan Wolfe, GVFI's pioneering mission is to prevent future pandemics before they occur. The GVFI team maintains satellite laboratories around the world, monitoring hot spots where viruses are most likely to jump from animals to humans."

221 Rhoda Wilson, "Who is the Virus Hunter Dr. Nathan Wolfe?," *The Exposé*, April 13, 2022. https://expose-news.com/2022/04/13/who-is-the-virus-hunter-dr-nathan-wolfe/

"A few days before the end of March, Russian Foreign Ministry spokeswoman Marija Zakharova published a timeline of U.S.-Ukraine bioresearch headed 'BioBiden.' Of the 23 timeline points she listed, Nathan Wolfe or organisations associated with him – Metabiota and Global Viral – were explicitly mentioned in 8 of them."

and bring new insurance products to market. Metabiota is supported by Google Ventures, DCVC, and other leading investors and serves some of the most respected customers in the corporate, insurance and sovereign sectors. Wolfe received his doctorate in Immunology & Infectious Diseases from Harvard in 1998. He has been honored with a Fulbright fellowship and the NIH Director's Pioneer Award. He is a World Economic Forum Young Global Leader and a National Geographic Emerging Explorer. Wolfe has published over 100 scientific publications and his work has been published in or covered by *Nature, Science, The New York Times, The Economist, NPR, The New Yorker, The Wall Street Journal* and *Forbes* among others. His critically acclaimed book, *The Viral Storm,* has been published in six languages and was shortlisted in 2012 for the Royal Society's Winton Prize. In 2011 he was named as one of the hundred most influential people in the world by *Time* magazine; *Rolling Stone* named him one of the "100 Agents of Change" in 2009; and *Popular Science* recognized him as one of their "Brilliant 10" in 2006. Following the 2014 coup d'état in Ukraine followed by the subsequent infiltration of the Ukrainian energy sector by Americans, the Russian Ministry of Defense revealed that Wolfe's Metabiota and Burisma (now under the protection of the Biden clan) had announced the beginning of a joint venture bearing on an "unnamed scientific project in Ukraine." Metabiota's top executive invited Hunter Biden to partake in the company's activities in Ukraine, stressing the need to "affirm Ukraine's cultural and economic independence from Russia."[222]

222 Josh Boswell, "EXCLUSIVE: Hunter Biden DID help secure millions in funding for US contractor in Ukraine specializing in deadly pathogen research, laptop emails reveal, raising more questions about the disgraced son of then vice president," *Daily Mail,* March 25, 2022 (updated March 27, 2022). https://www.dailymail.co.uk/news/article-10652127/Hunter-Biden-helped-secure-millions-funding-military-biotech-research-program-Ukraine.html?fr=operanews

"That month, Metabiota vice president Mary Guttieri wrote a memo to Hunter outlining how they could 'assert Ukraine's cultural and economic independence from Russia'. 'Thanks so much for taking time out of your intense schedule to meet with Kathy [Dimeo, Metabiota executive] and I on Tuesday. We very much enjoyed our discussion,' Guttieri wrote. 'As promised, I've prepared the attached memo, which

It was in this context that Wolfe's Metabiota, a private company specialized in the risks of pandemic and offshoot of the previously-mentioned GV, announced the naming on its board of Neil Callahan and John DeLoche (both employees of Hunter Biden's Rosemont Seneca Partners).[223] GV and Metabiota then began to aggressively lobby the U.S. Department of Defense for funding.[224] Between 2014 and 2016, Metabiota notched several contracts with DOD, including one project in Ukraine valued at $300, 000.[225]

Metabiota

According to Bulgarian independent journalist, Dilyana Gaytandzhieva:

> The U.S. Army regularly produces deadly viruses, bacteria and toxins in direct violation of the UN Convention on the prohibition of Biological Weapons. Hundreds of thousands of unwitting people are systematically exposed to dangerous pathogens and other incurable diseases. Bio warfare scientists using diplomatic cover test man-made viruses at Pentagon bio laboratories in 25 countries across the world. These U.S. bio-laboratories are funded by the Defense Threat Reduction Agency (DTRA) under a *$2.1 billion military program*—Cooperative Biological Engagement

provides an overview of Metabiota, our engagement in Ukraine, and how we can potentially leverage our team, networks, and concepts to assert Ukraine's cultural and economic independence from Russia and continued integration into Western society."

223 In 2005, Christopher Heinz, the son-in-law of then-U.S. Senator John Kerry co-founded Rosemont Capital, which in 2009 became Rosemont Seneca Partner when he joined forces with Hunter Biden. Heinz would depart the company in 2014 as the scandal of Hunter's joining the board of Burisma was becoming impossible to keep away from the media.

224 Freddy Ponton for 21st Century Wire, "Pentagon-Ukraine Bio Labs: The Hunter Biden Connection," *Europe Reloaded*, March 24, 2022. https://www. europereloaded.com/pentagon-ukraine-bio-labs-the-hunter-biden-connection/

"Metabiota has two board members, Neil Callahan and John Deloche. Both Callahan and Deloche are both a part of Rosemont Seneca."

225 Joseph Mercola, "U.S. Firm With Ties to WEF, DOD Implicated in Bioweapons Cover-Up," *The Defender*, April 8, 2022. https://childrenshealthdefense. org/defender/u-s-firm-with-ties-to-wef-dod-implicated-in-bioweapons-cover-up/

"The Global Virome Project which reportedly paid (or was planning to pay) Metabiota $341,000 to conduct a cost-benefit analysis."

Program (CBEP), and are located in former Soviet Union countries such as Georgia and Ukraine, the Middle East, South East Asia and Africa... Metabiota services include global field-based biological threat research, pathogen discovery, outbreak response and clinical trials. Metabiota Inc. had been contracted by the Pentagon to perform work for DTRA before and during the Ebola crisis in West Africa and was awarded *$3.1 million (2012–2015) for work in Sierra Leone*—one of the countries at the epicenter of the Ebola outbreak.

A July 2014 report "...drafted by the Viral Haemorrhagic Fever Consortium, accused Metabiota of failing to abide by an existing agreement on how to report test results and for bypassing the Sierra Leonean scientists working there. The report also raised the possibility that Metabiota was culturing blood cells at the lab, something the report said was dangerous, as well as misdiagnosing healthy patients. All of those allegations were denied by Metabiota."[226]

Meanwhile, Metabiota's lobbying efforts undertaken in cooperation with Rosemont Seneca Partners in 2014 yielded results such the DTRA's main integrator, Black & Veatch, opting to award Metabiota a subcontract to support its mission in Iraq in 2018.[227]

As stated by Mary Guttieri, executive vice president of Science and Microbiology at Metabiota:

Metabiota has deep ties to the global health community and has been working hand-in-hand with U.S. Government stakeholders and partner nations for almost a decade... As a result, our team knows what it takes to help countries assess risk and facilitate earlier detection of outbreaks. Working with Black & Veatch on these task orders will help

226 Dilyana Gaytandzhieva, "The Pentagon Bio-weapons," *Dilyana.bg,* April 29, 2018. https://dilyana.bg/the-pentagon-bio-weapons/
227 "Metabiota Gains Government Momentum with Black & Veatch Sub-Contracts for Defense Threat Reduction Programs," *Markets Insider,* August 8, 2018. https://markets.businessinsider.com/news/stocks/metabiota-gains-government-momentum-with-black-veatch-sub-contracts-for-defense-threat-reduction-programs-1027442834

us continue to leverage our analytics and deep scientific knowledge to improve the world's resilience to epidemics.[228]

George Webb is an investigative journalist who has been tracking the links existing between DARPA and the various private entities engaged in the setting up of hundreds of biolabs across the world.[229] On March 10, 2022, he tweeted: "Black & Veatch's Odessa facility seems to be the biolab that triggered Russia."[230]

Webb estimated that B&V and DTRA had managed to obtain contracts worth an accumulated $215.6 million on construction and operation of biolabs in countries such as Ukraine, Azerbaijan, Cameroon, Thailand, Ethiopia, Vietnam and Armenia, and that per the Georgia and Ukraine contracts alone, Black & Veatch subcontractor Metabiota received a $18.4 million federal contract.

Owing to Nathan Wolfe's close relationships with investors dating back to his founding of GFVI, and this despite Metabiota having subsequently committed a series of costly mistakes during the 2014 Ebola outbreak that swept across West Africa: the company kept receiving millions in funding from USAID, Google and the Skoll Foundation, among others.[231]

A Nexus of Investors Linked to the Uniparty

Rumours abound that EcoHealthAlliance created SARS-CoV-2.[232]

The revelations emanating from Andrew Huff, a former VP at EHA turned whistle-blower, tended to establish that the company had engaged in financing of gain-of-function research while

---

228 Ibid.

229 "George Webb Investigates Ukraine. Again.," *Radio Patriot,* March 10, 2022. https://radiopatriot.net/2022/03/10/george-webb-investigates-ukraine-again/

230 Sunny Lan, "U.S. Company Metabiota Links Biolabs in Africa and Ukraine to the Pentagon's DTRA [Part I]," *Sunny Lan* [blog], March 23, 2022. https://sunnylanblog.wordpress.com/2022/03/23/us-company-metabiota-links-biolabs-in-africa-and-ukraine-to-the-pentagons-dtra-part-i/

231 Ibid.

232 Noah Y. Kim "Ask PolitiFact: What's going on with EcoHealth Alliance, the NIH and coronavirus research?," *PolitiFact,* October 28, 2021. https://www.politifact.com/article/2021/oct/28/ask-politifact-what-does-nih-letter-say-about-gain/

keeping Congress in the dark as related to its being funded by the U.S. Department of Defense.[233]

Huff published a series of tweets voicing his concerns about sinister ties existing between the company he had once worked for and the Central Intelligence Agency, implying that head of EHA Peter Daszak worked for the Agency, pointing to the EHA as essentially "a CIA front organization." He also contended that Daszak acted as double agent in the pay of the Chinese government. These allegations highlighted that it was the United States of America, not China, that created the COVID virus, with the latter being "the result of a scientific R&D program merely transferred to China."[234]

In order to support its research projects, EHA fielded financial support from a variety of donors such NIH, NIAID, private entities and foundations such as Google, the Wellcome Trust, and the Gates Foundation.

As if this wasn't deemed sufficient to ring a few alarm bells, William Karesh, EHA's Executive Vice President, had long-time ties with the U.S. biodefence establishment: a claim not denied by EHA policy advisor, David R. Franz, a former commander at U.S. bioweapons lab at Fort Detrick.[235] WIV's notorious Dr. Shi Zhengli had also collaborated with EHA's Daszak on bat-related studies. Daszak and Zhengli began research on SARS-like coronavirus in bats back in 2005.

Neil Callahan was one of the players at the heart of the network of companies engaged in the funding of biological research in Ukraine

---

233 Aneeta Bhole, "Whistleblower US scientist who worked with Wuhan lab claims COVID WAS genetically engineered and leaked from the site – and says 'the US government is to blame' because it funded the research," *Daily Mail,* December 3, 2022. https://www.dailymail.co.uk/news/article-11498155/Whistleblower-worked-funded-Wuhan-lab-claims-Covid-genetically-engineered-leaked.html

"Dr Andrew Huff, the former vice president of EcoHealth Alliance, called the pandemic 'one of the greatest cover-ups in history' and the 'biggest U.S. intelligence failure since 9/11.'"

234 William Ebbs, "Many Russians Think America Created the Wuhan Coronavirus, and the Reasons May Shock You," *CNN,* September 23, 2020. https://www.ccn.com/many-russians-think-america-created-the-wuhan-coronavirus/

235 "William B. Karesh, DVM, Executive Vice President for Health and Policy, EcoHealth Alliance," *Our Team,* Bipartisan Commission on Biodefense. https://biodefensecommission.org/teams/william-b-karesh-dvm/

following the Maidan coup d'état.[236] Callahan was most instrumental for he had served both as CEO of Pilot Growth Management, the leading investor in Metabiota, and as Managing Director and co-founder of Rosemont Seneca Technology Partners (RSTP), an offshoot of Rosemont Seneca Partners. His position as CEO of Pilot Growth Management, not to mention his close proximity with Hunter Biden, led to his appointment on Metabiota's Board of Advisors

In 2014–2015, Rosemont Seneca Partners voted to invest $30 million in Metabiota, with RSTP providing the bulk of the funding. Of note, RSTP had started financing Metabiota back in 2008, when Black & Veatch and DTRA signed several contracts for the construction and operation of biolabs in various countries.[237]

Another investor in Matabiota was In-Q-Tel, founded by the CIA back in 1999. Initially going by the name of Peleus, IQT mostly sought to invest in tech companies, thus allowing the CIA to remain up to date with the latest hardware in the field of information technologies. IQT is notably behind the financing of such Internet giants such as Google Apps and Facebook.[238] Google started out as a CIA project via Stanford University and eventually went on to purchase "Keyhole," a company once funded by...IQT.

---

236 "Neil Callahan, Founder & Managing Partner," Pilot Growth. https://www.pilotgrowth.com/neil-callahan/

237 Natalie Winters, "Hunter Biden Invested In A Pandemic Firm Collaborating With Daszak's EcoHealth and The Wuhan Lab." *The National Pulse,* 2021. https://thenationalpulse.com/archive-post/hunter-biden-invested-in-ecohealth-wuhan-partner/

"Rosemont Seneca Technology Partners – an investment firm led by Hunter Biden – was a lead financial backer of Metabiota, a pandemic tracking and response firm that has partnered with Peter Daszak's EcoHealth Alliance and the Wuhan Institute of Virology."

238 Michael Chary, "In-Q-Tel; The CIA is Investing in Technology Startups," *Gaia,* August 23, 2017. https://www.gaia.com/article/what-is-cia-in-q-tel

"In-Q-Tel, since its inception in 1999, continues to fund start-ups in the tech world ranging from skincare lines to novel drone technology, but much of its investment goes into data mining. These tools collect, store, and analyze data to create profiles on individuals, groups, and events that are of interest to the CIA, law enforcement, and corporations. Often these programs mine platforms like Twitter, Facebook, and Instagram to monitor activist protests, influential 'decision-makers,' and trends. One day these algorithms surveil our personal data and activity, and the next they're being sold to corporations for advertising."

Turning Ukraine into a Biological Powder Keg

One of the first media outlets to cover the U.S. spawning of biolab facilities throughout Ukraine was the Serbian newspaper PECAT. In a 2017 article titled: "Why is the U.S. turning Ukraine into a biological bomb?," the newspaper reported:

> These military laboratories, where they are mainly engaged in the study and production of viruses and bacteria, are located in the following cities: Odessa, Vinnitsa, Uzhgorod, Lviv (three), Kharkov, Kyiv (three), Kherson, Ternopil. There are several such laboratories near Crimea and the Lugansk People's Republic. All the heads of these military laboratories are from the ranks of intelligence officers, U.S. military personnel, or proven American politicians. Also, these laboratories are often run by experts in biological weapons and biological terrorism.[239]

In 2018, *News Front,* a website based in Crimea, released a piece titled "CyberBerkut: USA taking control over biological research in Ukraine." The article related the following:

> The USA is gaining total control over biological research facilities, researchers and stocks of deadly viruses in Ukraine. This will allow the USA to control the epidemiological situation in the region, get access to every development in the sphere and manipulate population size while increasing American pharmaceutical corporations' profit. The Pentagon has got access to Ukrainian biological research facilities under the plausible pretext of preventing the proliferation of biological weapons. The biological projects are sponsored and supervised by the U.S. Defence Threat Reduction Agency (DTRA), which is operating through its office in the U.S. Embassy in Kyiv, headed by Joanna Wintrol. The American engineering firm Black & Veatch is covering construction and maintenance of

---

239 "Why is the U.S. turning Ukraine into a biological bomb?," *Inosmi.ru,* August 12, 2017. https://inosmi.ru/20170812/240033801.html

biological facilities and conducting biological researches under special projects. By a lucky chance, Metabiota, a subcontractor, is sharing the building with Black & Veatch in Kyiv.[240]

A History of Suspicious Outbreaks

Bulgarian journalist Dyliana Gaytandzhieva has written extensively about the nefarious nature of the U.S. Department of Defense's activities in Ukraine.[241] In a 2018 article, Gaytandzhieva described a Ukraine transformed into a mere U.S. satrap whereupon:

> ...Ukraine has no control over the military bio-laboratories on its own territory. According to the 2005 Agreement signed between the U.S. DoD and the Ministry of Health of Ukraine, the Ukrainian government is prohibited from public disclosure of sensitive information about the U.S. program and Ukraine is obliged to transfer to the U.S. Department of Defense (DoD) **dangerous pathogens for biological research.** The Pentagon has been granted access to certain state secrets of Ukraine in connection with the projects under their agreement... Among the set of bilateral agreements between the U.S. and Ukraine is the establishment of the Science and Technology Center in Ukraine (STCU)—an International organization funded mainly by the U.S. government which has been accorded diplomatic status.[242] [emphasis added]

The handling of these "dangerous pathogens" seemingly did not go without a series of disturbing incidents leading up to suspicious outbreaks in the population of Ukraine and neighboring Russia.

---

240 "CyberBerkut: USA taking control over biological research in Ukraine, *NewsFront,* October 3, 2018. https://en.newsfront.info/2018/10/03/cyberberkut-usa-taking-control-over-biological-research-in-ukraine/

241 Dilyana Gaytandzhieva, "The Pentagon Bio-weapons," *Dilyana.bg,* April 29, 2018. https://dilyana.bg /the-pentagon-bio-weapons/

242 Ibid.

As early as 2011, Ukraine was the scene of a cholera outbreak during which over 30 patients were rushed to the hospital after experiencing severe bouts of diarrhea.[243]

A similar incident occurred in 2014 resulting in the exposure to cholera of nearly 800 people.[244]

That same year, the pathogen was identified in the wake of an outbreak in Moscow following a study conducted by the Russian Research Anti-Plague Institute which concluded that the two strains shared remarkable characteristics. The strain was later identified as Vibrio Cholera.[245]

An additional 100 new cases were diagnosed in 2015 in the city of Mikolaiv.

It was eventually uncovered that a company by the name of Southern Research Institute (SRI) had been conducting a research project at several bio-facilities in Ukraine which focused on cholera, influenza and the Zika virus.

---

243 Interfax-Ukraine, "Area in Ukraine hit by cholera outbreak," Kyiv Post, July 24, 2011. https://www.kyivpost.com/post/8970
"A medical authority said one more person had been diagnosed with cholera and hospitalized in Mariupol, Ukraine, bringing the total number of cases in the current local outbreak to 24."

244 AP, "UKRAINE: ODESSA: BEACHES CLOSED TO COMBAT SPREAD OF CHOLERA," news video [2:22], posted on YouTube July 21, 2015. https://www.youtube.com/watch?v=K47S1DarhTE

245 Konstantin V Kuleshov et al., "Comparative genomic analysis of two isolates of Vibrio cholerae O1 Ogawa El Tor isolated during outbreak in Mariupol in 2011," *Infection, Genetics and Evolution* 44 (Oct. 2016): 471-478. https://pubmed.ncbi.nlm.nih.gov/27480918/
"An outbreak of cholera was registered during May-July 2011 in Mariupol, Ukraine, with 33 cholera cases and 25 carriers of cholera. Following this outbreak, the toxigenic strain of V. cholerae 2011EL-301 was isolated from seawater in the recreation area of Taganrog city on the territory of Russia. The aim of our study was to understand genomic features of Mariupol isolates as well as to evaluate hypothesis about possible interconnection between the outbreak of cholera in Mariupol and the single case of isolation of V. cholerae from the Sea of Azov in Russia. Mariupol isolates were phenotypically characterized and subsequently subjected to whole genome sequencing procedure. Phylogenetic analysis based on high-quality SNPs of V. cholera O1 El Tor isolates of the 7th pandemic clade from different regions showed that clinical and environmental isolates from Mariupol outbreak were attributable to a unique phylogenetic clade within wave 3 of V. cholera O1 El Tor isolates and characterized by six clade-specific SNPs. Whereas Taganrog isolate belonged to distantly related clade which allows us to reject the hypothesis of transmission the outbreak strain of V. cholerae O1 from Ukraine to Russia in 2011."

Not unlike Black & Veatch and Metabiota, SRI had not only benefited from its business dealings with DTRA since 2008: it also had been identified as a privileged subcontractor acting on behalf of the U.S. biological Weapons Program going back to the late 1950s![246]

Records revealed that the company's lobbying featured the wiring of $250,000 to then Sen. Jeff Sessions in order to secure a range of contracts just as the DOD was rolling out its biolabs programs in Ukraine. The lobbying revolved around issues bearing on "research and development for U.S. intelligence" and "defense related research and development."[247] Incidentally, SRI's senior director was none other than Watson Donald, who had once served as Jeff Sessions's personal aide on the Hill.[248] In total, Southern Research Institute spent over a million dollars in lobbying activities over a ten-years period between 2006 and 2016.[249]

In 2016, Ulana Nadia Suprun was named acting Health Minister of Ukraine. During her watch, the interface between the U.S. Department of Defense and the Ukrainian Ministry of Health increased dramatically.[250] Like Nataly Jaresko, Suprun was a U.S. citizen of Ukrainian descent whose forefathers had once figured amongst the most fanatic Banderists during the War: an ideal Biden appointee.[251]

In January 2016, another serious outbreak of a strain of swine flu occurred within the walls of one of the Ukrainian Ministry of Defense

---

246 "Southern Research Institute Continues to Play a Role in U.S. Government's Program to Make World Safer," Southern Research, October 25, 2012. https://southernresearch.org/southern-research-institute-continues-to-play-a-role-in-u-s-governments-program-to-make-world-safer/

"Southern Research Instituteis a not-for-profit 501(c)(3) scientific research organization founded in 1941 that conducts preclinical drug discovery and development, advanced engineering research in materials, systems development, and environment and energy research. More than 520 scientific and engineering team members support clients and partners in the pharmaceutical, biotechnology, defense, aerospace, environmental and energy industries."

247 Dilyana Gaytandzhieva, "The Pentagon Bio-weapons," *Dilyana.bg,* April 29, 2018. https://dilyana.bg/the-pentagon-bio-weapons/

248 Ibid.

249 Ibid.

250 Jonathan Pimm, "Ulana Suprun: the accidental reformer," *The Lancet* 392, no. 10149 (September 1, 2018): 727. https://www.thelancet.com/journals/lancet/article/PIIS0140-6736(18)31855-5/fulltext

251 yalensis, "Ulana Suprun – The MRI Shows Bandera On Her Brain," *Awful Avalanche* [blog], January 29, 2017. https://awfulavalanche.wordpress.com/2017/01/29/ulana-suprun-the-mri-shows-bandera-on-her-brain/

bio-facilities in the town of Kharkov. The leak resulted in 20 casualties over 48 hours, while an additional 200 cases were rushed to intensive care.[252] The story was left unreported in local media, while over the next two months the outbreak tallied up 364 fatalities throughout the country. It was eventually discovered that the strain responsible for the lethality rate was identical to the H1N1 strain which had triggered worldwide panic way back in 2009.[253]

The story was eventually reported on by DONI, a media operating from the self-declared independent Popular Republic of Donestk. It stated:

> Donetsk People's Republic intelligence has reported that Californian Flu is leaked from the same place where research of this virus has been carried out. The laboratory is located near the city of Kharkov and its base for U.S. military experts. Information from threatening epidemic is announced by Vice-Commander of Donetsk Army, Eduard Basurin… "According to the medical personnel of the AFU units (Ukrainian troops) there were recorded mass diseases among the Ukrainian military personnel in the field. Physicians recorded the unknown virus as a result of which the infected get the high fever which cannot be subdues by any medicines, and in two days there comes the fatal outcome… We keep registering new facts of growing the epidemics of acute respiratory infections among the Ukrainian military. Just since the beginning of this week more than 200 Ukrainian military have been taken to civil and military hospitals of Kharkov and Dnepropetrovsk. It

---

252 "Dozens Killed By Deadly Swine Flu Virus In Ukraine," *Radio Free Europe/ Radio Liberty,* January 14, 2016. https://www.rferl.org/a/dozens-killed-deadly-swine-flu-virus-ukraine/27486815.html

"The areas worst hit include Kyiv, Kharkiv, Vinnytsia, and Odessa, lawmaker Irina Sysoyenko wrote on her Facebook page. She said 28 people have died from flu in Odessa and 25 in Vinnytsya."

253 "Ukraine Ministry of Defense: 300 people have died from swine flu in Donbas region," *UAWire,* January 25, 2016. https://uawire.org/news/ukraine-reported-about-death-of-300-people-from-swine-flu-virus-in-donetsk-region

"On January 24th, the Ministry of Defense of Ukraine reported that approximately 300 people were killed by the H1N1 swine flu virus or acute respiratory viral infections (ARVI) in Donetsk."

is important to repeat that the DPR intelligence previously reported the research being carried out in a private laboratory in the locality Shelkostantsiya, 30 km away from the city of Kharkov, and involving U.S. military experts.[254]

Between June 2017 and January 2018, a series of Hepatitis A outbreaks affected dozens of inhabitants of areas not coincidently located in South East Ukraine where most of the U.S. DOD biolabs were located. First, it was recorded that 60 people had to be rushed to the Zaparozhia hospital in June 2017. No official cause for the outbreak was ever released.[255] That same month, 19 children from an orphanage were admitted in intensive care following another Hepatitis A outbreak, this time near the city of Odessa.[256]

It was then the city of Kharkov's turn to report 29 cases in November 2017. While this time the virus had been identified in the drinking water, this incident again cast a pale of suspicion on what Ukrainian authorities knew of the circumstances leading up to such a pathogen finding its way into the water supply. Again, a U.S. biolab (the same responsible for the Swine Flu outbreak a year earlier) happened to be located in the Kharkov area.[257]

Finally in January 2018, police launched an investigation into another outbreak of Hepatitis A leading to the hospitalization of 37

254 Sean Adl-Tabatabai, "Mysterious Deadly Virus Leaked From U.S. Laboratory Kills 20," *The People's Voice,* January 25, 2016. https://thepeoplesvoice.tv/mysterious-deadly-virus-leaked-from-us-laboratory-kills-20/

255 Ruslan Rovik, "The outbreak of hepatitis in Mykolaiv will be investigated by the police," *Today,* January 4, 2018. https://www.segodnya.ua/regions/others/vspyshkoy-gepatita-v-nikolaeve-zainteresovalas-policiya-1103357.html

"Earlier, an outbreak of Hepatitis A was recorded in Zaparojie. More than 60 people were admitted to hospital beds there, while doctors have not yet been able to establish the source of infection."

256 Nino Khetsuriani et al., "Seroprevalence of hepatitis B virus infection markers among children in Ukraine, 2017," *Vaccine* 39, no. 10 (March 2021): 1485–1492. https://www.sciencedirect.com/science/article/abs/pii/S0264410X2100133X

257 "Viral hepatitis recorded in Kharkiv region," *Kharkiv News | Today* November 2, 2017. https://www.segodnya.ua/regions/kharkov/v-harkove-strashnyy-virus-prodolzhaet-porazhat-lyudey-1068974.html

"In the village of Andreevka, Balakliya district, people continue to suffer from viral hepatitis. This was reported in the State Institution, Kharkiv Regional Laboratory Center of the Ministry of Health of Ukraine."

people in the city of Mikolaiev, where a hundred cases of cholera had been recorded three years earlier.[258]

Gaytandzhieva also pointed out that while "...officially the research and development of ethnic bio-weapons have never been publicly confirmed. Documents show that the U.S. collects biological material from certain ethnic groups (Russian and Chinese), raising fears in Moscow of a covert U.S. ethnic bio-weapons program."[259]

She added that "... Apart from Russians, the U.S. has been collecting biological material from both healthy and cancer patients in China. The National Cancer Institute has collected biological samples from 300 subjects from Linxian, Zhengzhou, and Chengdu in China."[260]

Last but not least, Russia claimed to have uncovered DTRA documents pertaining to the U.S. issuing a patent purporting to show the existence of drone delivery technology referred to as Toxic Mosquito Aerial Release System (TMARS): a system described as an unmanned aerial vehicle operating via remote control. Titled "Advantageous Effects of Invention," the documents reveal the following:

> With the Toxic Mosquito Aerial Release System, large masses of people can be immunized or enemy troops can now be wiped out or rendered useless without having to risk or endanger our own troops. The Toxic Mosquito Aerial Release System is extremely low cost and can easily accomplish what a billion dollars in medical interventions and airstrikes cannot do. The mosquitos in the Toxic Mosquito Aerial Release System can be contaminated with various types of genetically altered bacteria to activate the immune system, or contaminated with toxic sickness agents depending on the objectives. For military purposes, the mosquitos may be used to deliver an agent such as malaria to create sickness, or they could use much more toxic or highly contagious agents and viruses. A highly contagious

---

258 Ruslan Rovik, "The outbreak of hepatitis in Mykolaiv will be investigated by the police."

"Earlier we reported that over the past few days in Mykolaiv, 37 people were hospitalized with a diagnosis of hepatitis A, including six children."

259 Dilyana Gaytandzhieva, "The Pentagon Bio-weapons."

260 Ibid.

virus could wipe out 100% of the enemy troops because the ones that did not get bitten will be contaminated by their fellow soldiers.[261]

The three personalities mentioned in the DTRA document included Dr. Robert Pope, a former DTRA Director, Dr. Rhys M. Williams, the in-office DTRA Director, and Joanna Wintrol, who was then the Head of the DTRA in charge of all DTRA projects in Ukraine until 2021.

Black & Veatch, which had received substantial funding from Rosemont Seneca (Biden's investment fund), also partnered up with the DTRA on biological weapon projects, including UP-1, UP-2, and UP-8.

The three executives working for B&V in Ukraine included Steven Edwards, the CEO, Lance Lippencott, the project manager and implementer, and David Mustra, the biosafety recruitment manager in Ukraine.[262]

As far back as 2018, investigative Bulgarian reporter Dyliana Gaytandzhieva reported that

The Pentagon has invested at least $65 million in gene editing. The U.S. Defense Advanced Research Projects Agency (DARPA) has awarded 7 research teams to develop tools for genome engineering in insects, rodents and bacteria under DARPA's Sage Genes Program using a novel CRISPR-Cas9 technology. Under another military program (Insect Allies), GM insects are engineered to transfer modified genes to plants. The $10.3 million DARPA project includes both gene editing in insects and in the viruses that they transmit. Ecological Niche-Preference Engineering is a third ongoing military program for genome engineering in insects. The Pentagon's stated objective is to engineer GM organisms so that they can resist certain temperatures, change their habitat and food sources.[263]

---

261 Ibid.
262 Ibid.
263 Ibid.

These revelations seem relevant as the use of insects has fed into rumors that Kiev may unleash mosquitoes infected with malaria on Russian troops.[264]

Game's Up

Russia's launching of its Special Military Operation on February 24, 2022, triggered a flurry of activities aimed at concealing the nature of the work being carried out in the U.S.-operated biolabs located in Ukraine.

Immediately, the World Health Organization issued an advisory to Ukrainian authorities and to that country's Health Ministry, enjoining them to "destroy high-threat pathogens housed in the country's public health laboratories in order to prevent 'any potential spills' that would spread disease among the population." The WHO stressed that "it had collaborated with Ukrainian public health labs for several years to promote security practices that help prevent 'accidental or deliberate release of pathogens'"[265]

---

264 Danielle Ong, "Russia Claims Ukraine Is Using 'Infected Mosquitos' To Attack Russian Soldiers With 'Dangerous Infection,'" *International Business Times,* June 19, 2023. https://www.ibtimes.com/russia-claims-ukraine-using-infected-mosquitos-attack-russian-soldiers-dangerous-infection-3700878

"Igor Kirillov—the head of the Russian Radiation, Chemical and Biological Protection Troops—this week claimed that Ukraine is using infected mosquitoes to transmit infections among Russian troops in the Kherson region amid the flooding caused by the collapse of the Nova Kakhovka Dam. "The Kyiv regime's planned flooding of Kherson region's territory may complicate the situation, including the situation with arbovirus infections. After the fall of the water level, the formation of mosquito-borne diseases, especially West Nile fever, is possible," Kirillov said, per translations from Advisor of Internal Affairs of Ukraine Anton Gerashchenko, who claimed Moscow is using the insects to cover up the outbreaks caused by the flooding. "The high technical level of U.S. preparedness for the use of the carriers is evidenced by the patent for an unmanned aerial vehicle designed to spread airborne infected mosquitoes. When bitten, the mosquitoes are capable of infecting the military with a dangerous infection such as malaria. An infected serviceman is not capable of performing front-line combat missions."

265 Jennifer Rigby and Jonathan Landay, "EXCLUSIVE WHO says it advised Ukraine to destroy pathogens in health labs to prevent disease spread," *Reuters,* March 11, 2022. https://www.reuters.com/world/europe/exclusive-who-says-it-advised-ukraine-destroy-pathogens-health-labs-prevent-2022-03-11

"The WHO would not say when it had made the recommendation nor did it provide specifics about the kinds of pathogens or toxins housed in Ukraine's laboratories. The agency also did not answer questions about whether its recommendations were

Disputing Russian allegations of foul play in Ukraine, the UN commission tasked with Disarmament Affairs reported to the Security Council through its High Representative that it was "not aware" of any biological programs in Ukraine. It reminded the Council that such activities are in any event prohibited under the Biological and Chemical Convention: a treaty ratified by over 180 countries (including Ukraine and the United States) whose cooperation the Commission stated is essential to secure "the safe and secure disposal of any pathogens they come across, and to reach out for technical assistance as needed."[266]

In panic, Washington and its allies stridently rejected Moscow's allegations, dismissing them as a maneuver aimed at concealing their intention to proceed with their own launching of biological or chemical attacks, according to Undersecretary of State Victoria Nuland.

In the face of Washington's sempiternal accusations of "Russian disinformation," Russia began providing the Security Council with documents and other evidence collected in the wake of its military operations in Ukraine.

Russian President Vladimir Putin then joined the fray by issuing a comprehensive address on the issue:

> There was a network of dozens of laboratories in Ukraine, where military biological programs were conducted under the guidance and with the financial support of the Pentagon, including experiments with coronavirus strains, anthrax, cholera, African swine fever and other deadly diseases... frantic attempts are underway to conceal the traces of these secret programs.[267]

Always the consummate negotiator, Putin invited impartial countries to take part in an international investigation along with representatives of international organizations in order to provide additional evidence.[268]

---

followed."

266 Ibid.

267 "Evidence shows U.S. labs in Ukraine develop biological weapons: Putin," video [17:54], CGTN, May 17, 2022. https://news.cgtn.com/news/2022-05-17/Evidence-shows-U-S-labs-in-Ukraine-develop-biological-weapons-Putin-1a6UxcOuTT2/index.html

268 UN Security Council, "United Nations unaware of any biological weapons

This consensual approach contrasted with Washington's unease which in turn led to increased concerns amongst UN Member-States that there might just be some truth to Moscow's claims.

The U.S. is on record as having rejected the monitoring protocol intended to strengthen the Biological Weapons Convention (BWC), so that in essence there exists no oversight mechanism which might be applied to activities conducted in biolabs it operates around the world.

Legal experts point to the accidents related to these labs, as well as Washington's documented use of biological and chemical weapons in Southeast Asia, as evidence that pressure should be exerted on the United States to accept the protocols to the BWC in order to prevent the deploying of WMDs on foreign soil.[269]

The Chinese also expressed their concerns about the U.S. biolabs through its Permanent UN Representative.

> The international community have already been raising concerns about the U.S. military biological activities. They have 336 laboratories around the world. This number comes from the information provided by the U.S. to the Conference of Parties of the BWC (Biological Weapons Convention). The U.S. always claim they advocate transparency. If they believe the relevant information is fake, they can just

programmes in Ukraine, top disarmament official affirms, as Security Council considers new claims by Russian Federation," *ReliefWeb,* May 13, 2022. https://reliefweb.int/report/ukraine/united-nations-unaware-any-biological-weapons-programmes-ukraine-top-disarmament

"When the floor opened for Council members, the representative of the Russian Federation said his delegation has accumulated a lot of materials that directly indicate that the United States and Ukraine are violating the Convention by carrying out dangerous biological projects in the centre of Eastern Europe and on the western borders of his country. Highlighting project 3007 in which Ukrainian specialists, supervised by United States colleagues, have carried out collections of water samples from rivers flowing through Ukraine, he said their aim is to establish specific dangerous pathogens and determine their ability to incapacitate. As soon as the collection of materials is complete, he said, they will be presented to the Council for investigation, so that his country can finally cut off the military-biological activities that threaten international peace and security. Further, given the United States' refusal to engage in a constructive discussion, he added, his delegation plans to use the mechanisms under articles V and VI of the Biological Weapons Convention."

269 *Report of the International Science Commission for the Investigation of the Facts Concerning Bacterial Warfare in Korea and China* (Peking, 1952). https://www.documentcloud.org/documents/4334133-ISC-Full-Report-Pub-Copy.html

provide us with relevant data for clarification, so that the international community can draw a conclusion by itself."[270]

Experts from civil society contributed to the discussion.

Du Kaiyuan, a Shanghai-based military commentator, highlighted that "the tests for biological weapons need live tests which might cause legal problems in the U.S., but it can get enough samples from other countries."[271]

Sheradil Baktygulov, a Kyrgyz political analyst based in Bishkek, told the *Global Times* that "the formal explanations of the U.S. authorities on more than 300 U.S. biolabs activities around the world do not match the real situation on the ground. The truth is much darker as has been shown by many independent investigations since 2018... There were numerous mysterious outbreaks of human illnesses and losses of livestock in Georgia, Ukraine and Russian provinces bordering that country since 2007. Moreover, the U.S. is keeping its bioweapons in violation of international treaties."[272]

As the controversy gained momentum, Russia's Permanent UN Representative announced that Russia would exercise its prerogatives under the Biological Weapons Convention and activate Articles 5 and 6 which allow for an investigation. He added that his country had accumulated sufficient incriminating evidence supporting the claim that both the U.S. and Ukraine had violated the BWC.[273]

This recommendation received the support of UN deputy arms chief Thomas Markram who recommended that the BWC's investigative mechanisms be activated to address Russia's concerns over the bio-labs in Ukraine.[274]

The Convention's text calls *inter alia* for Signatory-States to abide by the following:

---

270 U.S. biolabs a clear and present danger: China Daily editorial," *China Daily,* March 13, 2022. http://www.chinadaily.com.cn/a/202203/13/WS622dd159a310cdd39bc8c45f.html

271 GT staff reporters, "International voices urge U.S. explanation for bioweapons accusations," *Global Times,* March 17, 2022. https://www.globaltimes.cn/page/202203/1255185.shtml

272 Ibid.

273 Ibid.

274 Ibid.

- Never to develop, produce, stockpile, or otherwise acquire or retain: 1) biological agents or toxins of types and in quantities that have no justification for peaceful uses; and 2) weapons, equipment, or means of delivery designed to use such agents or toxins for hostile purposes (Article I).

- To destroy or divert to peaceful purposes all agents, toxins, weapons, equipment, and means of delivery specified in Article I in their possession, or under their jurisdiction or control (Article 2).

- Not to transfer or in any way to assist, encourage, or induce any entity to manufacture or otherwise acquire any of the agents, toxins, weapons, equipment or means of delivery specified in Article I (Article 3).

- To take any necessary measures to prohibit and prevent the development, production, stockpiling, acquisition, or retention of any of the agents, toxins, weapons, equipment, and means of delivery specified in Article I under its jurisdiction or control (Article 4).

Article 5 of the BWC stipulates that "The states, parties to this Convention, undertake to consult one another and to co-operate in solving any problems which may arise in relation to the objective of, or in the application of the provisions of, the Convention. Consultation and co-operation pursuant to this Article may also be undertaken through appropriate international procedures within the framework of the United Nations and in accordance with its Charter."

Article 6 states that "any state party to this Convention, which finds that any other state party is acting in breach of obligations deriving from the provisions of the Convention, may lodge a complaint with the Security Council of the United Nations. Such a complaint should include all possible evidence confirming its validity, as well as a request for its consideration by the Security Council."[275]

The Russian Defense Ministry, moreover, presented evidence highlighting Hunter Biden's correspondence with employees of

---

275 United Nations Office for Disarmament Affairs, *Biological Weapons Convention.* https://disarmament.unoda.org/biological-weapons/

the Defense Threat Reduction Agency and Pentagon contractors in Ukraine.[276]

As such, these documents revealed the following:

- Hunter Biden was a key player in providing financing to support research work on various pathogens through the raising of funds for Black & Veatch and Metabiota.

- The Vice President of Metabiota wrote an email to Hunter Biden in which she enthused that the Vice-President's son's partnership with Metabiota would ensure the *"cultural and economic independence of Ukraine from Russia."*

- Other Investors in the biological facilities located in Ukraine featured Hunter Biden, Rosemont Seneca, George Soros, and his Open Society Foundations.

- The Pentagon entered into several contracts with subcontractors Metabiota, Black & Veatch, and CH2M Hill.

- U.S. specialists were engaged in perfecting modes of delivery in order to disseminate poisonous radioactive and narcotic substances.

- A Director Robert Pope and Ukrainian Health Minister, Ulyana Suprun, highlighted the close cooperation existing between U.S. and Ukrainian officials in their common search to achieve certain "objectives," which included the survivability of substances of very high concern (SVHC), the strengthening and consolidating of the SVHC, the need to identify a suitable location to store the biological weapon into one depository in Ukraine, as well as the finding of a way to isolate and dispose of the SVHC.

Another letter indicated that Ukrainian aircraft manufacturer, Motor-Sich, had approached Turkish defense company, Baykar, asking the latter whether their UAVs could travel over 300 km in order to

---

276 Al Mayadeen, "Russia releases documents on U.S.-funded bio-weapons, Hunter Biden exposed," *Al Mayadeen*, March 31, 2022. https://english.almayadeen. net/news/politics/russia-releases-documents-on-us-funded-bio-weapons-hunter-bi

"spray aerosols with a capacity of more than 20 liters" (Baykar replied in the negative).[277]

Elements bearing on the entanglement of the Biden clan in Ukraine's murky politics likely featured prominently on Donald Trump's mind as he made that July 2019 phone call to that country's recently elected president, Volodymir Zelenskiy.

Trump's potential proximity with the comedian-turned-head of state prompted the Washington Establishment to go all-out in preventing the incumbent president from lifting the veil of corruption, and so a battle began centered on impeaching the forty-fifth president.

277 Ibid.

PART III

Election 2024:
Woe to the Vanquished

IN TYPICAL FASHION, the Democrats spun the narrative around Trump's first impeachment as one pertaining to his allegedly seeking to "use the powers of his office to solicit foreign interference on his behalf in the 2020 election."[278]

Eerily previewing the content of Andrii Derkach's own 2020 allegations of interference by Ukrainian officials in the 2016 U.S. presidential election, the impeachment inquiry report released in December 2019 sought to characterize Trump's July 2019 phone call to his Ukrainian counterpart as evidence that the U.S. president's inquiry into the existence of an investigation concerned "a discredited theory (thanks to Democrats sitting on the House Intelligence Committee) that it was Ukraine, not Russia, that interfered in the 2016 presidential election."[279]

Even more intriguing is the report's barely-veiled reference to Biden as "a political rival that he (Trump) apparently feared the most."[280]

No objective explanations support such affirmation. By December 2019, not only had Joe Biden not yet clinched his Party's the nomination; his campaign was not galvanizing crowds, and so it seems reasonable to suggest that "the facts were being made to fit the policy."[281]

If anything, the zeal exhibited by the Democrats in their pursuit of the impeachment contrasted dramatically with the pace of another investigation bearing on Hunter Biden's own turpitudes.

---

278 Zachary B. Wolf and Sean O'Key, "The Trump-Ukraine impeachment inquiry report, annotated," *CNN,* December 3, 2019. https://edition.cnn.com/interactive/2019/12/politics/trump-ukraine-impeachment-inquiry-report-annotated/

279 Ibid.

280 Ibid.

281 Bob Locke, *"The Downing Street Memo* and the Mass Media's attempt to suppress coverage of it." https://webpages.csus.edu/~boblocke/locke/mymandowning.html

"This memo was, in fact, the minutes of a meeting between the Prime Minister of England, Tony Blair, and his highest ranking members of MI 5, England's equivalent to the CIA."

A Slow-moving Tax Investigation

Hunter could have sat quietly at Burisma for years while earning a $50,000 monthly salary.

However, the Burisma story revealed unsightly facts and far more significant amounts of money. To be sure, these documents figure in no less a source than the U.S. Senate report published in September 2020. The report is still on the Senate website under the title "Hunter Biden, Burisma, and Corruption: The Impact on U.S. Government Policy and Related Concerns."[282]

The report is based on both public sources and confidential documents that shed light on the financial dealings of Biden and his associated firms. As such, it gives the reader a comprehensive inside-out insight into the relationship between Burisma and the Biden family. It was prepared by two Republican senators, Ron Johnson and Chaco Greslia. The report may today be undeservedly forgotten, but who knows when it might again receive the merited public attention? When it came out in the midst of the U.S. presidential campaign, Biden's campaign staff described it as another attempt to "hurt a political opponent and interfere with the election process." Joe Biden, for one, never forgot it, which in turn explains the virulence of his actions against Andrii Derkach. What was so explosive in that Senate report?

The authors managed to get information pertaining to all payment transactions between Zlochevsky's Burisma and Hunter Biden (on page 65). The April 15, 2014 transfers, (before Hunter Biden joined the board of Burisma Holdings) are particularly relevant: totaling $112,758.15, they were made out to Rosemont Seneca Bohai LLC, a company owned by Hunter's business partner and Burisma colleague Devon Archer. Then on May 7, 2014, a $250,000 payment was made from Burisma to the Washington law firm of Boies, Schiller and Flexner LLP (Boies Schiller), where Hunter Biden was at the time still employed. Just a week later, on May 12, 2014, Biden would join Burisma's board of directors. Then, on September 16, 2014, another

---

282 U.S. Senate Committee on Homeland Security and Governmental Affairs and U.S. Senate Committee on Finance, Majority Staff Report, *Hunter Biden, Burisma, and Corruption: The Impact on U.S. Government Policy and Related Concerns,* September 23, 2020. https://www.finance.senate.gov/imo/media/doc/ HSGAC - Finance Joint Report 2020.09.23.pdf

payment of $33,039.77 would again be made to the account of the law firm Boies Schiller.[283]

The transfers would eventually be effected on a regular basis. Between 15 May 2014 and February 12, 2016, Burisma paid 48 additional tranches to Rosemont Seneca. Of note, 39 of the 48 transfers (each totaling $83,333.33) were paid out for consulting services. One can't help but wonder why Hunter Biden was collecting fees for "consulting services" in addition to his remuneration for his work on the board of directors, for even a solid company like Burisma could make no such large-scale remunerations.[284]

Where did these substantial fees ultimately go after they were transferred to Rosemont Seneca? The answer is obvious: between June 5, 2014 and October 5, 2015, Rosemont Seneca made 38 payments totaling $701,979 to Hunter Biden's three personal accounts. According to the Ukrainian investigators, Burisma transferred $4,817,000 to Rosemont Seneca between May 2014 and October 2015.

---

283 Ibid.

"On April 15, 2014, Burisma Holdings (Burisma), a Ukrainian private oil and gas company owned by corrupt Ukrainian oligarch Mykola Zlochevsky, sent two wires totaling $112,758.15 to Rosemont Seneca Bohai LLC. Rosemont Seneca Bohai is an apparent shell entity owned by Hunter Biden's long-time business associate, Devon Archer, which was first registered in Delaware on Feb. 13, 2014. According to Real Clear Politics, on the following day, April 16, 2014, Archer visited Vice President Biden at the White House. One week later, on April 22, 2014, Vice President Biden appeared with Ukrainian Prime Minister Arsemy Yasenyuk and addressed Ukrainian legislators in Kyiv regarding Russia's actions in Crimea. That same day, Burisma announced that Archer had joined its board of directors. In the wake of Vice President Biden's visit, the press described him as "the public face of the administration's handling of Ukraine." The earliest payment from Burisma related to Hunter Biden appears to have been made to Boies, Schiller, and Flexner LLP (Boies Schiller), the Washington law firm where he was employed as a counsel in 2014. On May 7, 2014, mere weeks after Vice President Biden took lead of the Obama administration's Ukraine policy, Burisma sent Boies Schiller a payment of $250,000. Approximately one week later, on May 12, 2014, Hunter Biden joined Archer on Burisma's board of directors. Burisma made a second payment to Boies Schiller on Sept. 16, 2014, in the amount of $33,039.77. Both the May 7 and Sept. 16 payments state in the transaction notes that they were 'for Legal and Consulting Services.'"

284 Ibid.

"Between May 15, 2014 and Feb. 12, 2016, Burisma sent another 48 wires to Rosemont Seneca Bohai, totaling $3,489,490.78. Of the 48 transactions, 39 are described as 'Consulting Services' and 39 of the 48 are in the amount of $83,333.33, with the last of the payments occurring on Feb. 12, 2016."

Then suddenly, the money transfer scheme from Zlochevsky to Biden changed. The reason was that in May 2016, Biden's friend and partner Devon Archer, himself a director on Burisma's board, was arrested on suspicion of securities fraud. The SEC accused Archer and six of his partners of defrauding investors by selling more than $43 million in sham bonds issued in 2014 and 2015. As a result, beginning January 25, Burisma began remitting fees to Hunter's law firm, Owasco PC. Between January and November 16, 2016, Hunter would collect a total of $752,054, 99. to complement his base salary. Questions arose as to why Burisma was rewarding Hunter so generously, for it is not clear how a lawyer could possibly provide such added value to an oil and gas corporation, a sector in which Biden had no expertise.[285]

Biden also had no expertise in ways to cover up suspicious transactions.

The details of financial transactions between Burisma and Hunter Biden's firms were presented in another portion of Andrii Derkach's exposé of November 11, 2019, during which he revealed the existence of a statement from Morgan Stanley Bank, which was involved in these financial transactions. "Morgan Stanley is one of the largest bank holdings in the United States," Derkach explained, showing the public that very statement.[286] That statement showed that between May 2014

---

285   Joshua Rhett Miller, "Federal appeals court reinstates convictions for Hunter Biden's ex-business partner," *New York Post,* October 9, 2020. https://nypost.com/2020/10/09/federal-appeals-court-reinstates-convictions-for-hunter-bidens-ex-business-partner/

"Wednesday's ruling by a three-judge panel of the U.S. Court of Appeals for the Second Circuit found that Archer—who previously partnered with Biden and served with him on the board of a Ukrainian natural gas firm, Burisma Holdings—'knew at least the general nature and extent of the scheme and intended to bring about its success,' according to the Journal."

286   "MP Derkach says Biden Jr. received Burisma payments via mediators," *Interfax-Ukraine,* November 11, 2019. https://en.interfax.com.ua/news/general/623992.html

"Starting from May 2014 to October 2015 Burisma company transferred to Rosemont company $4.817 million, and the latter transferred a payment amounted to $871,000 to the account of Hunter Biden, son of former U.S. Vice President Joe Biden, reported MP Andriy Derkach in a video blog on Facebook. 'This is the official statement from Morgan Stanley. Morgan Stanley is one of the biggest bank holdings in the USA. Here you can see a cash flow of Rosemont Seneca Boa company owned by Devon Archer, for a year and a half (from May 2014 to October 2016). According to the bank statement, starting from May 2014 to October 2015 Burisma company transferred to Rosemont company $4.817 million, and the latter transferred a payment and October 2015, Burisma transferred $4,817,000 to Rosemont, of which $871,000 was then transferred to Biden's accounts.

Derkach also produced materials from a Latvian financial intelligence report which revealed the transfer of funds from Burisma in favor of two offshore shell companies owned by Hunter Biden and partners. *The total amount of these payments was about 16.5 million dollars.*[287]

It is interesting that Derkach's materials were obtained not from the Russian FSB printer, but from the Baltic States, which are considered friendly to Ukraine and the United States. Moreover, the Latvian financial intelligence unit also uncovered evidence of Ukrainian corruption in the movement of the $16.5 million dollars. "The Financial Intelligence Unit of Latvia, referred materials to the GPU (General Prosecutor's Office) and the State Financial Monitoring of Ukraine that Robert Hunter Biden may be involved in corrupt practices," Derkach said.[288]

---

that amounted to $871,000 to the account of Biden,' said Derkach, adding an official statement from Morgan Stanley."

287 Andrii Derkach, Member of Ukrainian Parliament, "Andrii Derkach won the trial against Burisma for the second time," 2021. https://web.archive.org/web/20211127030639/https://www.derkach.com.ua/en/publications/andrii-derkach-won-the-trial-against-zlochevskys-burisma-for-the-second-time/

"Representatives of Burisma demanded a refutation of the information that they paid $900 thousand for lobbying activities to the former Vice-President, and now the U.S. President Joe Biden, and $16.5 million to his son Hunter Biden, along with Aleksander Kwasniewski, Alan Apter and Devon Archer. 'The Pechersk Court noted that Burisma does not dispute the fact of payments to Biden and his son. The Company does not agree that such amounts were paid through the Rosemont Seneca Bohai company' – MP Derkach commented on the decision. According to Derkach, the ongoing tax audit of Hunter Biden's operations in the United States will confirm that the money that the son of the President of the United States wrote about in his new book and which was used as payment for the services of the Bidens was withdrawn from Ukraine and laundered through the shell companies Digitex Organization LLP and Wirelogic Technology A.S. 'As have already mentioned and shown in the previous documents at the disposal of the Prosecutor's General Office of Ukraine contained in the files of criminal proceedings, as well as data from the financial monitoring of Ukraine, Latvia and Cyprus, there are all traces of the movement of funds and payments, and Burisma used the same "dirty" money to pay for services of KROLL Associates UK LTD in the amount of at least $300 thousand,' the MP said."

288 LETA, "Document leak: what ties Latvia's ex-president, Biden's son and PrivatBank together?," *Baltic News Network,* October 3, 2019. https://bnn-news.com/document-leak-what-ties-latvia-s-ex-president-biden-s-son-and-i-privatbank-i-together-205937

Although the story did not develop until later, all these documents provided by Morgan Stanley and Latvian financial intelligence have never been refuted by anyone. Neither the State Department, nor the White House, nor any member of the Biden family ever sued Derkach for defamation. On the contrary, Andrii Derkach won his case against Burisma, which had accused him of slander. Per the Ukrainian court's ruling, the payments from Burisma were authentic.[289]

Even assuming that the Morgan Stanley bank statements and Latvian reports Derkach produced originated from the FSB printers, how would one reconcile this version of a Russian ploy with the fact that Hunter Biden did fail to pay taxes on the money he received from Zlochevsky's company? In the United States, failure to pay taxes is very serious, and so it befuddles one to think that the American media waited until December 2020 to finally report on the U.S. Justice Department and the Delaware State Attorney's Office's investigation into Hunter's transactions from previous years.

Earlier in 2019, the U.S. Internal Revenue Service (IRS) had filed claims of unpaid taxes against Biden and his wife over undeclared revenues estimated at $400,000 from his Ukrainian royalties.[290]

"Last year, the now ex-President of Latvia Raimonds Vējonis had attended a forum in Monaco organized by an associate of Ukraine's ex-president Viktor Yanukovich and owner of Burisma Holdings Mykola Zlochevsky."

289 "MP Derkach reiterates about external control of Ukraine by United States, related corruption," *Interfax-Ukraine,* September 16, 2020. https://en.interfax.com.ua/news/press-conference/688404.html

"At a press conference in Kyiv on Wednesday, he announced that he won a court case against Burisma last week. 'By the way, if Burisma again wants to whiten Biden in court, I want to notify that I already won one lawsuit regarding payments from Burisma to Biden last week. By the way, Burisma's lawyers, trying to whiten Biden, did not dispute the fact of payments. They were embarrassed only by the indicated amount of payments to Biden. This fact was also noted in the court's decision,' he said, presenting a photocopy of the decision of Kyiv-based Pechersky District Court."

290 Bart Jansen, "Hunter Biden's taxes under investigation by U.S. attorney's office," USA Today, December 9, 2020. https://eu.usatoday.com/story/news/politics/2020/12/09/hunter-bidens-taxes-under-investigation-u-s-attorneys-office/3869793001/

"A central point of the article refers to an email from Vadym Pozharskyi, an adviser to Burisma, who thanked Hunter Biden for 'giving an opportunity to meet your father and spent (sic) some time together.' If true, the claim would undercut Joe Biden's repeated assertions that he never spoke to his son about business dealings in Ukraine."

The source for Hunter's own e-mail correspondence was Rudolph Giuliani's lawyer, Robert Costello, who had received files figuring on the laptop that Hunter had failed to pick up from the repairman. In another email, Rosemont Seneca Partners president Eric Schwerin is reported to have told Hunter: "In 2014, you joined the Burisma board of directors, and we still need to amend your 2014 return to reflect the unreported Burisma income."[291]

The income, according to the letter, was a solid $1.2 million, including $400,000 received from Burisma. Curiously, the letter is dated January 16, 2017, the date of Joe Biden's last visit to Kiev. It would appear that against the backdrop of Joe's imminent departure from the Vice-Presidency, Schwerin instructed his lawyers to start mopping up any rough edges that could lead to serious problems in the future. However, Hunter dropped the ball.

To date, neither the DOJ or any IRS official has ever acknowledged the existence of a mistake, which would lead to the conclusion that Biden's finances were in in fact in order. If anything, it clearly became impossible to cover up the bribes without the threat of withdrawing loan guarantees to Ukraine still dangling over the heads of that country's officials.

At this writing, the U.S. Justice Department has announced that Hunter had pled guilty to two counts of failing to pay over $100,000 in taxes on a $1.5 million dollar income in each of the years 2017 and 2018.[292]

---

291 Tom Winter, "Email to Hunter Biden raises fresh questions about his tax dealings," *NBC News,* December 11, 2020. https://www.nbcnews.com/politics/politics-news/email-hunter-biden-raises-fresh-questions-about-his-tax-dealings-n1250973

"The email goes on to note that Hunter Biden, who is now the subject of a federal tax probe, netted more than $1.2 million for the year. The earnings include the $400,000 from Burisma as well as income from Rosemont Seneca Advisors and a legal firm."

292 Kara Scannell, Evan Perez and Paula Reid, "Hunter Biden to plead guilty to federal tax charges, strikes deal on gun charge," *CNN Politics,* updated June 20, 2023. https://edition.cnn.com/2023/06/20/politics/hunter-biden/index.html

"As part of the plea agreement, the Justice Department has agreed to recommend a sentence of probation for the two counts of failing to pay taxes in a timely matter for the years 2017 and 2018, according to sources. Hunter Biden owed at least $100,000 in federal taxes for 2017, and at least $100,000 in 2018, but did not pay what was due to the Internal Revenue Service by the deadlines."

Biden's not guilty plea to a gun charge stemming from his being in possession of a Colt Cobra .38 Special, despite being a drug user, was the result of the collapse of a plea-bargain agreement negotiated between the DOJ and Hunter's lawyers. The judge took exception to the blanket immunity granted Hunter for all future crimes when it was conceded by Biden's own counsel that his client was being investigated over possible FARA violations.

Hunter was arraigned in early October just when Trump's civil fraud case in New-York got underway. He entered a no guilty plea on the gun charges while tax charges remain pending.

A Weaponized Justice Department

Obviously owing to Joe Biden's bid to run for president, the DOJ opted to put its investigation on hold ahead of an election during which Joe Biden's political foes would come to focus on Hunter's work as a board member of Burisma as well as his involvement in a series of investments with Chinese companies.[293]

With government watchdogs and pundits having broadly taken issue with the ethical implications of his foreign business dealings, the federal probe posed a real threat to Hunter's influence-peddling ventures.

Zoe Kestan, one of Hunter's former girlfriends, had secretly testified before a grand jury empaneled in Wilmington, Delaware, that she had been spending time with Biden at a variety of high-end hotels in Manhattan and Los Angeles, including the Four Seasons, Mercer, SIXTY SoHo, and Soho Grand, as well as the Hollywood Roosevelt, NoMad, and celebrity-friendly Chateau Marmont.[294]

293 Emma Colton, "Prosecutor investigating Hunter Biden stalled to avoid alerting public about probe ahead of election: Report," *Fox News,* July 16, 2021. https://www.foxnews.com/politics/federal-proscutor-investigating-hunter-biden-stalled

"By the time investigators were ready to issue grand jury subpoenas and search warrants, election season was in full swing and Weiss reportedly feared the public knowing about the investigation and it would become politicized."

294 Elizabeth Rosner and Bruce Golding "Ex-girlfriend tells Hunter Biden grand jury about lavish spending," *New York Post,* updated February 22, 2022. https://nypost.com/2022/02/21/ex-girlfriend-tells-hunter-biden-grand-jury-about-lavish-spending/

"The probe reportedly involves Hunter Biden's controversial, overseas business

Kestan moreover testified about Hunter telling her to withdraw "thousands of dollars at a time" from ATMs, while giving her cash to buy clothing, meals, and other items although she had "no idea how he obtained the money."

Hunter, for his part, stated: "I take this matter very seriously but I am confident that a professional and objective review of these matters will demonstrate that I handled my affairs legally and appropriately, including with the benefit of professional tax advisers," the president's son argued in a statement at the time."[295]

A Neutralized Whistleblower

Just as the saga bearing on the federal case filed against Hunter was coming to a close owing to the announcement of a plea-bargain agreement with the Justice Department, the story took on a new twist when an IRS whistleblower decided to go public about what he claimed were instances of obstruction during the investigation.

Gary Shapley, a 14-year veteran of the Internal Revenue Services, went on television to detail the pattern of obstructing measures seemingly emanating from the FBI and the Department of Justice which he said prevented the investigation from going after Biden in order to gather evidence required to prosecute the President's son to the full extent of the law.[296]

Highlighting the fact that he was repeatedly prevented from taking steps considered routine in other cases, Shapley stressed the

---

dealings. Last month, a partial copy of a subpoena surfaced that showed JPMorgan Chase Bank was ordered to turn over records related to any transactions involving him and the Bank of China."

295 Chris Strohm and Laura Davison, "Cloud Looms Over Biden Presidency With Son Under Criminal Probe," *Bloomberg,* December 10, 2020. https://www.bloomberg.com/news/articles/2020-12-10/cloud-looms-over-biden-presidency-with-son-under-criminal-probe

296 Annie Grayer and Sara Murray, "IRS veteran goes public as whistleblower in Hunter Biden criminal probe," *CNN Politics,* May 25, 2023. https://edition.cnn.com/2023/05/24/politics/irs-whistleblower-hunter-biden/index.html

"'There were multiple steps that were slow-walked – were just completely not done – at the direction of the Department of Justice,' Shapley told CBS News chief investigative correspondent Jim Axelrod in an interview Tuesday. 'When I took control of this particular investigation, I immediately saw deviations from the normal process. It was way outside the norm of what I've experienced in the past.'"

importance in his view to avoid a perception among the public that the justice system could be tempted to show favorable bias towards certain defendants, stating: "We have to make sure as a special agent for IRS Criminal Investigation that we treat every single person the same... And that just simply didn't happen here."[297]

While Sharpley described himself as a Republican, he dismissed any notion that he acted out of political motive, refuting the claim that he'd ever been engaged in partisan politics. He stated that the five-year investigation uncovered conduct that he said should have resulted in additional charges.[298]

Back in April, a lawyer for the IRS whistleblower had submitted to the Committee a letter explaining that his client had worked as an IRS criminal supervisory special agent "who has been overseeing the ongoing and sensitive investigation of a high-profile, controversial subject since early 2020 and would like to make protected whistleblower disclosures to Congress."[299]

The letter aimed to underline that "the protected disclosures: (1) contradict sworn testimony to Congress by a senior political appointee, (2) involve failure to mitigate clear conflicts of interest in the ultimate disposition of the case, and (3) detail examples of preferential treatment and politics improperly affecting decisions and protocols that would normally be followed by career law enforcement

---

297 Jim Axelrod, "IRS whistleblower says he was stopped from pursuing leads in Hunter Biden probe," *Yahoo! News,* June 27, 2023. https://news.yahoo.com/irs-whistleblower-says-stopped-pursuing-230200650.html

"'It is almost embarrassing that the tax division of the Department of Justice apparently approved this sweetheart of tax deals,' says former federal prosecutor Gene Rossi. 'Should he have gotten a felony? Absolutely yes.'"

298 Andrew Feinberg, "IRS 'whistleblower' who claimed Hunter Biden case was mishandled won't cooperate with Senate probe," *The Independent,* May 26, 2023. https://www.independent.co.uk/news/world/americas/us-politics/irs-whistleblower-gary-shapley-hunter-biden-b2346365.html

299 Sarah Fitzpatrick and Zoë Richards, "IRS agent wants whistleblower protections to discuss Hunter Biden probe," *NBC News,* updated April 20, 2023. https://www.nbcnews.com/politics/politics-news/irs-agent-wants-whistleblower-protections-discuss-hunter-biden-probe-rcna80564

"House Ways and Means Committee chair Jason Smith, R-Mo., said in a statement that his panel looks forward 'to sitting down promptly with this individual to better understand the scope and detail of the concerns raised. The Committee takes seriously any allegations of misconduct by government officials or offices and will, on behalf of American taxpayers, look into concerns that are brought to our attention.'"

professionals in similar circumstances if the subject were not politically connected."[300]

House Oversight Committee Chair James Comer (R-Ky.) issued a statement expressing the following view: "It's deeply concerning that the Biden Administration may be obstructing justice by blocking efforts to charge Hunter Biden evasion. We've been wondering all along where the heck the DOJ and the IRS have been. Now it appears the Biden Administration may have been working overtime to prevent the Bidens from facing any consequences."[301]

Biden's attorney retorted that "It is a felony for an IRS agent to improperly disclose information about an ongoing tax investigation… The IRS has incredible power, and abusing that power by targeting, embarrassing, or disclosing information about a private citizen's tax matters undermines Americans' faith in the federal government."[302]

The Biden Influence-peddling Investigation

In the wake of the 2022 midterm elections, the Comer/Grassley-led House Judicial Oversight Committee proceeded to lay out evidence that U.S. President Biden's son, Hunter, had engaged in influence peddling while his father was serving as vice president.

The president's participation in enriching his family is, in a word, abuse of the highest order, I want to be clear:

---

300 Ibid.

301 Kaitlin Lewis, "IRS Whistleblower's Hunter Biden Allegations Add Fuel to James Comer's Fire," *Newsweek,* April 19, 2023. https://www.newsweek.com/irs-whistleblowers-hunter-biden-allegations-add-fuel-james-comers-fire-1795469

302 Kristinn Taylor, "Smash Mouth: Hunter Biden Lawyer Accuses IRS Whistleblower of Committing Felony by Disclosing "Information About an Ongoing Tax Investigation,'" *The Gateway Pundit,* April 20, 2023. https://www.thegatewaypundit.com/2023/04/smash-mouth-hunter-biden-lawyer-accuses-irs-whistleblower-of-committing-felony-by-disclosing-information-about-an-ongoing-tax-investigation/

"Throughout his nearly 30-year long legal career, Clark has represented hedge fund clients in precedent setting matters involving Section 5 of the Securities Act, Rule 105 of Regulation M and the rules regarding insider trading. He successfully defended Mark Cuban at his insider trading trial in SEC v. Mark Cuban and represented Elon Musk in SEC v. Elon Musk, an investigation and resolution of selective disclosure allegations. Clark also currently represents Hunter Biden in an investigation regarding tax issues."

> This is an investigation of Joe Biden, and that's where our focus will be next Congress...I want to make it very clear that from this point on, this is no longer the Hunter Biden investigation. This is the Joe Biden investigation.[303]

As a first order of business, Comer announced that the Commission would send letters to the heads at the National Archives and Records Administration, Federal Bureau of Investigation and Treasury Department requesting them to hand over documents bearing on the nature of the Biden family business both at home and abroad. Comer added that the letters would enquire about the nature of the relationship and communication existing between the Bidens and named individuals purported to have engaged with the Bidens such as Eric Schwerin, Edward Prewitt and Georges Bergès.[304]

As a response, White House Spokesperson Ian Sams' office released the following communiqué:

> Instead of working with President Biden to address issues important to the American people, like lower costs, congressional Republicans' top priority is to go after President Biden with politically motivated attacks chock full of long-debunked conspiracy theories. President Biden is not going to let these political attacks distract him from focusing on Americans' priorities, and we hope congressional

303 "Rep. James Comer: 'This Is an Investigation of Joe Biden,'" *Daily Signal,* November 17, 2022. https://www.dailysignal.com/2022/11/17/this-is-an-investigation-of-joe-biden-house-gop-lawmaker-says-in-announcing-probe/

"Comer highlighted two items found on Hunter Biden's abandoned laptop computer—a map of the U.S. written in Chinese and an email about related D.C. office space that includes the names of the president, first lady Jill Biden, and the president's brother."

304 Deirdre Walsh and Ximena Bustillo, "GOP Rep. Comer says pending probes will show Hunter Biden peddled influence," *NPR,* November 17, 2022. https://www.npr.org/2022/11/17/1137197668/republicans-have-won-the-house-now-theyre-promising-to-investigate-the-bidens

"Comer told NPR on Wednesday that Biden has said publicly he never met some of his son's associates, but his investigation has produced photos, emails and bank records. He suggested that some of the evidence shows that bank accounts between Hunter and his father were 'co-mingled.' Comer said Jordan will show how whistleblowers brought evidence about improper financial dealings to the FBI and DOJ but they didn't pursue any investigations."

Republicans will join us in tackling them instead of wasting time and resources on political revenge.[305]

Comer decided to focus on actions alleged to constitute "influence peddling" on behalf of foreign governments in violation of the Foreign Agent Registration Act (FARA), adding that he believed "that there's ample evidence to prove that Joe Biden knew about Hunter's shady business dealings… he may have been involved financially in some of those business dealings, but at the very least, we believe we need to investigate to see if these shady business deals have compromised this White House."[306]

President Biden acted somewhat smugly in dismissing the content of the allegations, even though some of the evidence showed that bank accounts between Hunter and himself were *"co-mingled."*

Comer added that House Republican and Member of the Committee Jim Jordan would moreover provide evidence that both the FBI and DOJ had refused to pursue any investigations despite probable cause that foul play had taken place per the testimonies of the two IRS whistleblowers.

The Committee's investigation began in earnest on January 11, 2023, with a renewed push to obtain information related to the Bidens' international financial transactions from the Treasury Secretary, Janet Yellen. Comer alluded specifically to having Suspicious Activity Reports (SARs) handed over to the Committee.[307]

---

305 Sam Cabral, "House Republicans say 'top priority' is to probe Biden family," *BBC News,* November 17, 2022. https://www.bbc.com/news/world-us-canada-63665351

306 Ryan King, "James Comer suggests GOP may have evidence Joe Biden knew of Hunter's business dealings," *Washington Examiner,* February 12, 2023. https://www.washingtonexaminer.com/news/house/james-comer-suggests-gop-evidence-biden-knew-hunters-dealings

"'The difference between Jared Kushner and Hunter Biden is that Kushner …. was interviewed by investigators. So he's already been investigated,' he added. 'Thus far, Hunter Biden's attorneys, the president's attorneys, the president's White House, they're doing everything they can to block our investigation.'"

307 "Comer Requests All Burisma-Related Suspicious Activity Reports," *Total News,* June 29, 2023. https://totalnews.com/comer-requests-all-burisma-related-suspicious-activity-reports/

"U.S. banks flagged more than 150 SARs from Hunter and James Biden, including 'subtantial' funds that were subject to further review by the Treasury Department. SAR can include evidence of potential criminal activity such as money

That same day, the Republican also issued letters to Vijaya Gadde, James Baker, and Yoel Roth, three former employees of tech giant Twitter, in order to have them testify under oath before Congress about the censorship of anything related to the *New York Post's* story retracing the Biden family's alleged influence peddling.[308]

> For the past two years, the Biden Administration and Big Tech worked overtime to hide information about the Biden family's suspicious business schemes and Joe Biden's involvement. Now that Democrats no longer have one-party rule in Washington, oversight and accountability are coming. For years, the Biden family peddled influence and access around the world for profit, often at the expense of our nation's interests. The American people must know the extent of Joe Biden's involvement in his family's shady business deals and if these deals threaten national security and his decision-making as president. This investigation is a top priority for House Republicans during the 118th Congress. The investigation will inform legislative solutions to protect Americans' First Amendment right to freedom of speech and press and prevent public officials and their family members from using public office to enrich themselves.[309]

A couple of days later, on January 13, the House judiciary committee announced another investigation, this time into the discovery of

laundering and fraud, according to a 2020 Senate report."

308 Andrew Goudsward, "Ex-Twitter execs lawyer up as GOP probes drive white-collar work," *Reuters,* February 8, 2023. https://www.reuters.com/legal/government/ex-twitter-execs-lawyer-up-gop-probes-drive-white-collar-work-2023-02-08/

"Gadde, Baker and Roth were all senior executives at Twitter when the company decided to temporarily prevent users from posting a 2020 New York Post article on Hunter Biden's business dealings in Ukraine based on information purportedly found on his personal laptop. The former executives said during the hearing Wednesday that blocking the story was an error that they reversed within 24 hours. Gadde said it appeared at the time that the article may have been based on hacked materials. The company's decision has come under renewed scrutiny from congressional Republicans and Twitter CEO Elon Musk, who has criticized decisions by prior company management as infringing on free speech rights."

309 U.S. House Committee on Oversight and Accountability, "Comer Announces New Actions in Biden Family Investigation," January 11, 2023. https://oversight.house.gov/release/comer-announces-new-actions-in-biden-family-investigation/

classified documents at Joe Biden's Delaware home and former office in Washington, D.C.[310]

Underscoring a profound sense of distrust in the Department of Justice headed by Merrick Garland, Jim Jordan stated:

> We are conducting oversight of the justice department's actions with respect to former vice-president Biden's mishandling of classified documents, including the apparently unauthorized possession of classified material at a Washington DC private office and in the garage of his residence in Wilmington… On 12 January 2023, you appointed Robert Hur as special counsel to investigate these matters. The circumstances of this appointment raise fundamental oversight questions that the committee routinely examines. We expect your complete cooperation with our inquiry.[311]

In a veiled allusion to the FBI raid launched in August 2022 on the private residence of Donald J. Trump, former U.S. President and putative Biden political opponent for the next election. Jordan called out the Justice Department on its unwillingness to act as promptly in

---

310 Ken Tran, "House GOP launches investigation into Biden's classified documents," USA Today, January 13, 2023. https://eu.usatoday.com/story/news/politics/2023/01/13/house-republican-biden-classified-documents/11047999002/

"'The American people deserve transparency and accountability from our most-senior executive branch law enforcement officials,' the letter reads, requesting the Justice Department to provide the documents no later than Jan. 27."

311 Kelly Laco, "Jim Jordan launches first investigation as Judiciary chair into Biden classified docs scandal," House of Representatives Judiciary Committee, January 13, 2023. https://judiciary.house.gov/media/in-the-news/jim-jordan-launches-first-investigation-as-judiciary-chair-into-biden-classified

"'We are conducting oversight of the Justice Department's actions with respect to former Vice President Biden's mishandling of classified documents, including the apparently unauthorized possession of classified material at a Washington D.C. private office and in the garage of his Wilmington, Delaware, residence,' Jordan and Rep. Mike Johnson, R-La., wrote in a letter sent Friday to Garland."

"'It is unclear when the Department first came to learn about the existence of these documents, and whether it actively concealed this information from the public on the eve of the 2022 elections,' Jordan wrote. 'It is also unclear what interactions, if any, the Department had with President Biden or his representatives about his mishandling of classified material. The Department's actions here appear to depart from how it acted in similar circumstances.'"

the case of Biden and demanded that Garland turn over documents related to the Biden investigation by the end of January.

The judiciary committee also requested the White House to provide information about whether Hunter Biden had access to the garage at the Delaware residence.[312]

> We have doc[ument]s revealing this address appeared on Hunter's driver's license as recently as 2018, the same time he was cutting deals with foreign adversaries. Time for answers.

Referring to the alleged influence-peddling scheme, Jordan added:

> Right now there are tons of questions. A lot of those I think will be answered in the intelligence committee and the oversight committee. But we'll be looking at the justice department component.

On the issue bearing on classified documents found at Biden's private residence in Delaware, Mike Rogers, the chair of the House Armed Services Committee, announced that letters would be sent to officials at the Department of Defense.[313]

Ten days later, in an interview with Maria Bartiromo on January 22, Jim Comer demurred:

---

312 Caitlin Doornbos, Miranda Devine and Samuel Chamberlain, "Drug-addled Hunter Biden lived at Delaware home where classified docs were kept," *New York Post,* January 13, 2023. https://nypost.com/2023/01/13/hunter-biden-lived-at-delaware-home-where-classified-docs-were-kept/

313 Brooke Singman, "Biden classified records: Rogers asks DOD if improper handling of docs caused 'damage to national security,'" *Fox News,* January 12, 2023. https://www.foxnews.com/politics/biden-classified-records-rogers-dod-improper-handling-docs-caused-damage-national-security

"'I write to inquire whether you have been contacted to cooperate with U.S. Attorney Lausch's review and/or are conducting an independent investigation based on your own authorities,' Rogers wrote. He said it is 'critical to assess whether possible national security damage, particularly to DOD equities, resulted from any improper storage, handling, or disclosure of classified information stored in a closet of a non-governmental entity like the Biden Center.'"

When Joe Biden was a U.S. senator, in 1977, he worked with Republicans to thwart Jimmy Carter's nominee for the CIA director because he had inadvertently taken classified documents home. So, when Joe Biden says he has no regrets, I mean, this is very concerning here. We need to know who had access to those documents, because this is an ongoing investigation for influence peddling. And the evidence continues to build that this family has not only profited off the Biden family name, but also that our national security could be at risk… This would be a lot easier if the White House would work with us. But not only are they stonewalling our investigation. They're constantly -- if you watched that press conference with Ian Sams, who is their guy they brought into to fight back against the investigators, which is preposterous, because this is an Oversight Committee. We're supposed to provide oversight to the federal government and the executive branch. It's nothing but slurs.[314]

Concerned about the risks of its appearing to obstruct the investigation in the wake of Comer's remarks, the Biden legal team relented and invited a team of federal investigators to conduct a thorough search of the president's Delaware residence.

Unaware that the eventual discovery of classified items would subsequently unleash a barrage of subpoenas, the Democrats were left reeling as Illinois senator Dick Durbin remarked that Biden should be "embarrassed by the situation" while Senator Tim Kaine, a Democrat of Virginia, also pondered: "How many documents are we talking about? Dozens? A handful or hundreds? How serious are they? Why were they taken? Did anyone have access to them? And then, is the president being cooperative?"[315]

---

314 "Maria Bartiromo to House Oversight Chairman James Comer: Did President Biden Commit Treason With Classified Docs?", video [8:36], *RealClear Politics,* January 22, 2023. https://www.realclearpolitics.com/video/2023/01/22/maria_bartiromo_to_house_oversight_chairman_james_comer_did_president_biden_commit_treason_with_classified_docs.html

315 Bob Hoge, "Dem Senator Dick Durbin Slams Biden's Handling of Classified Documents, Calls It 'Outrageous' and 'Unacceptable,'" *RedState,* January 22, 2023. https://redstate.com/bobhoge/2023/01/22/dem-senator-dick-durbin-slams-bidens-handling-of-classified-documents-calls-it-outrageous-and-unacceptable-n692635

Biden, when queried on the subject, adopted a defiant tone and provided aloof statements to the effect that "… you're going to find there's nothing there. There's no 'there' there," which resulted in further angering certain members of his own party, including Senator Joe Manchin, a West Virginia Democrat, who lamented: "I think he should have a lot of regrets."[316]

Veteran Washington operator Lanny Davis, having once served as Bill Clinton's former Special Counsel, noted that there often existed an "inherent disconnect" between the legal team and the staff tasked with communicating on behalf of the White House as to the nature of the content suitable to enter the public domain."[317]

To be sure, the alleged "mishandling" of classified documents has plagued senior politicians on both sides of the aisle as aides to former Vice-President Mike Pence also discovered classified-marked documents at his Indiana home: a revelation that James Comer rushed to minimize while lauding Pence's "transparency which stands in stark contrast to Biden White House staff who continue to withhold information from Congress and the American people."[318]

"Well, I'm concerned. There's a standard that we follow when it comes to members of Congress and classified information. The door to my office is closed. The person who presents the document to me takes it out of a locked briefcase, hands it to me and watches as I read it, when I finish reading it, and he takes it back and puts it in the briefcase and leaves the scene. I mean, that's how carefully we review these documents. To think that any of them ended up in boxes in storage one place or the other is just unacceptable."

316 Summer Concepcion, "Sen. Joe Manchin criticizes Biden's handling of classified documents: 'Irresponsible,'" *NBC News,* January 22, 2023. https://www.nbcnews.com/politics/joe-biden/sen-joe-manchin-criticizes-bidens-handling-classified-documents-irresp-rcna66899

"'It's just hard to believe that in the United States of America, we have a former president and a current president that are basically in the same situation. How does this happen?' he said, adding that he recalls being asked whether he was 'clean' of secure documents upon leaving a sensitive compartmented information facility."

317 Lauren Gambino, "Biden claims 'no regrets' but classified papers case could come back to bite him," *The Guardian,* January 26, 2023. https://www.theguardian.com/us-news/2023/jan/26/joe-biden-classified-documents-democrat-response-2024

"Davis, whose 1999 White House memoir, *Truth to Tell,* was aptly subtitled: *Tell it Early, Tell it All, Tell it Yourself,* said he understood the Biden team's initial instinct not to disclose the revelations publicly out of deference to the justice department. But he wondered, 'with the wisdom of hindsight' and the caveat that he is not privy to internal deliberations, why Biden's team hadn't been more forthcoming, especially with the findings it knew would be made public."

318 Jamie Gangel, Jeremy Herb and Evan Perez, "First on CNN: Classified

The political theatre continued when on January 30 the Committee undertook to conduct its first public hearing on the Biden family business, just one day following the incumbent's State of the Union Address.

The White House promptly accused Comer of "setting the stage for divorced-from-reality political stunts" while "handing the keys of oversight to the most extreme MAGA members of the Republican caucus."[319]

By early March, the Committee remained faced with institutional inertia, which in turn led to the holding of an additional hearing to spotlight the Department of the Treasury's own refusal to disclose material bearing on the banking transactions of members of the Biden family. In an attempt to denounce the Treasury Department's withholding of documents, Comer disclosed their content, emphasizing his own willingness to take into account matters considered sensitive to Department officials.

Addressed to Isabella More, deputy assistant secretary for oversight at the treasury Department, the letter read:

> Given the amount of time that has passed since our initial request and Treasury's inability to provide a projected timeframe when the SARs will be produced, the Committee believes Treasury may be delaying its production to hinder our investigation and operating in bad faith.[320]

---

documents found at Pence's Indiana home," *CNN Politics,* January 24, 2023. https://edition.cnn.com/2023/01/24/politics/pence-classified-documents-fbi/index.html

"The discovery of classified documents in Pence's residence marks the third time in recent history in which a president or vice president has inappropriately possessed classified material after leaving office. Both Biden and Trump are now being investigated by separate special counsels for their handling of classified materials."

319 Brett Samuels, "White House rips appointment of 'extreme MAGA members' to House Oversight panel," *Yahoo! News,* January 18, 2023. https://news.yahoo.com/white-house-rips-appointment-extreme-162531881.html

"'House Republican leaders should explain why they are allowing these individuals to serve on this Committee and reveal transparently once and for all what secret deals they made to the extreme MAGA members in order to elect a Speaker,' Sams said in a statement, urging Republicans to focus on issues such as inflation instead."

320 Letter from James Comer, Chairman, House Committee on Oversight and Accountability, to Isabella More, Deputy Assistant Secretary for Oversight, Department of the Treasury, February 24, 2023. https://oversight.house.gov/wp-

In a letter responding to Comer, the Treasury Department assistant secretary for legislative affairs, Jonathan C. Davidson, fired back, stressing that the department "already completed significant work to identify and review potentially responsive records."[321] Davidson figured on the list of individuals slated to appear before the Committee and he awkwardly attempted to convey the message that a public hearing "would likely not be the most effective venue for an update."[322]

Comer immediately smelled blood:

> Biden's Treasury Department continues to make excuses for its failure to provide the suspicious activity reports that are critical to our investigation of the Biden family's business schemes… At next week's hearing, a Treasury Department official can explain to Congress and the American people why the department is hiding critical information.[323]

The Department caved in, albeit not without doing everything to insulate Biden from public scrutiny.

On March 13, Comer held a press conference during which he announced:

> After two months of dragging their feet, the Treasury Department is finally providing us with access to the suspicious activity reports for the Biden family and their associates' business transactions. It should never have taken us threatening to hold a hearing and conduct a transcribed interview with an official under the penalty of perjury for Treasury to finally accommodate part of our request. For over 20 years, Congress had access to these reports but the

content/uploads/2023/02/2023-02-24-Letter-Treasury.pdf

321 Annie Grayer, "House Oversight panel will hold hearing on probe into Biden family financial dealings," CNN Politics, March 4, 2023. https://edition.cnn.com/2023/03/04/politics/house-oversight-hearing-probe-hunter-biden/index.html

"'The Department has consistently engaged with the Committee in good faith on this matter,' Davidson wrote. 'These are the same processes, and similar timelines, that the Department followed when it received requests from committee chairs in the prior Congress.'"

322 Ibid.

323 Ibid.

Biden Administration changed the rules out of the blue to restrict our ability to conduct oversight...According to bank documents we've already obtained, we know one company owned by a Biden associate received a $3 million dollar wire from a Chinese energy company two months after Joe Biden left the vice presidency. Soon after, hundreds of thousands of dollars in payouts went to members of the Biden family. We are going to continue to use bank documents and suspicious activity reports to follow the money trail to determine the extent of the Biden family's business schemes, if Joe Biden is compromised by these deals, and if there is a national security threat. If Treasury tries to stonewall our investigation again, we will continue to use tools at our disposal to compel compliance.[324]

Down the Biden Rabbit Hole

The stonewalling of Janet Yellen retrospectively made sense as the existence of a $3 million wire-transfer led to questions as to *how many* members of the Biden family profited from the scheme.

Comer proceeded to expose the following facts:

"The very next day after that wire was received, the Walker account started transferring money into three different Biden family members' accounts, including a new Biden family member that's never before been identified as someone being involved in the influence-peddling scheme," adding that the money transfer was "just the first wire that we've actually been able to obtain bank records on. There are many, many more...There are more family members involved in this than just the president's son. And what they've said in the media, 'Oh, this was for business.' We can't identify any business. It appears it went into their personal account."[325]

---

324 U.S. House Committee on Oversight and Accountability, "Comer: Treasury Department Caves, Provides Access to Biden Family & Their Associates' SARs" [press release], March 14, 2023. https://oversight.house.gov/release/comer-treasury-department-caves-provides-access-to-biden-family-their-associates-sars/

325 Steven Nelson, "Comer subpoenaed 14 years of bank records in Hunter

At this point, no less than four additional Biden family members entered the fray. First, Joe Biden's brother, James, attracted attention for his sudden naming as vice-president of HillStone International, a mere three weeks after HillStone International president Kevin Justice's own visit to the White House in November 2010, a visit that featured a meeting with an adviser to then-Vice President Joe Biden.

Biden's brother explained that Hill asked him to be their representative in meetings with Saudi officials in 2012, conceding that "... of course, the name didn't hurt."[326]

Then Biden's son-in-law, Dr. Howard Krein (married to first daughter Ashley Biden), coincidently launched his StartUp Health investment consultancy at the same time his father-in-law was vice president.[327] Krein's company executives were seen attending a large health care tech conference organized by the Department of Health and Human Services, before frequently visiting the White House while Joe Biden was vice president.[328]

Then, it was discovered that Frank Biden, the president's youngest brother, ran a solar energy company, Sun Fund Americas.[329] Against

---

Biden probe: Raskin," *New York Post,* March 13, 2023. https://nypost.com/2023/03/13/comer-subpoenaed-14-years-of-bank-records-in-hunter-biden-probe-raskin/

326 Caroline Downey, "Biden's Brother Was Paid to Settle Business Dispute with Saudis during VP Tenure," *Yahoo! News,* February 14, 2023. https://news.yahoo.com/biden-brother-paid-settle-business-034758132.html

"'I asked specifically if he had attended a meeting with the Saudi Ministry of Trade in mid-February 2012 to receive the final payment for the work Hill had performed,' Sullivan said of his conversation with Jim Biden. 'He answered that, to the best of his memory, he had been at such a meeting, and that the reason he had attended was "because of his position and relationship" with his brother.'"

327 Mark Moore, "Biden's son-in-law Howard Krein's health care work reportedly draws ethical scrutiny," *New York Post,* February 9, 2021. https://nypost.com/2021/02/09/bidens-son-in-law-krein-reportedly-raises-ethical-questions/

"'Howard Krein is playing with fire,' Meredith McGehee, executive director of Issue One, a nonpartisan ethics watchdog group, told ABC News. 'If he gets too close to that flame—if he is trying to either cash in on his relationship with the president, or he is trying to influence policy—the flame is going to get him. And it is not worth it to him or to Biden.'"

328 Ibid.

"'I happened to be talking to my father-in-law that day and I mentioned Steve and Unity were down there [in DC],' Krein said. '[Biden] knew about StartUp Health and was a big fan of it. He asked for Steve's number and said, "I have to get them up here to talk with Barack." The Secret Service came and got Steve and Unity and brought them to the Oval Office.'"

329 Victor Nava, "Speculation mounts over ID of 'new' Biden family

all odds, Sun Fund Americas entered into an agreement to develop alternative sources of energy with the Ministry of Public Education of Costa Rica, a country that Joe Biden regularly visited on behalf of the Obama administration while handling the Administration's portfolio of "Overseas Private Investment Corporation Loans" provisioned for the clean energy agenda.[330]

Last but not least, Valerie Biden Owens, Joe Biden's younger sister was identified as working as a senior partner of the firm Joe Slade White & Company. a consulting firm specialized in "political messaging." Valerie's work on her brother's campaigns in 1988 and 2008 had led to Slade, White & Company receiving $2.5 million in the context of their consultancy during Joe Biden's 2008 presidential bid.[331]

To date, the Committee's investigation had not alluded to Howard Krein, Valerie Biden or Sara Biden (James' wife). Then on March 16, the Committee released financial records pointing to Biden family members receiving over $1 million in 2017 from an account owned by Rob Walker, one of Hunter's associates known to have contracted with a Chinese energy company.[332]

Comer proceeded to expose how the Committee had requested Bank of America to produce "all financial records" for three Biden business associates starting on Jan. 20, 2009, which marked the start of Joe Biden's tenure as vice president, before detailing how the investigation zeroed in on John R. Walker.

The money trail showed that a Shanghai-based company called State Energy HK Limited had funneled millions of dollars to the account of Robinson Walker LLC and that from 2015 to 2017, Hunter Biden, the president's brother James, and Mr. Biden's daughter-in-law Hallie through their companies, altogether received $1.3 million from

member who got cut of $3M wire," *New York Post,* March 14, 2023. https://nypost.com/2023/03/14/speculation-mounts-on-who-the-new-biden-family-member-is-that-got-a-cut-of-3-million-wire-transfer-in-2017/

330 Ibid.

331 Ibid.

"Finally, Valerie Biden Owens, Joe's younger sister who ran all of his Senate campaigns and his presidential campaigns in 1988 and 2008, was also a senior partner in the political messaging firm Joe Slade White & Company, according to Schweizer, and the firm received large fees from those campaigns, including $2.5 million alone from Joe Biden's 2008 presidential bid."   ·

332 Steven Nelson, "Comer subpoenaed 14 years of bank records: Raskin."

Mr. Walker. The records specifically revealed that over $1 million of that money was paid in 2017, in the wake of Mr. Walker's receipt of $3 million from State Energy HK Limited.[333]

Comer conceded that on its face the payment failed to show unlawful behavior but he remained puzzled as to the "consideration" extended in exchange for these payments.

> The Oversight Committee is concerned about the national security implications resulting from President Biden's family receiving millions of dollars from foreign nationals...We will continue to follow the money trail and facts to determine if President Biden is compromised by his family's business schemes and if there is a national security threat.[334]

Democrats through their own representatives on the Committee openly railed against their Republican colleague.

> Chairman Comer's memo proved once again that, after four years of investigations by Senate and House Republicans into Hunter Biden, they have found no connection to the president of the United States or indeed any government official at all.[335]

While as many as 11 additional business transactions with China came to be identified on the heels of the $3 million wire transfer,

---

333 Victor Nava, "Speculation mounts."

334 U.S. House Committee on Oversight and Accountability, "Comer Reveals Biden Family Members Receiving Payments from Chinese Energy Company" [press release], March 16, 2023. https://oversight.house.gov/release/comer-reveals-biden-family-members-receiving-payments-from-chinese-energy-company/

335 Nick Mordowanec, "Republicans Tout 'New Evidence' Against Joe Biden's Children," Newsweek, March 16, 2023. https://www.newsweek.com/republicans-tout-new-evidence-against-joe-bidens-children-1788354

"Former federal Prosecutor Neama Rahmani told Newsweek there's a reason the Treasury Department flagged some the Bidens' transactions as suspicious. 'It's a lot of money,' he said. 'You're talking about more than a million dollars to Hunter Biden Hallie and others. This was after one of their associates receives $3 million from a Chinese company. When I was a federal prosecutor, I always followed the money.'"

Comer kept lamenting the Committee's incapacity to find a smoking gun.

> We don't know what the Bidens did in return for this money. The lawyer said that it was capital for a business… We haven't been able to find a business… Right now, it looks like the Biden family just pocketed this money.[336]

Hunter Biden's lawyers defended their client's prerogatives to collect monies in the context of legitimate business dealings:

> Hunter Biden, a private citizen with every right to pursue his own business endeavors, joined several business partners in seeking a joint venture with a legitimate energy company in China… Hunter received his portion of good faith seed funds which he shared with his uncle, James Biden, and Hallie Biden … and nobody else.[337]

Comer meanwhile attempted to focus on the fact that Hunter and his father always seemed to be together when the then-Vice President traveled on official business.

> We know that when the president was vice president in the Obama administration, he made several trips to China. He brought his son and some of these associates with him… They met in different places with some of these people that the president claimed he never met with. So we know the president hasn't been truthful about his involvement when he was vice president.[338]

---

336 Allie Griffin, "Rep. James Comer: Bidens, China may have had 11 additional deals," New York Post, March 19, 2023. https://nypost.com/2023/03/19/rep-james-comer-bidens-china-may-have-had-11-additional-deals/

"'In the beginning, the White House denied having any knowledge or the fact that their family was involved in any sort of way, shape or form with the CCP,' Comer said. 'But now we have bank records that reveal otherwise.'"

337 Ibid.

338 Amie Parnes and Mychael Schnell, "Hunter Biden probes put GOP under some pressure," The Hill, March 27, 2023. https://thehill.com/homenews/house/3917317-hunter-biden-probes-put-gop-under-some-pressure/

"'They're asking the right questions. The question is, are they going to get any

The investigation still seemed to go nowhere when a month later Comer briefed the media after examining additional documents at the headquarters of the Treasury Department.

> "Thousands of pages of financial records related to the Biden family, their companies, and associates' business schemes were made available to members of the House Committee on Oversight and Accountability, which confirm the importance of this investigation," Comer said in a statement.... "The Biden family enterprise is centered on Joe Biden's political career and connections, and it has generated an exorbitant amount of money for the Biden family. We've identified six additional members of Joe Biden's family who may have benefited from the Biden family's businesses that we are investigating, bringing the total number of those involved or benefiting to nine," he said.[339]

Concerning the thousands of pages of financial records, the Oversight Committee announced:

> "The Oversight Committee will continue to pursue additional bank records to follow the Bidens' tangled web of financial transactions to determine if the Biden family has been targeted by foreign actors and if there is a national security threat," Comer said. "We will soon provide the public with more information about what we've uncovered to date. The American people need transparency and accountability, and the Oversight Committee will deliver much needed answers."[340]

---

answers,' said Republican strategist John Feehery, a former House GOP aide. 'If you can make a direct link to what his business dealings were, that becomes a much more interesting story.'"

339 Victor Nava, "Six more Bidens may have gained from family business schemes: Comer," *New York Post,* April 17, 2023. https://nypost.com/2023/04/17/six-more-bidens-may-have-gained-from-family-business-schemes-comer/

340 Ibid.

Ben Whedon, "House GOP investigating 9 Biden family members for connections to business dealings," *Just The News,* April 17, 2023. https://justthenews.com/politics-policy/house-gop-investigating-9-biden-family-members-connections-family-business

With frustration growing, Marjorie Taylor-Greene, a vocal opponent of the Bidens, lashed out in alleging that the Bidens were involved in human trafficking.

Taylor-Greene took to Twitter after reviewing over 2,000 pages of financial records:

> I just saw evidence of human trafficking. This involves prostitutes, not only from here in the United States but foreign countries like Russia and Ukraine.[341]

As the investigation entered its fifth month, the Republicans were clearly getting bogged down, that is, until there arose the revelation that a whistleblower inside the FBI purported to establish that the current President of the United States was involved in a "criminal scheme" while serving as VP in the Obama administration.

The Committee announced that a subpoena had been delivered to the FBI, prompting the nation's top enforcement agency to hand over a FD-1023 report bearing on a bribery scheme involving a foreign national in "a country other than China."

> Based on these disclosures, it has come to our attention that the Department of Justice (DOJ) and the Federal Bureau of Investigation (FBI) possess an unclassified FD-1023 form that describes an alleged criminal scheme involving then-Vice President Biden and a foreign national relating to the exchange of money for policy decisions.[342]

---

341 David McAfee, "Marjorie Taylor Greene claims she saw 2,000 pages of evidence on 'Biden crime family,'" *Raw Story,* April 18, 2023. https://www.rawstory.com/marjorie-taylor-greene-2659875409/

"Greene added that the American people deserve to know about the Biden family's 'crimes,' and noted that the GOP House Committee on Oversight and Accountability has a 'much bigger investigation to do than thought.'"

342 Letter from Rep. James Comer and Senator Charles Grassley to U.S. Attorney General Merrick Garland and FBI Director Christopher Wray, May 3, 2023. https://www.documentcloud.org/documents/23796566-comer-grassley-fbi-documents

"The DOJ and the FBI appear to have valuable, verifiable information that you have failed to disclose to the American people. Therefore, Congress will proceed to conduct an independent and objective review of this matter, free from those agencies' influence."

The letter sent to the FBI alongside the subpoena detailed how "it has been alleged that the document includes a precise description of how the alleged criminal scheme was employed as well as its purpose. Based on the alleged specificity within the document, it would appear that the DOJ and the FBI have enough information to determine the truth and accuracy of the information contained within it. However, it remains unclear what steps, if any, were taken to investigate the matter."[343]

The White House replied that:

> For going on five years now, Republicans in Congress have been lobbing unfounded, unproven, politically-motivated attacks against the President and his family without offering evidence for their claims or evidence of decisions influenced by anything other than U.S. interests... That's because they prefer floating anonymous innuendo, amplified by the megaphone of their allies in rightwing media, to get attention and try to distract and deflect from their own unpopular ideas and lack of solutions to the issues the American people actually care about... When it comes to President Biden's personal finances, anybody can take a look: he has offered an unprecedented level of transparency, releasing a total of 25 years of tax returns to the American public.[344]

Chuck Grassley emphasized that "this comes from credible and unclassified whistleblower disclosures, this possible criminal activity when Biden was vice president, and we want this information. The Justice Department, the FBI needs to come clean to the American people about what they did with the document, because we know the document exists."[345]

---

343 Ibid.

344 Kelly Laco, "Biden's 'criminal BRIBERY scheme' with a foreign national: Whistleblower claims FBI and DOJ have file detailing Joe's 'exchange of money for policy decisions' when he was VP," *Daily Mail,* May 3, 2023, updated May 4, 2023. https://www.dailymail.co.uk/news/article-12043299/Bidens-criminal-BRIBERY-scheme-foreigner-GOP-claims-VP-offered-cash-access.html

345 Steven Nelson, "House subpoenas FBI file on Biden role in 'criminal scheme' as new whistleblower emerges," *New York Post,* May 3, 2023, updated May 4, 2023. https://nypost.com/2023/05/03/fbi-file-links-joe-biden-to-criminal-scheme-

The country "that is not China" was soon revealed to be Ukraine where "Just days after Hunter joined the board, White House national security adviser Jake Sullivan, at the time a vice presidential aide, told reporters on Air Force Two en route to Kyiv that Joe Biden would push for U.S. support to Ukraine's natural gas industry, which later that year was awarded $50 million by Congress."[346]

As it turns out, federal visitor logs revealed that Joe Biden had met Devon Archer in 2014 soon after both Hunter Biden and Archer joined the Burisma board.[347] Another entry pertained to then-VP Biden attending an April 16, 2015, dinner at DC's Cafe Milano along with Burisma executive Vadym Pozharskyi, and some of Hunter's associates from Russia and Kazakhstan.[348]

The confrontation between the Committee and the FBI soon escalated to unprecedented levels as the Committee Chairman threatened Wray with contempt before Wray finally relented, albeit not without redacting the document:

> The FBI has continually demonstrated its commitment to accommodate the committee's request, including by producing the document in a reading room at the U.S. Capitol... This commonsense safeguard is often employed in response to congressional requests and in court proceedings to protect important concerns, such as the physical safety of sources

---

per-whistleblower-comer-subpoenas/

346 Steven Nelson, "Post confronts Jake Sullivan over ex-WH stenographer 'corrupt' claim," *New York Post,* April 24, 2023, updated April 25, 2023. https://nypost.com/2023/04/24/post-confronts-jake-sullivan-over-ex-wh-stenographer-corrupt-claim/

"'On Ukraine, I wanted to give you the opportunity to respond to a former White House stenographer who this month outed you as [the] anonymous senior administration official who briefed reporters on Air Force Two en route to Ukraine in 2014,' a Post reporter began asking Sullivan."

347 Steven Nelson, "Biden releases first White House visitor logs, but some will remain secret," New York Post, May 7, 2021. https://nypost.com/2021/05/07/biden-releases-first-white-house-visitor-logs-but-some-will-remain-secret/

348 "Hunter Biden's 'close friend' charged with treason in Kazakhstan," *Washington Examiner,* January 10, 2022. https://www.washingtonexaminer.com/news/white-house/hunter-bidens-close-friend-charged-with-treason-in-kazakhstan

"Emails among Hunter Biden, his Rosemont Seneca business partner and fellow Burisma board member Devon Archer, and Ukrainian Burisma official Vadim Pozharskyi show their desire to work out a deal with Massimov."

and the integrity of investigations. The escalation to a contempt vote under these circumstances is unwarranted.[349]

It was thus decided that the viewing of the FD-1023 would take
place in a secure room on Capitol Hill.

It would eventually be made public that the FD-1023 was the
product of a comprehensive file provided to the Justice Department
in 2020 by former New-York Mayor and Trump attorney, Rudy
Guliani.[350] Guliani had personally visited Ukraine during the last year
of Trump's term in search for evidence bearing on the relation between
Biden and Burisma.

Former Trump Attorney General William Barr had then entrusted
the opening of an investigation to a U.S. attorney in Pittsburgh, as
Barr was concerned that the content of the file provided by Guliani
would somewhat interfere with the tax investigation of Hunter Biden
taking place in Delaware.[351] Insofar as the content of the FD-1023
was concerned, it alleged that the foreign national allegedly paid $5
million in exchange for a specific policy to be adopted.[352]

---

349 Reese Gorman, "Oversight Chairman Comer to hold FBI director in
contempt of Congress over Biden document," *Washington Examiner,* June 5, 2023.
https://www.washingtonexaminer.com/news/house/oversight-chair-comer-hold-fbi-
director-contempt-of-congress-biden-document

350 Hayes Brown, "All roads lead to Giuliani in the GOP's quest for Biden dirt"
[opinion], MSNBC, June 2, 2023. https://www.msnbc.com/opinion/msnbc-opinion/
james-comer-house-republicans-fbi-biden-investigation-giuliani-rcna87269

"'Former Pittsburgh U.S. Attorney Scott Brady oversaw the FBI investigation of
the Giuliani claims. The FD-1023 document being demanded by Comer is among the
products of that investigation,' CNN reported."

351 Ibid.

"The material in question was dubious enough that Barr 'directed that they be
reviewed by a U.S. attorney in Pittsburgh,' in part because Barr was concerned that
Giuliani's document tranche could taint the ongoing Hunter Biden investigation
overseen by the Delaware U.S. attorney."

352 Aaron Johnson, "Joe Biden Allegedly Paid $5 Million by Burisma
Executive in 'Pay-for-Play' Bribery Scheme, FBI Document Reveals," Radar Online,
June 8, 2023. https://radaronline.com/p/joe-biden-paid-burisma-executive-bribery-
fbi-document/

"The Burisma executive allegedly asked the confidential source about gaining
the rights to U.S. oil and how to get involved with a U.S. oil company. The executive
also reportedly discussed Hunter's role on the board, revealing the now first son was
'dumb' when asked by the source why they needed his or her advice if they had
connections to Biden's son."

Addressing the Senate on June 13th, Committee Co-Chairman Chuck Grassley conveyed that he had had the opportunity to view the document and that it featured the claim that the Burisma executive had kept no less than 15 recordings of his conversations with Hunter Biden and an additional two with Vice President Joe Biden as "a sort of insurance policy for the foreign national in case he got into a tight spot."[353]

Republican Senator Ron Johnson urged caution, musing that the claim bearing on the existence of the tapes "should be taken with a grain of salt. This could be coming from a very corrupt oligarch. He could be making stuff up. We really don't know whether the tapes even exist. We just don't know that whether this was a bluff on (the part) of whoever the executive was. We think it was Mykola Zlocheskiy, the CEO, the corrupt oligarch. But we really don't know."[354]

It would eventually be confirmed that the FBI informant was indeed Zlocheskiy and it begs the question as to whether the Committee will attempt to get him to testify under oath and/or provide the recordings.[355]

At writing, no decision has been made in favor of doing so.

---

353 Brooke Singman, "Grassley: Burisma executive who allegedly paid Biden has audio recordings of conversations with Joe, Hunter," *Fox News,* June 12, 2023. https://www.foxnews.com/politics/grassley-burisma-executive-who-allegedly-paid-biden-has-audio-recordings-of-conversations-with-joe-hunter

"A source familiar said according to the document, the $5 million payments appeared to reference a kind of 'retainer' Burisma intended to pay the Bidens to deal with a number of issues, including the investigation led by Shokin. Another source referred to the arrangement as a 'pay-to-play' scheme."

354 "Sen. Ron Johnson: Take Allegation About Biden/Burisma Tapes 'With A Grain Of Salt,'" video [1:29], *RealClear Politics,* June 15, 2023. https://www.realclearpolitics.com/video/2023/06/15/sen_ron_johnson_we_dont_know_if_biden_tapes_exist_take_it_with_a_grain_of_salt.html

355 Margot Cleveland, "FD-1023 Exposes Biden Bribery Details, Teases More Evidence," *The Federalist,* July 20, 2023. https://thefederalist.com/2023/07/20/explosive-fd-1023-exposes-more-biden-bribery-dirt-and-teases-damning-evidence-to-come/

"According to the FD-1023 report, in 2019, the CHS had offered to assist Zlochevsky if he wanted to speak to the U.S. government about the Bidens and what Zlochevsky claimed was their coercion of Burisma to pay the bribes. Did anyone ever ask the CHS to contact Zlochevsky? If not, why not?"

Asked to comment on the alleged existence of incriminating recordings, White House Press Secretary Karine Jean-Pierre smugly echoed Biden's claim that this was all *"malarkey."*[356]

The Committee was increasingly looking as if it was on a fishing expedition. As of early July, the Committee had issued requests to officials from the FBI and the Justice Department to testify as to the reasons why the IRS investigation and anything related to Biden family business abroad seemed to encounter obstruction at every corner.

At this stage, the Committee hoped to build a case designed to establish that Biden's Attorney General Merrick Garland should be impeached for refusing to investigate Hunter Biden. To do so, the Committee announced that it would first hold hearings with two former IRS employees on the issue of obstruction from DOJ.[357] These two IRS whistleblowers testified that the FBI had "slow-walked" the investigation into Hunter Biden's failure to pay taxes. IRS Criminal investigator, Joseph Ziegler, described how "It appeared to me, based on what I experienced, that the U.S. attorney in Delaware in our investigation was constantly hamstrung, limited and marginalized by (Justice Department) officials as well as other U.S. attorneys."[358]

Get Trump!

The entire Justice Department as well as the preeminent federal law enforcement agency have for years been sitting on evidence and/or have refused to appoint an independent Special Counsel to investigate these allegations against the sitting President and his son.

---

356 "Karine Jean-Pierre quotes Biden in response to question about Burisma recordings: 'It's malarky,'" press conference video [47:45], Fox News, livestreamed on June 13, 2023. https://www.youtube.com/live/BChemKm5Rx0

357 U.S. House Committee on Oversight and Accountability, "Hearing with IRS Whistleblowers About the Biden Criminal Investigation" [hearing], July 19, 2023. https://oversight.house.gov/hearing/hearing-with-irs-whistleblowers-about-the-biden-criminal-investigation/

358 Phillip M. Bailey, USA Today, "IRS whistleblowers lash out at federal officials in fiery Hunter Biden hearing: 5 takeaways," *Yahoo! News,* July 19, 2023. https://news.yahoo.com/irs-whistleblowers-lash-federal-officials-211028325.html

"Ziegler alleged David Weiss, the U.S. Attorney for Delaware, who was appointed by former President Donald Trump, previously agreed certain felony charges against Hunter Biden were warranted."

At the same time, these same agencies have now become weapons in the hand of the incumbent administration to prevent Donald J. Trump, the former president of the United States and leading opposition candidate, from running for reelection.

The country's descent into extreme political divisiveness following the 2016 election allowed for the rot of partisanship to infect every stratum of the federal and state bureaucracy.

Seeking to influence judicial practice, the Open Society Foundation provided substantial funding to candidates that have campaigned on the defunding of law enforcement.[359]

Some of these elected officials are now targeting the front-running Republican candidate: Donald J. Trump.[360] Soros has long advocated for a reshaping of American society under the aegis of a liberal agenda which aims to deconstruct society's structures. In so doing, Soros has participated in the financing of countless NGOs both in America and abroad. His Open Society Foundations are rumored to be behind countless "color revolutions."

In the United States, Soros openly claimed being the driving force behind the election of no less than seventy-five district attorneys who proceeded with a drastic overhaul of the laws on the book, often at the victims' expense. Manhattan District Attorney Alvin Bragg's name is often mentioned alongside that of George Soros.

---

359 Isabel Vincent, "How George Soros funded progressive DAs behind U.S. crime surge," *New York Post,* December 16, 2021. https://nypost.com/2021/12/16/how-george-soros-funded-progressive-das-behind-us-crime-surge/

"These legal arsonists have abandoned their duty to public safety by pursuing leniency even for the most heinous crimes, and they often flat-out refuse to charge criminals for shoplifting, vagrancy and entire categories of misdemeanors."

360 Shawn Langlois, "George Soros bashes President Trump, explains why he no longer participates in this market bubble," *MarketWatch,* August 12, 2020. https://www.marketwatch.com/story/george-soros-bashes-president-trump-explains-why-he-no-longer-participates-in-this-market-bubble-2020-08-12

"'Even in the United States, a confident trickster like Trump can be elected president and undermine democracy from within,' he said. 'But in the U.S. you have a great tradition of checks and balances and established rules. And above all you have the Constitution. So I am confident that Trump will turn out to be a transitory phenomenon, hopefully ending in November.' Until then, however, Soros warned that Trump 'remains very dangerous,' because 'he's fighting for his life and he will do anything to stay in power.' He added that Trump will be held accountable for his violations of the Constitution if he loses the presidency."

The height of this deconstruction agenda occurred during the Summer of 2020 in the wake of the George Floyd murder. Under the coordination of the Black Lives Matter movement, Seattle, Minneapolis, and Portland descended into mayhem and destruction and the mob targeted police with support from Democrats. With the protesters setting up so-called "autonomous zones," local officials stubbornly refused Trump's offer to deploy the National guard to quell violence. Looting and assaults became commonplace and impunity spread throughout the areas affected by the rioting, leaving regular bystanders to fend for themselves.

Bragg instructed his staff to remove prison terms for heinous crimes: a controversial move which led to an uproar when Bragg charged a shopkeeper with second-degree murder even though the defendant was found to have acted in self-defense. Obviously, New Yorkers weren't about to go like lambs to the slaughter despite the fact that Bragg's office has repeatedly refrained from filing charges in cases of reckless driving and theft, thus encouraging the crime rate to soar and destroy Rudy Guliani's legacy.

Chicago has also seen its crime rate soar to levels unseen since 1994 while Kim Foxx, a DA voted in with Soros funds, opted instead to engage in social engineering policies resembling those initiated by Bragg in New-York. Philadelphia has also followed the trend of giving impunity to felons with the election of Larry Krasner, another Soros protégé, with the outcome leading to, you guessed it, an upsurge in narcotic use and violent crimes.

To be sure, Soros never hid his disdain for Trump: a *"pitiful figure... whose narcissism has turned into a disease."*

Against this backdrop, Trump might still have been tempted to believe that the relentless pressure and smear campaigns unleashed during his administration would reach some closure upon his departure from the Oval Office.

Such was not to be the case.

The January 6 "Insurrection"

Unwilling to concede that the 2020 election, Trump rallied his supporters near the capitol building before enjoining them to "peacefully march on Congress" in order to prompt then Vice-President Mike Pence to refuse certification of the delegate count.[361]

> Republicans are constantly fighting like a boxer with his hands tied behind his back. It's like a boxer. And we want to be so nice. We want to be so respectful of everybody, including bad people. And we're going to have to fight much harder. And Mike Pence is going to have to come through for us. And if he doesn't, that will be a sad day for our country because you're sworn to uphold our Constitution.[362]

What ensued remains to this day a mystery, as some of Trump's supporters were somehow mysteriously granted access inside the building by Capitol police while Congress was in session.[363]

The Democrats rushed to portray the event as an attempted "insurrection" bent on overthrowing the Republic.[364] The aftermath saw scores of arrests take place across the country with suspects often being denied their elementary due process rights.[365]

---

361 "Transcript of speech by President Donald Trump on Jan. 6," *Arkansas Democrat Gazette*, January 14, 2021. https://www.arkansasonline.com/news/2021/jan/14/washington-post-transcript-of-speech-by-president/

"I know that everyone here will soon be marching over to the Capitol building to peacefully and patriotically make your voices heard. Today, we will see whether Republicans stand strong for the integrity of our elections. But whether or not they stand strong for our country—our country, our country has been under siege for a long time. Far longer than this four-year period."

362 Ibid.

363 Jack Gramenz, "Vision emerges of police moving barricades to allow rioters into US Capitol, taking selfies," *news.com.au*, January 8, 2021. https://www.news.com.au/technology/online/social/vision-emerges-of-police-moving-barricades-to-allow-rioters-into-us-capitol-taking-selfies/news-story/45a9be3adf9b447b53d23cf5536c5d02

364 Clayton Besaw and Matthew Frank, "Was it a coup? No, but siege on U.S. Capitol was the election violence of a fragile democracy," The Conversation, January 6, 2021, updated January 10, 2021. https://theconversation.com/was-it-a-coup-no-but-siege-on-us-capitol-was-the-election-violence-of-a-fragile-democracy-152803

365 Miranda Devine, "An egregious denial of due process for Jan. 6 protesters" [opinion], *New York Post*, March 8, 2023. https://nypost.com/2023/03/08/an-

In an instance of political theater reminiscent of the infamous "Moscow Trials," the Democratic party proceeded under the leadership of Liz Cheney to create the so-called "January 6th Commission."[366]

Eighteen months later, the "January 6th Commission" released a report, which called for the following:

- Such prohibition should extend to all those identified as having participated in the "insurrection."

- Congress should adopt legislation aimed at toughening criminal penalties against anyone opposed to the "peaceful transfer of power."

- Congress should impose harsh penalties against anyone deemed to have adopted a threatening demeanor towards election workers.

- Congress should "clarify" the role of the vice-president in stressing the purely "ceremonial" nature of his presiding over the tallying of the Electoral College Votes.

- Federal law enforcement agencies should be urged to pay particular attention to anti-government "extremist" groups.

Commenting on the conclusions of the Committee's report, former House Majority Speaker Nancy Pelosi declared that:

---

egregious-denial-of-due-process-for-jan-6-protesters/

"Contrary to what apologists have been saying since Carlson began airing the footage, all this material has not previously been made available to the J6 defendants, some of whom have been jailed without trial for two years, in violation of their constitutional right to a fair and speedy trial."

366 "Read: Liz Cheney's opening statement at Jan. 6 hearing," *Politico,* July 27, 2021. https://www.politico.com/news/2021/07/27/liz-cheney-opening-statement-jan-6-hearing-500836

"…We cannot leave the violence of January 6th – and its causes – uninvestigated. The American people deserve the full and open testimony of every person with knowledge of the planning and preparation for January 6th. We must know what happened here at the Capitol. We must also know what happened every minute of that day in the White House – every phone call, every conversation, every meeting leading up to, during, and after the attack. Honorable men and women have an obligation to step forward. If those responsible are not held accountable, and if Congress does not act responsibly, this will remain a cancer on our Constitutional Republic, undermining the peaceful transfer of power at the heart of our democratic system. We will face the threat of more violence in the months to come, and another January 6th every four years…"

As the Select Committee concludes its work, their words must be a clarion call to all Americans: to vigilantly guard our Democracy and to give our vote only to those dutiful in their defense of our Constitution.[367]

Culture Wars
Standing in the Way of Election Reform

Notwithstanding the glaring flaws related to the proper holding of a federal election, the debate over requiring voters to provide identification unsurprisingly descended into a partisan war.

The conservative view was summarized as follows:

Every individual who is eligible to vote should have the opportunity to do so. It is equally important, however, that the votes of eligible voters are not stolen or diluted by a fraudulent or bogus vote cast by an ineligible or imaginary voter. The evidence from academic studies and actual turnout in elections is also overwhelming that—contrary to the shrill claims of opponents—voter ID does not depress the turnout of voters, including minority, poor, and elderly voters. (Hans von Spakovsky, The Heritage Foundation, 2011)[368]

The Liberal approach indicated a contrary view:

Voter ID laws deprive many voters of their right to vote, reduce participation, and stand in direct opposition to our country's trend of including more Americans in the democratic process. Many Americans do not have one of the forms of identification states acceptable for voting. These voters are disproportionately low-income, racial and ethnic minorities, the elderly, and people with disabilities. Such

---

367 Select January 6th Committee Final Report and Supporting Materials Collection, *GovInfo.* https://www.govinfo.gov/collection/january-6th-committee-final-report

368 "Arguments for and against voter identification laws," *Ballotpedia.* https://ballotpedia.org/Arguments_for_and_against_voter_identification_laws

voters more frequently have difficulty obtaining ID, because they cannot afford or cannot obtain the underlying documents that are a prerequisite to obtaining government-issued photo ID card. (American Civil Liberties Union, 2017)[369]

To be sure, the nature of the arguments reflected a certain inclination on the part of both party's officials to cater to their respective bases.

On the one hand, conservatives appealed to their voters' propensity to adopt an orderly, law-abiding approach to the issue of ID requirement, for the latter was deemed to contribute to transparency in the electoral process and thus outweigh the risk of fraud hanging over elections.

Liberals, on the other hand, seemed keen on invoking the argument of "disenfranchisement," de facto barely concealing their beliefs that their electoral base somewhat couldn't be expected to possess, let alone carry, bona-fide means of identification.

Currently, only 35 states have adopted some sort of voter ID registration reform which leaves plenty of room for fraud to still occur on a massive scale in 2024.[370]

First Blood: the "Stormy Daniels" Indictment

The Establishment's primary objective has been to unleash the full power of the federal government against Trump in order to prevent him from even running in the first place.

The drive to neutralize Trump got a boost with the election of Alvin Bragg as Manhattan's district attorney in 2022, taking over for retiring District Attorney Cyrus Vance Jr. Bragg's focus centered

---

369 Ibid.

370 Jeff Cercone, "Rules vary, but 35 states require some form of ID to vote," PolitiFact, June 13, 2022. https://www.politifact.com/factchecks/2022/jun/13/nikki-haley/rules-vary-35-states-require-some-form-id-vote/

"According to the National Conference of State Legislatures, 35 U.S. States have laws that require or request some form of identification to vote. Those laws applied to about 59% of registered voters in the 2020 election, according to the U.S. Census Bureau. The laws vary in terms of whether they are strictly applied and whether a photo ID, or other forms of documentation, are accepted."

around a grand jury empaneled to look into hush money paid on Trump's behalf during the 2016 presidential campaign.[371]

As if to throw observers off-balance, Bragg initially relented to issue an indictment against the former President on account of what he believed was a weak case.

Although this foot-dragging led to the resignation of a couple of prosecutors who had been working on the case, the move was only temporary as Bragg would eventually issue an indictment against the former president. Bragg's legal theory was that by allegedly filing false entries into his business records to camouflage the payment of hush money to porn star Stormy Daniels, the former president committed a felony under New York's State law.[372]

Former Manhattan prosecutor Mark Pomerantz pointed out that no appellate court had ever resolved the issue bearing on whether one can be charged under the felony version of New York's false records law.[373]

Moreover, the language of the statute upon which the indictment was predicated was deemed ambiguous, which in turn raised questions of legal interpretation. The United States Supreme Court has held that when the meaning of a criminal statute is unclear, the Constitution sometimes requires that statute to be read narrowly. The rationale is to protect the constitutional rights of a defendant charged for having violated an unclear criminal law. This rule of "lenity" was thus adopted to foreclose the using of criminal statutes which fail to give potential defendants "fair warning" that their conduct was illegal.[374]

---

371 Jeremy Herb, Kara Scannell, and Paula Reid, "Trump hush money probe goes quiet after chaotic week," *CNN Politics,* March 23, 2023, updated March 24, 2023. https://edition.cnn.com/2023/03/23/politics/trump-bragg-grand-jury-new-york

"The district attorney's office is trying to determine whether to call back Trump's former lawyer and fixer, Michael Cohen, to refute the testimony provided earlier this week by lawyer Robert Costello – or to call an additional witness to buttress their case before the grand jurors consider a vote on whether to indict the former president, one source familiar with the investigation said."

372 *The People of the State of New York against Donald J. Trump* [indictment filed in the Supreme Court of the State of oNew York, County of New York]. https://www.politico.com/f/?id=00000187-4d9a-dc00-a3d7-4d9f97b40000

373 Jennifer Rodgers, "Former Manhattan prosecutor has given Trump a gift" [opinion], *CNN,* February 10, 2023. https://www.cnn.com/2023/02/10/opinions/bragg-pomerantz-fight-trump-gift-rodgers/index.html

374 Ian Millhiser, "The dubious legal theory at the heart of the Trump indictment, explained," *Vox,* April 4, 2023. https://www.vox.com/politics/2023/4/4/23648390/

Were this particular issue to make its way to the highest court in the land, it is likely that the case would be thrown out.

Crossing the Rubicon

In an act of political prosecution unprecedented in U.S. history, the U.S. Justice Department under the control of a sitting president called for a frontal attack on his putative leading opponent who happened to be the front-runner for the 2024 election.[375]

In August 2022 the Bureau of Federal Investigation mobilized dozens of agents to conduct a raid on Mar-A-Lago, the Miami private residence of the 45th president of the United States.

In requesting that Southern District of Florida Judge Bruce E. Reinhart issue a search warrant, officials at the Bureau provided a statement of facts and evidence purporting to establish probable cause that evidence of a crime was to be found at the former president's residence.[376]

---

trump-indictment-supreme-court-stormy-daniels-manhattan-alvin-bragg

"The Supreme Court has long held, under a doctrine known as the 'Rule of Lenity' that 'fair warning should be given to the world,' in language that the common world will understand, of what the law intends to do if a certain line is passed. Thus, when the meaning of a criminal statute is unclear, the Constitution sometimes requires that statute to be read narrowly because an unclear criminal law did not give potential defendants 'fair warning' that their conduct was illegal. The current Court is divided about when this rule of lenity should apply, and whether it provides much protection at all to criminal defendants. But, if the current slate of justices decide that they must have the final word on whether Bragg may prosecute Trump, they could easily invoke the rule of lenity to justify asserting the Supreme Court's jurisdiction over the case."

375 Tal Axelrod, "Trump's 3 indictments mark unprecedented moment in presidential history" *ABC News,* August 3, 2023. https://abcnews.go.com/Politics/trump-indictment-marks-unprecedented-moment-presidential-history/story?id=97948293

376 Miranda Devine, Mark Moore, and Samuel Chamberlain, "Judge who OK'd Mar-a-Lago raid Obama donor once linked to Jeffrey Epstein," *New York Post,* August 9, 2022.

"Reinhart was elevated to magistrate judge in March 2018 after 10 years in private practice. That November, the Miami Herald reported that he had represented several of Epstein's employees — including, by Reinhart's own admission to the outlet, Epstein's pilots; his scheduler, Sarah Kellen; and Nadia Marcinkova, who Epstein once reportedly described as his 'Yugoslavian sex slave.' Kellen and Marcinkova were among Epstein's lieutenants who were granted immunity as part of a controversial 2007 deal with federal prosecutors that allowed the pervert to plead guilty to state charges rather than federal crimes. Epstein wound up serving just 13

This immediately prompted a discussion bearing on the violation of Trump's rights under the Fourth Amendment. The U.S. Constitution protects "the right of the People to be secure in their houses and papers." As such, a search warrant must "particularly describe the place to be searched and the things to be seized."

With substantial redacting of the affidavit's content standing in the way of adequately informing the public, news organizations sought to get Reinhart to unseal the affidavit, but the Justice Department opposed the request, arguing that disclosure of the material at this stage "would jeopardize an active criminal investigation."[377]

In order to invalidate the warrant, Trump's lawyers requested the appointment of a "special master" tasked with conducting a review of the evidence submitted by the FBI per article 41 of the Federal Rules of criminal procedure which eventually allows for the recovery of property unlawfully seized by the government.

In a similar legal recourse, former Trump attorney John Eastman had failed to prevent law enforcement from accessing his communications with his client on account of the attorney-client privilege exception. The government overcame this exception by invoking an "exception to the exception": no criminal charges had yet been filed.

Similarly, here, this allowed the government to conduct its investigation under the shroud of secrecy. In the search of Mar-A-Lago a specially vetted group of law enforcement officials was able to conduct a review of the seized materials before deciding whether any of these could be used to further the criminal investigation.

The warrant's overbreadth allowed the FBI to seize "any other containers/boxes" that were "stored or found together with boxes containing classified documents," making it possible for the Feds to proceed with the seizure of 26 boxes on the account of their being merely located in the house.

---

months in county jail and was granted work release."

377 Patricia Mazzei and Alan Feuer, "Sealed Affidavit in Trump Search Should be Redacted, Judge Says," *The New York Times*, August 18, 2022. https://www.nytimes.com/2022/08/18/us/politics/trump-fbi-affidavit-warrant.html

"Judge Reinhart's decision in the closely scrutinized case appeared to strike a middle course between the Justice Department, which had wanted to keep the affidavit entirely under wraps as it continued to investigate Mr. Trump's retention of classified documents, and a group of news organizations, which requested that it be released in full to the public."

Trump's legal team however prevailed and a special master would eventually be appointed to potentially exclude some of the seized evidence in an echo of what had been decided back in 2018 when an overbroad search warrant had been served on former Trump attorney Michael Cohen.[378]

Violations of Attorney-Client Privilege

Another issue bearing on the perceived assault on civil liberties which has arisen in the context of the federal persecution of the former President of the United States centers on the alleged violation(s) of the attorney-client privilege.

The rules of evidence are governed by the concept of admissibility, which states that all relevant evidence is admissible while irrelevant evidence is deemed inadmissible. So, to be admissible, every item of evidence must tend to prove or disprove a fact at issue in the case. If the evidence is not related to a fact at issue in a case, it is irrelevant and is, therefore, inadmissible.

Relevance of evidence is limited by exceptions such as the attorney-client privilege. In order to sidestep this prohibition in the context of Trump's attorneys, federal courts have again invoked "an exception to the exception" now referred to as the crime-fraud exception.[379] The

---

378 "Read the judge's full ruling for special master to review Trump documents," *PBS NewsHour,* September 5, 2022. https://www.pbs.org/newshour/nation/read-the-judges-full-ruling-for-special-master-to-review-trump-documents

"'The Court is mindful that restraints on criminal prosecutions are disfavored, but finds that these unprecedented circumstances call for a brief pause to allow for neutral, third-party review to ensure a just process with adequate safeguards,' Cannon, a Trump appointee, wrote in her 24-page order."

379 David Schultz, "The Crime-Fraud Exception Is a Self-Regulating Tool for Attorneys" [opinion], *Bloomberg Law,* March 21, 2023. https://news.bloomberglaw.com/us-law-week/the-crime-fraud-exception-is-a-self-regulating-tool-for-attorneys

"Attorney-client confidentiality is a central concept of American law. Yet this privilege can hide, not enable, illegal behavior. There will be increased pressure to force lawyers to rat on their clients, unless the legal community is more serious about self-regulation to ensure attorneys don't give legal advice to clients to help them break the law. Attorney-client privilege exists to encourage individuals to seek legal advice. As Chief Justice William Rehnquist once stated, 'The observance of the ethical obligation of a lawyer to hold inviolate the confidences and secrets of his client not only facilitates the full development of facts essential to proper representation of the client but also encourages laymen to seek early legal assistance.'"

crime-fraud exception allows prosecutors to access privileged materials if and when it is believed that the legal advice(s) and/or service(s) rendered to the client were done in furtherance of a crime.[380]

This jurisprudential avatar was raised in the matter involving Evan Corcoran. Corcoran was another Trump attorney who had been summoned to testify before a federal grand jury impaneled to determine whether there existed grounds to issue an indictment against the former president in the matter dealing with the classified material seized by the FBI at Mar-A-Lago.

Issuing a ruling under seal, Chief Judge Beryl A. Howell, from the Federal District Court of the District of Columbia, determined that the federal government had met the threshold allowing it to overcome the attorney-client privilege, thus implying that Corcoran's legal advice to the former President amounted to participation in the commission of a federal crime.[381]

As expected, Trump's office vigorously criticized Howell's ruling:

> Whenever prosecutors target the attorneys, that's usually a good indication their underlying case is very weak. If they had a real case, they wouldn't need to play corrupt games with the Constitution... Every American has the

---

380 Ibid.

"Using the crime-fraud exception is an extreme tool. Attorney-client communications should be shielded. But its apparent increased use is a product of the legal profession and attorneys failing to self-regulate themselves and police their clients. In the last 25 years, stories of what legal advice was provided by Enron attorneys and those advising corporations involved in the 2008 financial meltdown raised questions about whether they turn a blind eye to bad client behavior and perhaps enable it. This is the question too with Trump's attorneys in New York, Washington, and perhaps in Georgia as rumors of a Trump indictment play out there too. What did they know and what type of legal advice or action did they take to try to discourage him from breaking the law? The same question no doubt will surface as the evolving story of bank failures continue to unfold."

381 Kaitlan Collins, Devan Cole and Katelyn Polantz, "Trump attorney ordered to testify before grand jury investigating former president," *CNN Politics,* March 17, 2023. https://www.cnn.com/2023/03/17/politics/evan-corcoran-testimony-trump-lawyer/index.html

"The Obama appointee has repeatedly green-lit Justice Department requests to pursue information about Trump's actions during her tenure as chief of the DC District Court, but she rotates out of the administrative role on Friday."

right to consult with counsel and have candid discussions — this promotes adherence to the law... We will fight the Department of Justice on this front and all others that jeopardize fundamental American rights and values.[382]

Recently appointed Special Counsel Jack Smith promptly used the ruling issued by Judge Howell to force Corcoran to testify before the federal grand jury, leading many observers to speculate as to whether Corcoran will invoke his right under the Fifth Amendment so as to not to incriminate himself.

Lawfare

On June 8, 2023, Special Counsel Jack Smith took the unprecedented step filing federal criminal charges against Donald J. Trump.[383] According to the indictment issued by the federal grand jury, the charges included "willfully retaining national defense secrets in violation of the 1917 Espionage Act, making false statements and conspiracy to obstruct justice."

Smith is also investigating the former president's alleged role in engineering the alleged insurrection conducted on Capitol Hill on January 6, 2021.[384]

---

382 Ibid.

383 John Santucci and Ivan Pereira, "Sweeping 37-count indictment alleges Trump hoarded national secrets, orchestrated obstruction of investigation," ABC News, June 9, 2023. https://abcnews.go.com/US/trump-federal-indictment-unsealed-classified-documents-probe/story?id=99963920

"The court papers allege that the classified documents included 'defense and weapons capabilities of both the United States and foreign countries; United States nuclear programs; potential vulnerabilities of the United States and its allies to military attack; and plans for possible retaliation in response to a foreign attack.'"

384 Melanie Zanona, Annie Grayer and Alayna Treene, "Trump strategizes with Hill allies to go on offense against January 6 criminal probe," *CNN Politics,* July 18, 2023. https://www.cnn.com/2023/07/18/politics/republican-allies-trump-january-6-probe/index.html

"Trump's Hill outreach comes on the heels of him announcing on Tuesday he had received a letter from Smith on Sunday indicating he is a criminal target, a sign he may be soon charged by the special counsel."

Reactions to the indictment reflected the intense partisanship that has characterized anything the former president has said or done since he first announced that he would compete in the 2016 presidential election.

Fox news pundit Mark Levin opined that the entire Federal government is being weaponized against the Republican putative nominee:

> President Trump is 76 years old. If the Department of Justice gets its way, he will die in federal prison, just by one of these counts—conspiracy to obstruct justice, which has a 20-year maximum sentence. This is a disgusting mark on American history for the future to come, by these bandits in the White House, by the Democrat party who don't play fair anymore. They don't want to just win elections, they want to take control of this country, they want one-party rule. They have used the Department of Justice and the FBI to get what they want. They are throwing all these process crimes and all these crimes that grow out of the criminal investigation against Trump. What did he do with the documents? Did he sell them to the enemy? No. That is why we have an Espionage Act—not to trip up a president... What did he do? Did he burn them all? No, the government has all the documents back, so there is no violation of the Presidential Records Act, at this point... But they throw the book at him? They go after his attorneys, they make them testify, their attorneys under the crime-fraud exception to attorney-client privilege. That means he didn't have due process."[385]

385 Andrea Blanco, "Fox host Mark Levin screams at camera in outrage at Trump indictment over secret papers," *Independent,* June 11, 2023. https://www.independent.co.uk/news/world/americas/us-politics/mark-levin-trump-indictment-secret-papers-b2355369.html

Special Counsel Jack Smith:
The "Perfect Man" for the Job?

Before being tapped to act as Special Counsel, Jack Smith once worked as Chief Prosecutor in Den Hague, Netherlands.[386] Merrick Garland hailed Smith as "...the right choice to complete these matters in an even-handed and urgent manner."[387]

Smith's track record is, however, deserving of a rather more nuanced assessment.

Smith had been assigned to the Department of Justice's Public Integrity Section from 2010 to 2015. This section had been tasked with the handling of investigations in cases dealing with public corruption.[388] In that capacity, Smith had the opportunity to initiate a series of prosecutions against some of America's most high-profile politicians, including former Virginia Governor Bob McDonnell, former North Carolina Senator and erstwhile presidential candidate, John Edwards, and former Senate Committee on Foreign Relations, Senator Bob Menendez...(against whom new charges of bribery have recently been filed) with mixed results.[389]

---

386 Sarah N. Lynch, "Who is Special Counsel Jack Smith in the Trump documents case?," *Reuters,* updated August 3, 2023. https://www.reuters.com/world/us/who-is-jack-smith-special-counsel-who-brought-trump-indictment-2023-06-08/

"In 2008, Smith left to supervise war crime prosecutions at the International Criminal Court in The Hague. He returned to the Justice Department in 2010 to head its Public Integrity Section until 2015. More recently, Smith returned to war crimes cases in The Hague, winning the conviction of Salih Mustafa, a former Kosovo Liberation Army commander who ran a prison where torture took place during the 1998-99 independence conflict with Serbia."

387 Jose Pagliery and Justin Rohrlich, "War Crimes Prosecutor Jack Smith Will Decide Whether Donald Trump Gets Charged," *The Daily Beast,* November 18, 2022. https://www.thedailybeast.com/attorney-general-garland-to-announce-special-counsel-for-donald-trump-criminal-probes

388 Zachary Cohen, Kara Scannell, Jeremy Herb, Katelyn Polantz and Chandelis Duster, "Who is Jack Smith, the special counsel named in the Trump investigations," *CNN Politics,* updated November 19, 2022. https://www.cnn.com/2022/11/18/politics/jack-smith-special-counsel/index.html

"Lanny Breuer, the former assistant attorney general for the DOJ's Criminal Division who recruited Smith, said his onetime employee was 'a terrific prosecutor' with a 'real sense of fairness.... If you are going to have a special counsel, in my view, and you want someone who is going to be fearless, but fair, and not going to be intimidated and not overly bureaucratic, that's Jack – he is all of these things,' Breuer told CNN."

389 Ibid.

The Trump legal team immediately denounced the appointment as politically motivated while Smith rejected the claim that the Justice Department had become a weapon against the Republican candidate, stating:

> I intend to conduct the assigned investigation and any prosecutions that may result from them independently and in the best traditions of the Department of Justice... I will exercise independent judgment and will move the investigations forward expeditiously and thoroughly to whatever outcome the facts and the law dictate.[390]

While in his case filed against McDonnell Smith had secured a 2014 conviction, the latter was unanimously overturned by the United States Supreme Court.

Writing on behalf of the Court, Chief Justice Roberts, a George W. Bush appointee, expressed his unequivocal dismay of the methods then used by the prosecution:

> The Government's expansive interpretation of "official act" would raise significant constitutional concerns. Conscientious public officials arrange meetings for constituents, contact other officials on their behalf, and include them in events all the time. Representative government assumes that public officials will hear from their constituents and act appropriately on their concerns. The Government's position could cast a pall of potential prosecution over these relationships. There is no doubt that this case is distasteful; it may be worse than that. But our concern is not with tawdry tales of Ferraris, Rolexes, and ball gowns. It is instead with the broader legal implications of the Government's boundless interpretation of the federal bribery statute. A more limited interpretation of the term "official act" leaves ample room for prosecuting corruption, while comporting with the text of the statute and the precedent of this Court.[391]

390 Ibid.
391 Lawrence Hurley and David Ingram, "U.S. top court overturns Virginia ex-governor's corruption conviction," Reuters, June 27, 2016. https://www.reuters.com/

In 2011, Smith's unit obtained an indictment from a federal grand jury, this time against former Democratic Party presidential hopeful John Edwards. The six-count indictment charged Edwards *inter alia* with participating "in a scheme to violate campaign finance laws," "Conspiracy," "issuing false statements to the Federal Election Commission," and "concealing illegal donations."

The case stemmed from $900,000 of campaign donations being funneled to Rielle Hunter, a supporter with whom Edwards was having an affair even as his wife Elizabeth was fighting cancer. A 2012 jury trial had ended in a deadlock with some of the impaneled jurors expressing their view that Smith and his team had failed to make their case.[392]

In 2017, Smith prosecuted Bob Menendez for allegedly having "accepted close to $1 million worth of lavish gifts and campaign contributions from Melgen in exchange for using the power of his Senate office to influence the outcome of ongoing contractual and Medicare billing disputes worth tens of millions of dollars to Melgen and to support the visa applications of several of Melgen's girlfriends."[393]

Following his acquittal, Menendez alluded to malicious prosecution if not outright prosecutorial misconduct: "The way this case started was wrong, the way it was investigated was wrong, the way

---

article/usa-court-mcdonnell-idUSL1N19J0RK/

"'The ruling opens the possibility that politicians could sell meetings and other forms of access without violating federal law,' said Randall Eliason, a former federal prosecutor. 'Accss can be very important, especially when it's being arranged by someone's boss,' said Eliason, who now teaches law at George Washington University."

392 Jen Smith, "The other politician who faced jail for hush payments to a 'lover': Democrat darling John Edwards beat campaign finance charges in 2012 over money he gave his pregnant mistress while his wife battled cancer," *Daily Mail,* March 20, 2023. https://www.dailymail.co.uk/news/article-11881261/How-John-Edwards-beat-charges-2008-payments-pregnant-mistress-Trump-faces-indictment.html

393 Mollie Reilly, "Mistrial Declared In Bob Menendez Bribery Trial," *HuffPost,* November 16, 2017. https://www.huffpost.com/entry/bob-menendez-mistrial_n_5a0dd3d5e4b0c0b2f2f8ae46

"Following the announcement of the mistrial, Senate Majority Leader Mitch McConnell (R-Ky.) called on the Senate Ethics Committee to investigate the case. 'Senator Menendez was indicted on numerous federal felonies. He is one of only twelve U.S. Senators to have been indicted in our history,' McConnell said in a statement. 'His trial shed light on serious accusations of violating the public's trust as an elected official, as well as potential violations of the Senate's Code of Conduct.'"

it was prosecuted was wrong, and the way it was tried was wrong as well."[394]

Incidentally, Menendez has recently been indicted on charges of conspiring to commit bribery and acting as an agent for the Egyptian government.[395]

On July 19, 2023, Trump took to his "Truth Media" platform to inform the public that he'd been the recipient of a target letter from the Office of the Special Counsel informing him that he had been "identified" in the context of a grand jury investigation bearing on his alleged participation in the "storming of the Capitol Building."[396]

Constitutional scholar Jonathan Turley opined:

> They have to really stick the landing so that no one will question it or few people would question it. That's going to require some very direct and strong evidence. We haven't seen that. So if Smith doesn't have that type of evidence, and he's moving forward largely on the speech, then I think he will fulfill the narrative of Donald Trump. He will be the federal version of Alvin Bragg in bringing that indictment. … Smith has a reputation of stretching the criminal code sometimes too far. This is not an occasion for that. If you're going to indict the former president over January 6, you're going to need a lot of evidence showing that he was doing more than engaging in a political speech. In my view, what Donald Trump said in the Ellipse is entirely protected under a case called Brandenburg and the First Amendment. Smith is going to need a lot more than that speech.[397]

---

394 Laura Jarrett and Sarah Jorgensen, "Bob Menendez trial ends in mistrial after jury deadlocks," *CNN Politics,* November 16, 2017. https://www.cnn.com/2017/11/16/politics/bob-menendez-trial/index.html

395 David Voreacos and Austin Weinstein, "Menendez Bribery Defense May Lean on 'Subtle' Pitch to Ex-NJ AG," *BNN Bloomberg,* November 17, 2023.. https://www.bnnbloomberg.ca/menendez-bribery-defense-may-lean-on-subtle-pitch-to-ex-nj-ag-1.2000305

396 Richard Luscombe, "Trump says he received target letter in federal January 6 investigation," *The Guardian,* July 18, 2023. https://www.theguardian.com/us-news/2023/jul/18/trump-letter-jan-6-jack-smith

397 "DOJ will need 'a lot more' evidence to indict Trump in Jan. 6 probe, Jonathan Turley says," *Fox News,* July 18, 2023. https://www.foxnews.com/media/doj-evidence-indict-trump-jan-6-probe-jonathan-turley-says

With yet another indictment bearing on Trump's alleged pressure to change the results of the 2020 election by calling the Secretary of State of Georgia to "find me some votes," legal experts are likely to be queried on the meaning of "computer trespass."[398]

A Disingenuous Approach to Trump's Prosecution

Smith's statement to the effect that "We have one set of laws in this country, and they apply to everyone" would somewhat not sound so hollow had the Department of Justice displayed the same alacrity in investigating and potentially indicting Joe Biden and members of his family.

As things currently stand, one cannot help but feel that there exists a two-tiered system, given the zeal shown by the government in going after Trump. Indictments against the former president keep piling up while Joe Biden escapes the Department of Justice's scrutiny on allegations of influence-peddling.

This double-standard was made all the more obvious as Smith's indictment was issued mere hours after an incriminating document was made public purporting to establish that Biden had received a $5 million payment from a foreign national.

One could trace this two-tiered system of selective prosecution with former Secretary of State and erstwhile presidential candidate, Hillary Rodham Clinton, escaping prosecution despite having admitted deleted over 30, 000 classified emails which she kept on a private server.[399]

---

398 Tom Boggioni "Trump to face a 'a sprawling racketeering indictment' in Georgia: report," *Raw Story,* July 21, 2023. https://www.rawstory.com/trump-georgia-racketeering-2662320017/

"The report adds that computer trespass charge, 'proecutors would have to show that defendants used a computer or network without authority to interfere with a program or data, that would include the breach of voting machines in Coffee county,' the two people said. The breach of voting machines involved a group of Trump operatives – paid by the then Trump lawyer Sidney Powell – accessing the voting machines at the county's election office and copying sensitive voting system data."

399 Maggie Haberman, "Hillary Clinton, Citing Her 'Mistake,' Apologizes for Private Email," First Draft | Political News, *The New York Times,* September 8, 2015. https://archive.nytimes.com/www.nytimes.com/politics/first-draft/2015/09/08/hillary-clinton-calls-private-email-server-a-mistake-says-im-sorry-about-that/

Thus, while Jack Smith may try to reassure himself that the "law applies to everyone," the U.S. justice system lost the public trust when Judge Cannon opted to hold a trial six months before the 2024 presidential election.[400]

To anyone tempted to believe that Cannon's decision was an isolated incident as relates to the Justice system's treatment of Trump, Fulton County District Attorney Fanni Willis's request that the former president's trial in Georgia be held a mere 90 days prior to the general election puts the case to rest.[401]

A few days following Hunter Biden's late July court appearance in front of a federal judge, Smith issued his second indictment against Donald J. Trump.[402] The timing of this indictment drew scrutiny in the wake of momentum generated by the Comer-led Oversight Committee investigation which revealed that Hunter had received 4 million dollars from "a Ukrainian company."[403] In this context, these revelations

400 Cristina Laila, "'Judge Cannon Blew It — Big-Time' – Mark Levin Reacts to Judge Cannon's Decision to Set Trump's Classified Docs Trial Date For May 2024 – 6 Mos Before Election," *Gateway Pundit,* July 21, 2023. https://www.thegatewaypundit.com/2023/07/judge-cannon-blew-it-big-time-mark-levin/

"'Judge Cannon blew it. Big-time. A criminal trial in the middle of a presidential election, when I believe most of the primary races are over (or many anyway). And if Trump is found guilty on a single charge, even if he appeals, he will have to carry that into the general election, should he be the GOP nominee. This is why Smith, with the backing of Garland, was hellbent on getting indictments in place and demanding an early trial. He got what he wanted (moving the trial from December to May is inconsequential). So, Cannon has now given her rubber stamp to the election interference scheme of the Biden DOJ and the Democrats. She just didn't have the guts to stare down the rogue prosecutors and tell them that they will have to wait until the election is over to start their trial, assuming none of the coming (hopefully) motions are not fatal to their case. There is literally no reason to have ruled this way. And every reason not to.' Mark Levin said in a tweet on Friday."

401 Mark Alfred, "Fani Willis' Proposed New RICO Trial Date Could Ruin Trump's 2024 Plans," *The Daily Beast,* November 18, 2023. https://www.thedailybeast.com/fani-willis-proposed-new-rico-trial-date-could-ruin-trumps-2024-plans

402 Tierney Sneed, Holmes Lybrand, Marshall Cohen, Zachary Cohen, Devan Cole, Hannah Rabinowitz, Katelyn Polantz and Casey Gannon, "Donald Trump has been indicted in special counsel's 2020 election interference probe," *CNN Politics,* August 1, 2023. https://edition.cnn.com/2023/08/01/politics/donald-trump-indictment-grand-jury-2020-election/index.html

403 Greg Farrell, "Hunter Biden Made Over $4 Million Amid 'Nonstop Debauchery,'" *Bloomberg,* August 2, 2023. https://www.bloomberg.com/news/articles/2023-08-02/hunter-biden-made-millions-amid-nonstop-debauchery-plea-says

brought an added perspective on the decidedly one-of-a-kind "sweet deal" negotiated between Hunter's lawyers and the Justice department.

Prior to the hearing scheduled to validate the plea-bargain agreement, people associated with the presidential son's legal defense called the Federal court's clerk and impersonated some fictitious character allegedly working on behalf of "a Republican lawyer." The call aimed at convincing the clerk to remove some tax documents deemed damaging to the defendant.[404]

The hearing itself went drastically wrong as Judge Noreika rejected the terms of the plea deal owing to the blanket immunity granted the defendant in the light of the ongoing congressional investigation bearing on Hunter's possible violations of the Foreign Agent Registration Act. This immunity clause was deemed to constitute a step too far for Judge Noreika and she promptly refused to rubber-stamp the deal.[405] The media's extensive coverage of the hearing fed into the narrative that the Justice Department went out of its way to shield the younger Biden.

It was hoped that the latest indictment to befall Trump in Georgia on RICO charges would shift the public's attention away from Hunter's travails in Pennsylvania.

On August 14, a Georgia grand jury issued an indictment against Trump and eighteen of his advisors and close collaborators (including the former president's own personal attorney, Rudolph Guliani).[406]

---

404 Josh Gersten, "Judge says member of Hunter Biden's legal team 'misrepresented her identity' on eve of plea deal hearing," Politico, July 25, 2023. https://www.politico.com/news/2023/07/25/hunter-biden-judge-plea-deal-phone-call-00108184

405 Ashley Oliver, "Hunter Biden plea: Foreign agent revelation helps unravel 'sweetheart' deal," *Washington Examiner,* July 26, 2023. https://www.washingtonexaminer.com/news/justice/hunter-biden-plea-foreign-agent-fara-revelation-collapse

"U.S. District Judge Noreika raised the hypothetical of a Foreign Agents Registration Act violation as the Department of Justice faces scrutiny for declining to enforce the act for the younger Biden... 'I don't really understand the scope' of the deal's immunity provisions, Noreika said at one point, making note of Hunter Biden's foreign business endeavors with Ukrainian and Chinese energy companies. She later brought up the FARA question, to which Leo Wise, an assistant U.S. attorney for Weiss, indicated that the department would not be precluded from charging the younger Biden with a FARA violation."

406 Andrew Prokop, "How Atlanta prosecutor Fani Willis took on Donald Trump" *Vox,* August 14, 2023. https://www.vox.com/trump-investigatio

The indictment alleged that the Defendants had engaged in a "criminal enterprise" (RICO Act) predicated on steps taken to force Georgia's then Secretary of State, Brad Raffenberger, to "invalidate" the election.[407]

Mainstream media then hurriedly began to shift their focus on the Defendants' upcoming arraignment at Fulton County jail.

Meanwhile, Republican party challengers gathered to meet for a first televised debate aimed at portraying Trump as an outcast. The former president had decided against participating in the event owing to his holding an unprecedented lead over all of the declared candidates.[408]

The hope was that the Republican debate (sans Trump) combined with the Georgia indictment would derail Trump's momentum. This strategy failed miserably as ratings of Trump's own separate interview held the same night with Tucker Carlson on X (formerly Twitter) eclipsed those of the primary debate with an audience estimated to have exceeded 230 million viewers.[409]

Sensing that the Administration's obsession with tarnishing Trump's image with the voters was backfiring, Carlson ventured to ask his guest whether he was concerned for his own life: a question which Trump refused to address directly, expressing instead his concerns about "a level of passion that I've never seen. There's a level of hatred that I've never seen. And that's probably a bad combination."[410]

---

ns/2023/8/14/23827150/trump-georgia-indictment-2020-election-giuliani-meadows

"On Monday, Fani Willis, the district attorney of Fulton County, charged Trump with 13 counts, including racketeering and conspiracy. And the former president had company. Several of his attorneys, campaign aides, and administration officials were charged as well, including Rudy Giuliani and former White House chief of staff Mark Meadows."

407 Ibid.

408 Maegan Vasquez, "8 presidential candidates qualify for first Republican debate," *The Washington Post,* August 22, 2023. https://www.washingtonpost.com/politics/2023/08/22/republican-debate-presidential-candidates-qualify/

409 Lisa Richwine, "Trump's debate counter-programming draws millions of views on X," *Reuters,* August 3, 2023. https://www.reuters.com/world/us/trumps-debate-counter-programming-draws-millions-views-x-2023-08-24/

410 Isaac Arnsdorf, "Trump suggests in Carlson interview that U.S. could see more political violence," *The Washington Post,* August 23, 2023. https://www.washingtonpost.com/politics/2023/08/23/trump-tucker-carlson-interview/

"Earlier in the interview, Trump repeatedly avoided Carlson's invitations to speculate on whether he could be targeted for assassination. 'The next stage

A week later, Trump showed up for his Georgia arraignment and the optics took Washington's establishment by surprise. The former president's motorcade was cheered by throngs of bystanders (including many African Americans) all the way to the county jail where Trump would undergo fingerprinting and be photographed in one of the most bizarre and surreal episodes in U.S. presidential history.[411]

The Trump "mugshot" became an instant collector's item. It featured a man determined to go after his opponents and helped rack in millions of dollars in campaign contributions.[412]

Then, on the same day it was revealed that Hunter had received 250 thousand dollars from a Chinese company, a New-York judge proceeded to evaluate Trump's Mar-A-Lago property at a paltry 18 million dollars.[413] This ruling fed into the New-York District Attorney's contention that Trump had lied about the value of his properties and thus defrauded banks and insurance companies.

Simultaneously, James Comer provided updates on the "money trail" involving payments benefiting no less than nine Biden family members for a total exceeding 20 million USD through 20 shell companies, with Comer musing that in his own estimate, the figure could well reach 50 million.[414]

The accumulated evidence involves emails, meetings (notably one featuring Burisma's Chief Financial Officer, its CFO and the spouse of a former Moscow Mayor, Hunter, and Devon Archer at Washington D.C. Café Milano), notes, financial records, including

is violence,' Calson said. 'Are you worried they're going to try to kill you? Why wouldn't they try to kill you?'"

411 Frankie Stockes, "Video: Black Atlantans Chant 'Free Trump' as Motorcade Rolls Through Inner City," *National File,* August 25, 2023. https://nationalfile.com/video-black-atlantans-chant-free-trump-as-motorcade-rolls-through-inner-city/

412 Faith E. Pinho, "How much is Trump's mug shot worth? Over $7 million, campaign says," *Los Angeles Times,* August 28, 2023. https://www.latimes.com/politics/story/2023-08-28/how-much-is-trumps-mug-shot-worth-over-7-million-campaign-says

413 Ben Kochman, "Judge revokes Trump's NY business licenses, finds he committed fraud by inflating wealth," *New York Post,* September 26, 2023. https://nypost.com/2023/09/26/trump-committed-fraud-by-inflating-wealth-ny-judge/

414 United States House Committee on Oversight and Accountability, "Comer: Oversight Committee Has Uncovered Mounting Evidence Tying Joe Biden to Family Business Schemes" [press release], September 13, 2023. https://oversight.house.gov/release/comer-oversight-committee-has-uncovered-mounting-evidence-tying-joe-biden-to-family-business-schemes/

a staggering 170 Suspicious Transactions Reports led the political winds to shift against the incumbent President.

A day before House Majority Speaker, Kevin McCarthy announced that House Republicans would initiate an impeachment inquiry against Biden, a not so widely covered article was published in the venerable *National Review*.[415] Entitled "Yes, Joe Biden is corrupt," the article authored by Rich Lowry reflected the traditional Republican establishment (RINO) willingness to jettison support for Joe Biden.

Moreover, Mitch McConnell's repeated public "freezes" showed a GOP leadership completely disconnected from its base ever since it refused to support Trump's challenge following the 2020 Election.[416]

This civil war within the Republican Party was further illustrated by McCarthy's announcement that the impeachment inquiry against Biden would proceed despite not being subjected to a vote, thus highlighting the growing power of the MAGA faction.

This insurrection within the GOP would again come to the fore as MAGA Republicans engaged in a no-holes-barred fight against McCarthy to refrain him from taking political credits in adopting four budget bills aimed at preventing a shutdown of the federal government.[417] The "populists" argued that issues of substantive importance should not be shirked in favor of political expediency. To allow for the Federal government to continue functioning, transparency and accountability in spending had to be addressed.[418]

In fact, MAGA Republicans aimed at preventing the continued funding of what they perceived as a "weaponized Justice Department," an out-of-control immigration policy (viewed as the DNC's ploy to naturalize migrants and turn them into Democratic voters), and a lack of accountability as relates to funds shipped out to Ukraine. (All this

415 Rich Lowry, "Yes, Joe Biden Is Corrupt," *National Review,* September 11, 2023. https://www.nationalreview.com/2023/09/yes-joe-biden-is-corrupt/

416 Erik Uebelacker, "Mitch McConnell Suddenly Freezes Again While Talking to Reporters," *Yahoo! News,* August 30, 2023. https://news.yahoo.com/mitch-mcconnell-suddenly-freezes-again-173405240.html

417 Li Zhou, "Another government shutdown? Republicans are threatening to make that a real possibility," *Vox,* September 11, 2023. https://www.vox.com/politics/2023/9/11/23868182/government-shutdown-republicans-house-freedom-caucus

418 Ibid.

while Zelensky was in town seeking to finalize the latest Ukraine $24 billion aid package.)[419]

It all came to a head as the MAGA faction initiated a successful coup against McCarthy and removed him from the speaker's position.

Justice For All?

The Department would soon find itself engulfed in controversy as Attorney General Merrick Garland faces a barrage of questions from the House Judiciary Committee.

The questions directed at the AG revolved around the circumstances surrounding the elevation of Delaware U.S. Attorney David Weis to the position of Special Counsel.[420] Recall that Weiss was tasked with handling the tax evasion investigation of Hunter Biden since being appointed to handle that case by the Trump administration back in 2018.

The House Judiciary Committee questioned Weiss's independence since for all intents and purposes he remained an employee of the Justice department. In order to deflect accusations of shielding Hunter (Weiss had de facto allowed the statute of limitations to out on some of the charges), Weiss rushed to indict the President's son on gun charges. (The arraignment took place on October 3, one day after Trump's $250-million bank and insurance fraud case began in New York.)[421]

Weiss's perceived procrastination had stood front and center during the two IRS whistleblowers testimonies earlier this year and Garland's role as the guarantor of the rule of law was increasingly

---

419 Ibid.

420 Glen Thrush, "Takeaways From Garland's Testimony Before the House Judiciary Committee," *The New York Times,* September 20, 2023. https://www.nytimes.com/2023/09/20/us/politics/garland-testimony-house-hunter-biden.html

"Republicans tried, and failed, to get Mr. Garland to explain why Mr. Weiss suddenly requested to be appointed Special Counsel in August. Weeks earlier, a plea deal that would have granted Hunter Biden broad immunity from future prosecution on weapons and tax charges had fallen apart under the withering scrutiny of a federal judge in Delaware."

421 "With less than a month to spare, David Weiss indicts Hunter Biden on his gun crime" [opinion], *Washington Examiner,* September 14, 2023. https://www.washingtonexaminer.com/opinion/with-less-than-month-david-weiss-indicts-hunter-biden-gun-crime

becoming the focal point of an inquiry aiming to determine whether he failed to maintain public trust in the U.S. justice system.

The heated House Judiciary hearings pointedly criticized Garland for his handling of cases involving individuals charged with violating federal laws while merely exercising their First Amendment right to call into question the results of an election.[422]

The Department's prosecutions of January 6th defendants have resulted in long prison sentences and involved defendants who, according to the FBI, never intended to engage in a plot to overthrow the Republic.[423]

To be sure, these lenghty sentences set a precedent, if and when Trump gets convicted for "sedition," prompting some pundits to draw parallels with the 1933 Reichstag Fire and the subsequent adoption of the infamous Enabling Act.[424]

Lest one forgets, the Federal government has ominously engaged in tarring a large swath of Americans as "right-wingers" and "domestic terrorists."[425] One can only recall the incendiary rethoric used in the President's speech pronounced shortly before the 2022 Midterm elections.[426]

Against this backdrop, Garland was grilled by members of the Committee on his Department's selected targeting of Catholic organizations and parents opposed to the progressive agenda promoted by school boards.[427]

---

422 Brittany Carloni, "U.S. Rep. Victoria Spartz criticizes Merrick Garland in House hearing," *IndyStar,* September 20, 2023. https://www.indystar.com/story/news/local/indianapolis/2023/09/20/congresswoman-victoria-spartz-criticizes-merrick-garland-house-hearing-weaponized-justice-system/70913747007/

423 Mark Hosenball and Sarah N. Lynch, "Exclusive: FBI finds scant evidence U.S. Capitol attack was coordinated – sources," *Reuters,* August 20, 2021. https://www.reuters.com/world/us/exclusive-fbi-finds-scant-evidence-us-capitol-attack-was-coordinated-sources-2021-08-20/

424 "Henningsen: 'J6 Was America's Reichstag Fire,'" *21st Century Wire,* September 24, 2023. https://21stcenturywire.com/2023/09/24/henningsen-j6-was-americas-reichstag-fire/

425 "DoJ creates unit to counter domestic terrorism after Capitol attack," *The Guardian,* January 11, 2022. https://www.theguardian.com/us-news/2022/jan/11/justice-department-creates-unit-counter-domestic-terrorism

426 Jeff Mason, "Biden warns election deniers pose threat, blames Trump," *Reuters,* November 2, 2022. https://www.reuters.com/world/us/biden-give-speech-democracy-wednesday-capitol-hill-adviser-2022-11-02/

427 Ryan King, "Garland fires back at House Republican who asked if FBI

As if to illustrate the notion that no government institution is spared by political warfare, Supreme Court Justice Clarence Thomas is now facing allegations that he exerted undue influence in his weighing of cases involving interests linked to the Koch brothers.[428] In point of fact, the Supreme Court has come under attack ever since it held states to be sole arbiters of issues related to abortion, thus putting an end to the federalization of *Roe v. Wade.*

The DNC is now angling to find any pretext to undermine the legitimacy of the Supreme Court for its current composition is viewed as the remaining institutional obstacle to progressive social engineering policies.[429] Ever since Trump appointed three Supreme Court justices, thus tilting the Court towards a solid conservative majority, there are talks on the Hill of curtailing the power of the judicial branch. Confirmation hearings under the Trump administration led to (Soros-financed) "Antifa" militias laying siege to Supreme Court Justice Kavanaugh's domicile without so much as an admonishing.[430]

This impunity came into full display in the wake of the George Floyd murder, as numerous Democrat-administered cities descended into utter anarchy.

Ukraine: My Country Right or Wrong

By all accounts, the Ukraine conflict has come to define the Biden presidency at the expense of all other issues deemed of interest to the American people. Biden's prospect for reelection seemed predicated on the perceived success of American support of Volodymir Zelensky's regime, even though reality is starting even now to tear a hole in the official narrative.

targeted Catholics: 'So outrageous,'" *New York Post,* September 20, 2023. https://nypost.com/2023/09/20/garland-grows-visibly-irate-at-gop-criticism-of-catholic-targeting/

428 Nina Totenberg, "New conflict of interest allegations surface about Justice Clarence Thomas," *NPR,* September 22, 2023. https://www.npr.org/2023/09/22/1201154440/clarence-thomas-koch-supreme-court

429 Naomi Lim, "Biden and Democrats take aim at the Supreme Court before 2024," *Washington Examiner,* July 4, 2023. https://www.washingtonexaminer.com/news/white-house/biden-democrats-take-aim-supreme-court

430 Dave Blount, "Abortion Fanatics Lay Siege to Kavanaugh Home," *Whatfinger News,* January 2023. https://linkshare.whatfinger.com/abortion-fanatics-lay-siege-to-kavanaugh-home/

The conflict has benefitted from a media campaign aimed at convincing the American public that Kiev deserves all the help it can get despite the reality on the ground.[431]

Seymour Hersh recently published an article which tends to establish that the national security circles have given up on Ukraine's much vaunted counter-offensive.[432]

Revealingly, the *New York Times* deviated from acting as Zelensky's cheerleader to divulge that the missile attack on a market located in a Ukrainian-controlled town was the result of Kiev's own doing, rather than Russia's, as Kiev had previously claimed.[433]

In addition, a rash of resignations of senior officials operating within Zelensky's first circle included his Minister of Defense on the heels of reports published in U.S. media bearing on the embezzlement of a significant amount of U.S. assistance.[434]

And so, it all comes back to Ukraine.

One can only wonder what prompted Joe Biden to double-down in his personal entanglement with that country upon becoming president, for in the final analysis the U.S. President's personal obsession with Ukraine ended up serving as the lever needed to promote a policy of open confrontation with Russia leading to a downgrading of American power.

---

431 Mariana Alfaro, "Conservative group launches campaign to push for GOP support for Ukraine," *The Washington Post,* August 15, 2023. https://www.washingtonpost.com/politics/2023/08/15/ukraine-us-aid-republicans-congress/

432 Seymour Hersh, "Zelensky's 'bad moment,'" *Seymour Hersh* [Substack blog], September 21, 2023. https://seymourhersh.substack.com/p/zelenskys-bad-moment

433 John Ismay et al., "Evidence Suggests Ukrainian Missile Caused Market Tragedy," *The New York Times,* September 18, 2023. https://www.nytimes.com/2023/09/18/world/europe/ukraine-missile-kostiantynivka-market.html

434 John Bacon and Jorge L. Ortiz, USA Today, "Ukraine fires 6 deputy defense ministers as allies demand accounting of aid: Updates," *Yahoo! News,* September 19, 2023. https://news.yahoo.com/ukraine-dismisses-deputy-defense-ministers-160609107.html

Conclusion

THE WORDS OF WARNING uttered by George Washington during his Farewell Address have come back to haunt the United States.

In its drive to expand its dominion to the far reaches of the globe, Washington's establishment has not only managed to wreck the lives of millions; it has unintentionally generated "blowback."[435]

While the internment of Japanese Americans, the Red Scare, Iran-Contra, Watergate, the Pentagon Papers, and the Iraq WMDs all shook the political class to its foundations, never before have the country's own institutions appeared so fragilized as a result of an unbounded and reckless foreign policy.[436] Grave as these precedents might have seemed at the time, none of them ever managed to significantly compromise the very institutions relied upon by the American public.

What occurred in Eastern Europe has now led to the discredit of the entire political establishment and the institutions of government are now perceived as damaged beyond repair.

Ominously, the message sent to the American public is that truth itself is deemed expendable if it threatens the interests of those willing to impose authoritarian rule domestically before going to a war with a nuclear-armed state in order to escape political retribution.[437]

---

435 "Chalmers Johnson: Empire v. Democracy," History News Network, January 30, 2007. https://historynewsnetwork.org/article/34881

436 Ibid.

437 Lauren Sforza, "Clinton warns Putin will try to meddle in 2024 election," *The Hill*, September 25, 2023. https://thehill.com/homenews/campaign/4221334-clinton-warns-putin-will-try-to-meddle-in-2024-election/

Glossary

BCWC: Biological and Chemical Weapons Convention

Biolabs: Research facilities operated jointly by The DTRA (using private contractors) and Ukraine's Ministry of Health

Black Box Notebook: The secret ledger allegedly kept by Former President Yanukovich's Party of Regions to remunerate political operatives (and in which Paul Manafort's name was alleged to figure)

Burisma: Ukrainian Gas Company at the center of Hunter and Joe Biden's allegations bearing on influence-peddling

Crossfire Hurricane: Code Name of the manufactured smear campaign directed and coordinated by several U.S. Federal Agencies in order to insinuate that the 45th President of the United States materially benefitted from assistance from the Russian Federation in order to Defeat Hilary Rodham Clinton in the 2016 U.S. general election

Democorruption: Term used by former Ukrainian PM Andrii Derkach to describe the U.S. Democratic Party's money-laundering operation in Ukraine

Donbass: Resource-rich provinces of Eastern Ukraine

Derkach Tapes: Series of recordings bearing on the "External-Management" scheme put in place in Ukraine by Democratic Party elites and their relays in Ukraine

External Management: Scheme put in place in Ukraine by Democratic Party elites and their relays in Ukraine

Gain of Function: Artificially enhanced pathogens produced in U.S.-run biolabs

Minsk Accords: Diplomatic process agreed upon by Russia, Kiev, France, and Germany between 2014–2022 to peacefully put a stop to Kiev's continued violations of its own citizens' fundamental rights and in so doing maintain Ukraine's territorial integrity

Mikola Zlochensky: Burisma CEO

NABU: National Anti-Corruption Bureau of Ukraine (institution created in the wake of the 2014 Maidan Coup by the American-controlled Kiev junta)

Naftogaz: Ukrainian gas company engaged the reverse-gas scheme

NATO: North Atlantic Treaty Organization

PGO: Office of the General Prosecutor of Ukraine

Party of Regions: Presidential Party during the Yanokovitch Administration

Rada: Ukrainian Parliament

Reverse Gas: Scheme which saw Russian Gas transiting through third parties to Russian-Ukrainian gas contracts rebranded as "European gas," thus justifying fraudulent price hikes by American-controlled Ukrainian elites

Revolution of Dignity: February 21, 2014 U.S.-engineered color revolution which ousted incumbent and legitimately-elected Ukrainian president Yanukovitch

Russiagate: Psychological operation aimed at convincing parts of the American Public that Donald Trump was a Russian agent

SBU: Security Bureau of Ukraine

Snaftogaz: Process by which Ukrainian officials embezzled upwards of $1 billion through the reverse-gas scheme

Special Military Operation: Military operation carried out by the Russian Federation's Armed Forces in accordance with the police powers bequeathed it under UN Resolution 2202

Steele Dossier: Forgery produced by disgraced former MI6 employee Christopher Steele, which was used to generate controversy and tar the President of the United States

Supervisory Boards: Executive bodies of government-owned Ukrainian companies at the heart of a reform adopted by the Ukrainian Rada allowing foreigners to seat on these companies' boards of administration in order to partake in strategic decision-making process

Index